T0199311

# Embedding Culture and Quality for High Performing Organizations

Edited by
Norhayati Zakaria and Flevy Lasrado

A PRODUCTIVITY PRESS BOOK

First edition published in 2020
by Routledge/Productivity Press
52 Vanderbilt Avenue, 11th Floor New York, NY 10017
2 Park Square, Milton Park, Abingdon, Oxon OX14 4RN, UK

© 2020 by Taylor & Francis Group, LLC
Routledge/Productivity Press is an imprint of Taylor & Francis Group, an Informa business

Printed on acid-free paper

International Standard Book Number-13: 978-1-138-48338-5 (Hardback)
International Standard Book Number-13: 978-1-351-05506-2 (eBook)

Visit the Taylor & Francis Web site at
http://www.taylorandfrancis.com

# Contents

# Foreword

Quality management as a universal set of precepts defining best practices has been an indispensable business strategy for all types of businesses over the past several decades. Despite its widespread adoption and potential to bring about a sustainable competitive advantage, it has fallen far short of its potential value and yielding sustained peak performance. While quality management initiatives could fail due to a myriad of reasons, there is a general consensus that the difference in the performance impact of quality management practices lies in the universalistic perspective of quality management and organizational performance: there is a linear correlation between total quality management (TQM) adoption and organizational performance and that the context-independent nature of TQM implies that contextual requirements play a passive or peripheral role in realizing TQM's deliverables. There has been massive amount of attention paid to the notion of the "context-dependent" nature of TQM. This implies that the performance impact of TQM initiatives is affected by contextual and cultural relevance and that TQM-driven organizations must understand the cultural context in which TQM initiatives are adopted and implemented. As such, the performance impact of TQM initiatives must be measured in a contextually and culturally relevant manner. That is precisely the aim of this edited book.

The edited book contains detailed theoretical discussion and empirical scrutiny of the adoption and diffusion of quality through the lens of culture at both organizational and national levels. It has been written to advance understanding of the multifaceted reality of TQM including why and how TQM initiatives and cultural norms should be aligned and work in unison to form a blueprint for sustained, long-term performance in domestic and international businesses, the importance of business ethics as a crucial parameter for supporting a culture of quality, developing a culture of quality by going above and beyond a mere respectful obedience to the edict from on high to encompass strategies that encourage employees to accept quality as a personal value, mentoring and coaching as effective mechanisms for helping employees adapt to the culture of quality and excel by having a sense of pride in quality work, the vital role of quality in the context of green supply chain management and the resulting effects on firm performance, opportunities, and challenges of TQM adoption in multinational corporations (MNCs) and the resulting performance impact, and creating a culture of quality with a particular focus on maximization of the interests of all stakeholders through the lens of ISO 26000 (integration of socially responsible behavior into the organization as a whole).

In essence, this edited book will thus be of immense help to all those wishing to understand how TQM can be effectively adopted in different cultural contexts and how cultural awareness enables organizations to capitalize on TQM as a strategic tool for achieving steady high performance over the long haul.

**Ebrahim Soltani**
*Professor of Quality Management*
*Hamdan Bin Mohammed Smart University*
*August, 2019*

# Acknowledgments

Our journey to recruit esteemed contributors has been a challenging one due to the unique theme of the book. Hence, we have hand-picked the contributors based on their aspiring research agenda which pose numerous questions on understanding the conceivability of unification between culture and quality for organizational excellence. Without their significant contributions, the launch of this book would be next to impossible. We would like to express our appreciation to all the contributors of this edited book who shared their expertise and took the time to offer insights on numerous important topics to be included in this book. Our appreciation is further extended to the Faculty of Business and Management, University of Wollongong in Dubai, for their encouragement in terms of time, support, and space. Nonetheless, a special thanks to the publishing team of Routledge—Kristine Mednansky and members; all whom has been extremely supportive throughout the initiative to embark on this project.

# About the Editors

**Norhayati Zakaria, PhD**, is an Associate Professor at the University of Wollongong in Dubai (UOWD), where she teaches undergraduate courses in responsible leadership, managing across culture, intercultural applications for socially innovative business, and sustainability developmental goals for a capstone class of integrated business as well as postgraduate courses such as managerial concepts and skills research project for HRM. Dr. Zakaria earned her PhD in Information Science and Technology from Syracuse University, USA, in 2016. Dr. Zakaria's research program aims at exploring on how and why cultural values shape people differently in terms of communication styles, leadership, and management practices. Specifically, she is interested in further exploring a research agenda with a key question of: what is the cross-cultural kit of intelligence needed for talented human resources to build cross-culturally competent individuals and how do people and leaders develop culturally versatile competency and technologically savvy skills to effectively perform in the novel virtual work structure such as global virtual teams. Her book *Culture Matters: Decision Making of Global Virtual Teams* was published in 2017 by CRC Press Imprint, Taylor & Francis Group, and marked her scholarly work in the area of research that integrates cross-cultural management and information science fields. In a similar line of passion, her latest book (2019) extends her research pursuits on the effects of culture on the expatriation process. Titled *Making Sense of Culture: Cross-Cultural Expeditions and Management Practices of Self-Initiated Expatriates in the Foreign Workplace*, and published by Routledge, it illustrates a lived-experience of challenges between *herself and others* as they relate to being expatriates. Hence, more than 20 years of scholarly and academic experience in both fields has led her to collaborate with many global scholars in the United States, Japan, South Africa, Malaysia, Saudi Arabia, and the UAE. Her globally recognized research was also supported by numerous international research grants like the Asian Office of Aerospace Research & Development, the Japanese Society for the Promotion of Sciences, the Heiwa Nakajima Foundation, and the Malaysia Fundamental Research Grant Scheme, both as principal investigator and research member. Over the years, more than 100 impactful publications have been produced, a research that was built to understand the effects of culture on human behaviors when people engage in global virtual teams, and when leaders manage expatriates' acculturation processes and build organizational culture to achieve excellence and sustainability.

**Flevy Lasrado, PhD**, is a high performing professional with 15+ years of experience in teaching business management subjects of innovation, human resources, business excellence, and operations management. Dr. Lasrado is a recognized industry leader with an extended skill set in the area of quality management and innovation. The value of Dr. Lasrado's dedicated efforts to contextualize quality practices in the region has been recognized in both her professional award from the American Society of Quality (ASQ) and Fellowship status with the Higher Education Academy, UK. Through her cutting-edge research in the field of business excellence, as well as the innovation field, she has authored several books that have been published by international publishers, such as Springer Germany, IGI global, Palgrave UK, and Routledge UK. As a future-thinking academic with a passion for teaching and learning, Dr. Lasrado has won several other accolades in her career and is dedicated to contributing to society through her continuous engagement with national awards such as the Dubai Quality Award, the UAE Innovation Awards and healthcare awards. She carries extensive experience working with international accreditation bodies (e.g., AACSB, ABET and NASAD). She is Certified Lead Auditor for ISO 9001:2008 and Certified EFQM Assessor and Six Sigma methodologies. Currently, Dr. Lasrado teaches the Master of Quality Management program at the Australian University of Wollongong in Dubai, UAE. For more information visit www.flasrado.com

# About the Contributors

**Faisal I. Hai, PhD**, is an Associate Professor in Water Quality. His group at the University of Wollongong (UOW), Australia, works at the nexus of water quality and its impact on public health and ecology. He is the director of the Strategic Water Infrastructure Laboratory (SWIL), which has a longstanding track record of delivering competitive grant- and industry-funded projects. He is also the coordinator of the SMART water theme at the SMART Infrastructure Facility, which is a multidisciplinary research hub at UOW.

**Froilan T. Malit, Jr.** is an Associate at the Gulf Labour Markets and Migration (GLMM) and Population Programme, a Research Fellow at the Centre International de Formation des Autorités et Leaders (CIFAL) (Philippines), and Visiting Researcher at Zayed University (UAE). Malit has published peer-review articles, book chapters, and technical reports for international organizations on migration policy issues in the Asia-Gulf migration corridor. He has also previously worked for governments, international organizations, and academic institutions in the wider Middle East and North Africa (MENA) region. He holds both undergraduate and graduate degrees from Cornell University and the University of Oxford, and a migration certificate from the European University Institute.

**Jenny Knowles Morrison, PhD**, is a Qualitative Researcher and Organizational Ethnographer, focused on examining the human dimensions of policy implementation processes, with methodological capacities in surveys, action research, narrative inquiry, focus groups, and in-depth interviews. Her dissertation, "From Global Paradigm to Grounded Policy: The Socio-Cognitive Construction of Participatory Development in Cambodia" examined the complex historical, political, and cultural nexus of collaborations between a range of international donors and local actors in developing countries. This work has spurred her long-term research interest in how diverse actors, particularly in complex multicultural environments, are able to cross sectoral and institutional boundaries to enact sustainable and impactful policy outcomes.

**Kristian Alexander, PhD**, is an Assistant Professor at the College of Humanities and Social Sciences, Zayed University, Abu Dhabi, UAE. He has a PhD in Political Science with a focus on International Relations and Comparative Politics. He previously taught at the University of Utah, the University of Wyoming in the United States, and the University of Wollongong, Dubai. His research examines the significance of social movements in the Middle East and security-related issues, especially pertaining to migration in the GCC. He has published in a number of journals and contributed book chapters to edited volumes.

**Meredith B. Henthorn** is a PhD student in Educational Human Resource Development at Texas A&M University. Her primary research interest is cross-cultural mentoring. Meredith's experience includes human resources roles with several multinational corporations. She holds certifications in organizational development and is a certified facilitator of various intercultural inventories.

**Mohd Nazari Ismail, PhD**, is a Professor at the Department of Business Policy and Strategy, Faculty of Business and Accounting, University Malaya, and the former dean of the faculty. His latest book is entitled *Till Debt Do Us Part: The Growth of The Global Banking Industry and Its Insidious Effects.*

**Nizam Abdullah, PhD**, is a Business Practitioner at an MNC and graduated from his doctoral studies in Management and Administration at the University of Malaya. He combines the best of the two worlds in his research to draw empirical experiential knowledge such as in the area of the parent-subsidiary dynamic relationship.

**Nigel Grigg** is Professor of Quality Systems at Massey University in New Zealand, where he leads the Department of Operations and Engineering Innovation. Among his research interests, he has led and helped supervise research projects examining the influence of culture on operations and quality management theory and practice. He is an Associate Editor of the international journal *Total Quality Management and Business Excellence*, a Fellow of the Chartered Quality Institute, Senior Member of the American Society for Quality, and Director of the New Zealand Organisation for Quality.

**Roslina Ab Wahid** is an Associate Professor of Quality Systems at the Arshad Ayub Graduate Business School, Universiti Teknologi MARA, Malaysia. Her areas of specialization include quality management systems, operational excellence, operations management, and service quality. Apart from books and journal articles, Roslina has written modules on Transition to ISO 9001:2015, Introduction to ISO 9001:2015, and Internal Audit based on ISO 9001:2015 for training. As Director of Quality Systems & Operational Excellence of her university, Roslina has successfully managed several major projects: Integrated Quality Management System, Operational Excellence through Process Improvement, and Transition to ISO 9001:2015.

**Venkata Yanamandram, PhD,** is the Director of Assurance of Learning at the Faculty of Business, University of Wollongong Australia. He is responsible for executing the faculty's plan for systematically collecting data on student learning outcomes and reviewing and using it to continuously develop and improve the faculty's academic programs. Venkata develops, maintains, and implements a strategy and action plan for effective assurance of student learning. Venkata has taught at MBA and EMBA as well as at first- and second-year undergraduate levels, both onshore and offshore. For his contribution to teaching and learning, Venkata has received university and faculty awards.

**Younis Hasan, PhD**, is a well-known author in the field of green supply chain management. He obtained his Doctor of Business Administration from the University of Wollongong in Dubai and worked in the field of supply chain management for more than two decades in private sector, semi-government, and government organizations in the UAE. He attended many international workshops and conferences in prestigious institutions including Harvard Business School and the Kellogg School of Business. He has published articles in the finest journals in the area of his study. His research interests include supply chain management, operations management, logistics and procurement, sustainability, and green supply chain management.

# 1

## The Unison between Culture and Quality to Promote High Performing Organizations: How Is It Significant?

*Norhayati Zakaria and Flevy Lasrado*

### CONTENTS

### CULTURAL MATERIALIZATION IN ORGANIZATIONS

Imagine the following cultural turbulence as you initially enter a new workplace. You observe a manager bestow precipitous instructions to his or her team members, goods and services are not delivered on time, meetings are not punctual and are carried out with unsystematic agendas, people perform chaotic tasks without proper planning, desks are cluttered and unorganized, and teams fail to collaborate in a reciprocal manner, refusing to share knowledge among themselves. You might begin to contemplate the culture of this organization. You might even reflect further: Why do things happen in such a way? Who causes such destruction? Why do the quality of the practices, processes, and procedures seem inefficient and ineffective? To understand culture means to identify an abundance of questions that arise from employees' minds, vulnerable feelings, and destructive behaviors. Additionally, the power of culture is magnified to the extent that it can influence people's behaviors and interactions in the workplace and thus provide forward directions to take.

In terms of organizational culture, it is both explicit and implicit. In that regard, culture can be illustrated using the metaphor of an iceberg introduced by Hall (1976), which signifies the level of implicitness and explicitness of cultural meanings. This metaphor also allows us to understand the intricacy of culture, all depending on the layers; some are visible and observable, while some are not visible and non-observable. Hall describes three main layers which are: (1) stories, rituals, language; (2) shared values; and (3) shared assumptions. In a similar vein, Zakaria (2019) introduces culture from three different layers of complexity based on the Onion Model (adopted from Hofstede, 1980), which she classifies as the observation level, the manifestation level, and the indoctrination level (refer to Figure 1.1). The outer layer is visible and signifies certain artifacts and symbols. Nonetheless, its meaning can only be gauged at a superficial level unless you peel the onion, layer by layer, to discover the uniqueness of the observed patterns of behaviors. Let us detail out the Onion Model to further explain about how a person can engage in cultural sensemaking.

First, the observation layer of culture is noticeable and evident yet often difficult to make sense of and interpret. Misunderstanding usually takes place as people misconstrue or misinterpret the practices, signs, and gestures observable in a workplace during the initial stage of acculturation. The explicitness of culture at this level lies in the eye of the observer. People can see what is happening, but the logic behind why and how it is happening requires entrenched cultural understanding and interpretations. In the abovementioned scenarios, we can only observe culture in the form of symbols, outcomes, and artifacts, which are all easily identifiable at a first glance and are amenable to creating one's first impression of the workplace. For example, a person may enter a new workplace, observe the aforementioned characteristics, and then sigh, "What a culture!" He or she may then quickly formulate a mental image based on impulsive emotions without wanting to clarify their observations with anyone. In short, the outer layer of the onion explicitly shows people's reactions to the symbols, signs, or artifacts they observe, and all observation is made at a superficial level. It contains implicit meanings, which are unexplainable to some extent. At this level, a person cannot fully grasp or comprehend the observed behaviors since he or she is newly acculturated to the work environment and learning the ropes of the system, practices, and procedures. The learning process is simply at the surface level, and people usually fail to make sense of either what is happening or why it is happening.

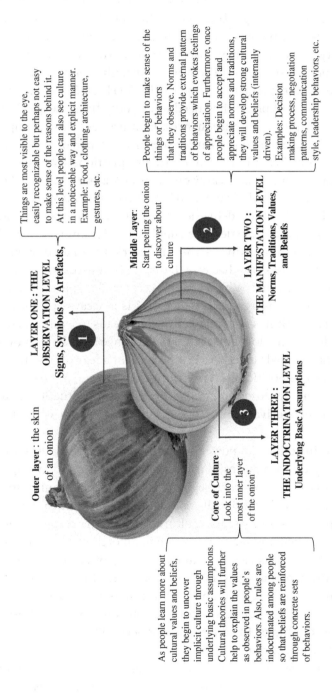

Things are most visible to the eye, easily recognizable but perhaps not easy to make sense of the reasons behind it. At this level people can also see culture in a noticeable way and explicit manner. Example: Food, clothing, architecture, gestures, etc.

**LAYER ONE : THE OBSERVATION LEVEL**
**Signs, Symbols & Artefacts,**

**Outer layer** : the skin of an onion

People begin to make sense of the things or behaviors that they observe. Norms and traditions provide external pattern of behaviors which evokes feelings of appreciation. Furthermore, once people begin to accept and appreciate norms and traditions, they will develop strong cultural values and beliefs (internally driven).
Examples: Decision making process, negotiation patterns, communication style, leadership behaviors, etc.

**Middle Layer**:
Start peeling the onion to discover about culture

**LAYER TWO :**
**THE MANIFESTATION LEVEL**
**Norms, Traditions, Values,**
**and Beliefs**

**Core of Culture :**
Look into the most inner layer of the onion"

**LAYER THREE :**
**THE INDOCTRINATION LEVEL**
**Underlying Basic Assumptions**

As people learn more about cultural values and beliefs, they begin to uncover implicit culture through underlying basic assumptions. Cultural theories will further help to explain the values as observed in people's behaviors. Also, rules are indoctrinated among people so that beliefs are reinforced through concrete sets of behaviors.

**FIGURE 1.1**
Using the Onion Model to make sense of culture. (From Zakaria, 2019.)

Second, the manifestation layer requires one to go into a deeper layer of cultural understanding. This level illustrates values, norms, and behaviors. Thus, making sense of culture becomes more intense because one's curiosity about what they observe requires further explanation. At this level, people also need to discover the meaning of culture that was indescribable or unexplainable at the earlier level. Once people observe a situation in the workplace, they need to not only think deeper but also reason out its causes and consequences. Culture needs to be unpacked at this layer. Let us refer to the earlier scenarios. A person will begin to formulate in his or her mind many pertinent questions: Why do people receive unclear instructions to carry out their tasks? Is it due to ineffective communication between the leader and his team members? Why are goods and services delayed in their deliveries? Is it caused by miscalculation and mishandling by affected parties like suppliers and manufacturers? Why do meetings run late, and why are they not carried out based on bulleted and established agendas? Is it because the leader is unfocused and inclined to engage in multitasking? Why do people create office spaces that are not neat and hence form disorganized structures? Is it because people are not trained to organize things systematically, which leads to waste and quality dysfunctionality? Why do teams refuse to exchange and share knowledge to achieve targeted goals together? Is it because of a fear of insecurity and betrayal, a threat to position in terms of role and power, or anxiety about information being disclosed to competitors? In those situations, culture introduces an inconceivable presence in an organization without one's realization.

Culture can introduce its power and presence in an organization in a subtle way yet produce a powerful impact on its workers and management team. At this layer, people will begin to unpack the reasoning for why things exist as they do, and culture becomes evident through norms, values, and practices and rituals. Culture can thus transfer its elements through both explicit and tacit knowledge in an organization. In essence, organizational culture is clearly defined as a way of doing things and is established through many layers of complexities. In the second layer, people become knowledgeable about why things happen the way they happen. People begin to understand the effects and forces of culture on the way people do things. In addition, at the second layer, people begin to appreciate and feel a culture.

Last, at the inner layer of the onion lies the basic, underlying assumptions that are shared among members in an organization. It is the core understanding of how culture transpires. Zakaria (2019) signifies this as a level of indoctrination, where the rules of a culture can be prescribed with the use of a theoretical lens. Hofstede (1980) asserts that culture is the software of the mind, where people's behaviors are programmed, thus leading to the display of behaviors. People can make accurate interpretations of organizational behaviors' manifestations through the interpretation of various theoretical, cultural lenses. With sound theories, basic assumptions provide a foundation that spells out why, when, and how people illustrate culture as a set of attitudes, beliefs, values, and behaviors that can be emulated and shaped by the owner of such a culture, for example, a leader in an organization. Schein (2004) defines culture as shared behaviors, beliefs, attitudes, and values that prescribe specific practices and certain ways of doing things in an organization. In this respect, we could explain culture concretely through empirical evidence by applying theories. Applying theoretical frameworks to measure and interpret observable behaviors, perceived thoughts, and expressed feelings facilitates the attainment of a deeper understanding of culture. Consequently, cultural sensemaking allows a person to unbundle the unknowns and avoid unrealistic assumptions of what was initially observed at a workplace. In fact, SERVQUAL dimensions are correlated with Hofstede's cultural dimensions (Furrer et al., 2000).

Coming back to the earlier scenarios, let us pick the example of lack of punctuality and justify the reasoning based on Trompenaar and Hampden-Turner's (1994) cultural theory of time orientation. For example, why does a manager start a meeting late? If we look at a culture where time is polychronic, time is considered elastic and non-urgent. People will take their time to schedule tasks because they are, by nature, multitaskers. Many things can be scheduled to operate at one time, thus making it inefficient for people to be delivering tasks on time. Polychronic-oriented people also have the tendency to take things in a laid-back manner: they procrastinate and are relaxed, and punctuality is not one of their best qualities. This clashes with monochronic cultures wherein time is considered linear: one thing happens at one time, and every task must be organized in an orderly manner to ensure efficiency. The key cultural questions here are as follows: How do you work with a manager who has different cultural values when quality needs to be prioritized, engaged, and followed through with to achieve sustainability? Is quality not equally as important as culture to be incorporated into organizations? Does quality itself not have its own values, characteristics, beliefs, and norms to be inculcated in team members? What if quality and culture are incongruent? Although the cultural factors underpinning different elements of total quality management (TQM) are dissimilar, even antagonistic, organizations can implement them in harmony (Prajogo and McDermott, 2005). In essence, this book is strongly emphasizing the premise that culture and quality need to be integrated; these two concepts need to be addressed as the main agenda in moving toward high performing organizations.

## QUALITY IS SIGNIFICANT: SO IS CULTURE!

"Culture" has around 160 varied definitions that have evolved over the decades based on different cultural theorists and scholars (Adler, 1997; Hall, 1976; Kluckhorn and Strodbeck, 1961; Hofstede, 1980; Trompenaars and Hampden-Turner, 2000; Zakaria, 2017), and the definition of quality has also evolved immensely over time (Juran, 1995; Deming, 1986; Crosby, 1995). In fact, the definitions of quality are still evolving. In the early period of the TQM field, the father of quality evolution, Edward Deming, introduced the concept of "continuous improvement" in manufacturing firms to show that a quality-oriented process needs to be incorporated if firms want to achieve a high level of efficiency and effectiveness. He famously and succinctly illustrated the principle of continuous improvement: "If you can't describe what you are doing as a process, you don't know what you're doing!" This quote represents a realistic way of operating in the manufacturing industry. Indeed, it sets the tone for the American history of developing a culture of quality, as Deming aptly asserts, "If the Japanese can do it, we can do it too!" Deming clearly realized and understood that culture can pave the way to make bold changes in the operating systems of any organization; culture sets the tone, and culture can make things happen. Culture can also enforce and reinforce quality to ensure that continuous improvement takes place at all levels of management (Lasrado, 2017).

Other scholars offer similar perspectives and argue that quality characterizes the efficiency and effectiveness of a process based on the management elements such as planning, implementation, and improvements (Cosby, 1980). As the field evolves, Deming affirms that quality is essentially about people, not product. Other scholars are supportive of this view and have begun to define quality as an assured process of making customers feel happy and satisfied with products and services (Juran, 1995). Contemporary organizations employ different mechanisms, systems, tools, and processes to achieve quality through their strategies and tasks, such as Quality Circle, Six Sigma, Kaizen, and Pareto Analysis, to ensure that employees in organizations adopt total quality management values as a way of doing things.

Given the meanings of both culture and quality, we argue that a high performing organization cannot formulate a sustainable vision, mission, and goal that incorporates the culturally oriented behaviors and actions of organizational members who practice quality values. Similarly, organizational culture is imperative to develop in any high performing organization because culture can support quality ideologies when it is well trained and inculcated in members. Powell (1985) strongly argues that total quality management tools singlehandedly are unable to provide competitive advantages. Instead, it is the organizational resources that produce certain tacit behaviors that are difficult to replicate and are hence unique to the organizations that practice them, such as open culture, employee empowerment, and executive commitment. Over time, such tacit behaviors become the norms of the members in organizations and become the accepted way of doing things which is to implement quality standards. However, without a strong quality culture embedded in the members in an organization, quality cannot be sustained over time. Hence, internalization of culture needs to be materialized in the effort of promoting quality in the pursuits of sustainability and organizational excellence (Lasrado and Zakaria, 2019).

If we argue that culture is the construction of an organization, in which a leader co-creates its values with its teams and develops standards of behavior, then what about quality management? What is quality in the context of organizational culture? Is it a process, is it state or a condition, is it a byproduct of a member in an organization, or is it an outcome that is born out a process or condition in an organization? How important is the effort of creating a culture that underlines quality exclusively? For many successful organizations, creating cultures that shape the values and behaviors of their members has resulted in high-performing outcomes (Al Mehairi and Zakaria, 2014). Similarly, creating a quality that prescribes values and formulates behaviors leads to high-performing outputs as well as achieving organizational excellence (Lasrado, 2017). In both contexts, culture and quality matter because they signify how organizations perform and function. However, how do each of these concepts matter in the context of contemporary organizations that aim for sustainability development as their long-term goals? Why it matters and how it matters will set the directions for how organizations can strategize their initiatives, efforts, and performance. Ironically, there seems to be too much focus on training people in tools and techniques and at the same time too little focus on understanding the human factor, i.e., how to build the right company culture (Dahlgaard and Dahlgaard-Park, 2006).

Thus, managing quality is a key concern for multinational corporations (MNCs), which face intense competition in a highly globalized and multicultural workplace. In order to promote high performance, MNCs must strategically build cultures based on shared values, norms, beliefs, and attitudes. It has become increasingly challenging for managers to achieve excellence because corporate structures have become highly diversified, and global teams rely on people with a variety of culturally oriented practices. Because different cultures define quality and excellence in different ways, the process of achieving excellence tends to involve different interpretations and outcomes. Therefore, it is essential that frameworks for high-performing MNCs be developed to embrace different cultural perspectives. Agreeably, a growing body of evidence links cultures and quality, but we need a more nuanced and sophisticated understandings of cultural dynamics (Mannion and Davies, 2018).

In the reality of contemporary organizations, management has different strategies and practices to attain organizational excellence. As the world experiences many global challenges, organizational excellence needs to be aligned with sustainability, which hinges on the three Ps—people, profit, and planet. Multiple stakeholders become the main targeted group of people that needs to be taken care of, and corporate social responsibility (CSR) is a desirable norm and culture for engaging in profit-making goals. Caroll's Pyramid Model (1999) illustrates CSR based on four different levels of engagement. First, at the foundation level, the firm has economic responsibility where all firms need to ensure profit making is their main agenda. Second, the legal responsibilities where firms need to be accountable, and hence strictly obey the law. Third, the ethical responsibilities wherein firms need to engage in ethical conducts no matter under what circumstances they encounter. Last, the highest level of social responsibility is achieved when firms engage in philanthropic activities and behaviors which is to become a good corporate citizen. Given the CSR activities, firms must also take heed of environmental factors, since it is equally important when aligning profit-making initiatives with the three Ps.

It has also been observed that TQM requires a quality-oriented organizational culture supported by senior management commitment and involvement, organizational learning and entrepreneurship, team working and collaboration, risk taking, open communication, continuous improvement, customers focus (both internal and external), partnership with suppliers, and monitoring and evaluation of quality (Mohammad, 2006) Therefore, not only internal strategies are important: organizations need to take into consideration external factors and parties to align their visions, missions, and goals with performance. The main questions that arise in achieving such goals are as follows: How does culture matter in efforts to implement total quality management in organizations? Specifically, why does culture need to be embedded along with quality management to build high performing organizations? In what ways can organizations develop cultures that are congruent with quality management? Taking into account many perspectives, we concede that both culture and quality need to be integrated to obtain high performing organizations.

We argue that organizational excellence in the workplace is not possible without quality management, yet this assertion sparks a further provocative question of how can excellence exist if a culture does not shape and inculcate quality management? Hence, we concur that culture and quality should be co-established to set a strong foundation for contemporary organizations in the modern age of achieving sustainability. Culture and quality need to complement each other in a partnership that strengthens the strategies and initiatives of organizations that aim to pursue excellence at all levels, at all costs, and at all times, with all the relevant people.

## THE AGENDA OF THIS BOOK

The aim of this book is to bridge two different areas of research, organizational culture and quality management, the combination of which can result in organizational excellence if managed effectively. We also proclaim that both areas of research are essential to build high performing organizations that thrive on innovation and sustainability. However, we are fully aware that building high performing organizations is challenging in a globalized business environment, particularly when sustainability goals are a priority. Thus, in this book, we would like to pose two key research questions: (1) What strategies do organizations need to promote to build high performing organizations; and (2) How does culture promote or hinder such strategies and initiatives? This book aims to integrate organizational and national cultural perspectives to promote sustainable quality management practices and build high performing organizations. Whereas most books currently on the market are based on organizational culture and quality management, this book uniquely considers cross-cultural impacts on organizational effectiveness and global human resource management for building high performing organizations to meet sustainable developmental goals.

We believe that this book fills a niche with its research on how quality management is strongly connected to the cultural values of a workplace. It is useful to note that the study of quality management and organizational excellence has been largely influenced by organizational culture. However, there is growing evidence that shows that national culture also has an impact on quality management practices because some cultures are more suitable to the implementation of specific quality programs than others (Wu and Huarng, 2015). An emergent body of research also highlights different aspects of culture that have facilitating or inhibiting consequences on the implementation of quality management (Kull and Wacker, 2010). Truly, managers need to be actively aware of the cultural characteristics of their organization before adopting quality techniques in order to benefit most from the use of these technique (Gambi et al., 2015). In fact, given that different culture profiles have different influences on QMS implementation (Willar et al., 2016), we envisage to discuss this quality and culture phenomena in light of the following objectives:

- Understand quality management practices in cross-culturally diverse work contexts based on cultural dimensions.
- Build on quality management principles by placing them within the context of culturally oriented practices that promote high performing organizations.
- Provide illuminating case studies and scenarios based on professional, hands-on experience that will be useful for leaders and practitioners.
- Provide a framework and models to management teams to develop relevant, quality-related attitudes and skills to compete in the global business world while showing quality and excellence.
- Develop theoretical or practical reflections and/or guidelines for discussing integrating culture and quality into high performing organizations.

## OVERVIEW OF CONTRIBUTING CHAPTERS

The book comprises eight (8) chapters contributed by 13 authors (including the editors) affiliated with universities located in Australia, Malaysia, United States of America, and the United Arab Emirates. We clearly assert that the integration between culture and quality is neither a new strategy nor a fad existing temporarily in organizations. In the last century, Demming, the Guru of Quality, exclusively advocated that culture without quality would make the achievement of organizational excellence impossible; in addition, quality without culture does not produce absolute accomplishment. Nevertheless, what is more challenging in this current century is that contemporary organizations need to focus on achieving sustainability and innovation. Sustainability requires responsible leadership to set different goals that offer diverse and dynamic strategies. Finally, as we have set out, culture can be identified and set out to provide users with a model of culture and to develop ways to apply the results of a cultural assessment, which would feed through into changes in a TQM program (Maull et al., 2001). The following summaries offer insights on the ways and practices that organizations are engaged in to achieve organizational excellence.

In the introductory chapter, Norhayati Zakaria and Flevy Lasrado as the editors establish a ground work on the concept of culture and how culture can be defined from three different levels through a metaphor called the "Onion Model" (Zakaria, 2019). The first chapter also explains the need for culture and quality integration and how such a unison is made possible due to its significance. The argument is clear, which is culture does exist and paves the construction of practices, norms, and common standards and procedures to be subscribed, complied, and shared by a group of people, for example, employees of an organization. While quality is a process that needs to be implemented wherein such practices need to be aligned accurately and relevantly with the culture that was constructed within an organization. Hence, the marriage between culture and quality is not a coincidence, instead, it needs to be integrated and embedded within a structure and system that allows harmonious relationships to ensure congruent outcomes, which is to develop a high performing organization.

In the second chapter, Roslina Wahab and Nigel Grigg suggest that not only does culture exist in organizations, but the emergence of subculture can also be as important. Their research work aims to understand how culture—both national and organizational—influences quality management practices when implementing ISO9001. They posed an interesting question on the applicability of ISO 9001 as a typical quality management practice, which is: can it be used as a universal standard or is there a need for regional variations of quality management that is more amenable to be applied based on the context. In short, they question whether or not such a phrase called "think local, act global" works more effectively when implementing quality standards instead of "think local, and act local" as a better measure for quality standard implementation. In fact, it is true, quality programs are not "one size fits all," rather, they are to be customized to the unique organizational settings. The chapter thus illustrates the influence of culture in relation to ISO 9001.

The third chapter, by Froilan Malit, Jenny Knowles Morrison, and Kristian Alexander, introduces ethical culture as the practice of promoting ethical values, behaviors, and practices (i.e., integrity, fairness, honesty, transparency) within an organization. Moreover, it also extends influence beyond organizational boundaries to external business practices. In light of the Asia-Gulf migration corridor, existing literatures suggest that Gulf-based construction MNCs have not only failed to uphold a strong ethical culture in their labor recruitment practices but instead collaborated with complex and multilevel recruitment (or subagencies) actors who have largely failed to uphold national and international labor recruitment laws and standards. After all, a high performing organization is not only a unison between organizational culture and quality. but also upholds the ethical stances that underpin performance and productivity. In essence, quality frameworks strongly compel "people" and "leadership" enablers to embrace ethical values, behaviors, and practices to achieve superiority on quality improvement

The fourth chapter by Venkata Yanamandram suggests that leadership is crucial when implementing change strategies to assure student learning outcomes. Yet, the imminent question is: in what ways could mid-level leaders create new capabilities that span several activities—i.e., using effective tools and methodology to get stakeholders to change their behaviors, routines, and activities? This chapter describes a change effort from the perspective of a mid-level leader (MLL) within the faculty of a large transnational university that operates across multiple locations. While there is not a one-size-fits-all approach to creating a culture of quality, the practice-informed recommendations are grounded within broad Kotter and Lawson models of organizational change management processes to lay the foundation for propagating a culture of assessment.

On the contrary, the fifth chapter by Meredith Henthorn and Jenny Knowles Morrison offers a framework for mentoring and coaching to promote organizational and workplace learning and gender inclusion in organizations using the European Foundation for Quality Management (EFQM) Excellence Model in the United Arab Emirates (UAE). The proposed approach varies from typical approaches to mentoring and coaching in three significant ways. First, the foundation of their framework rests on an inclusive approach to employee and organization development, in which they attempt to make male-dominated organizations more welcoming for women. Second, they integrate forms of mentoring and coaching into an overarching framework and offer guidance for application in quality-focused organizations. Third, they provide multiple formats, such as group mentoring, to align with the preference for group activities in collectivist cultures. Such frameworks are not only useful for managers but also provide a significant benefit to the academic community to advance the quality management practice in the UAE region. Earlier studies have also proposed frameworks and guides and illustrate the implementation benefits of quality models particularly to the UAE sector (Lasrado and Uzbeck, 2017; Lasrado, 2017); thus, the chapter further advances knowledge through their framework focusing on UAE.

Following on is a chapter from Hassan Younis, who talks about why and how industries attune their supply chain management based on quality culture and standards as part of a modern business strategy. The author provides an overview on the relationship between green supply chain management (GSCM) practices and corporate performance by examining the effect of the four main green supply chain management practices on four dimensions of corporate performance. The chapter defines green supply chain management and how it relates to sustainability, highlighting the main drivers and barriers of green supply chain management. The chapter also elaborates on ISO 14001 being one of the important GSCM certificates adopted by many businesses in the world. The nature of quality systems is then further elaborated in Chapter 8 while illustrating yet another ISO 26000 standard that organizations aspire to implement for achieving high performance and corporate reputation.

In the seventh chapter, Nizam Abdullah and Nazari Ismail present a chapter that examines the role of MNC managers as key actors in the implementation of center-led change initiatives. It studies the dynamism between center-subsidiary and subsidiary-subsidiary relationships of a Malaysian multinational corporation in the telecommunication sector. Data for this qualitative study were collected through in-depth direct interviews of key actors involved in a center-led change initiative. Through the sensemaking theoretical lens, themes and patterns arising from the data collected forms the core analytical part of the research. Subsidiaries that display a high level of communication intensity, adoption of change, and resolution to barriers throughout the development of change tend to show significant progress of those changes studied. Three unique patterns of sensemaking appear to drive the center-led initiatives from the planning/implementation to the business-as-usual phase, namely (1) communication intensity; (2) adoption to change; and (3) resolution to barriers. The results add knowledge to the sensemaking-in-change literature.

The concluding chapter of Flevy Lasrado and Faisal Hai discusses creating a culture for ISO 26000 to embrace corporate social responsibility. Focusing on the mining industry, the chapter provides an insight into the arena of CSR initiatives by ISO and sets the path for a future empirical investigation in this emerging and important area in relation to the mining industry. This chapter is an essential starting point for organizations that need a view on how the CSR standard works, where they stand in relation to it, and how they can work toward developing their CSR efforts. Thus, by connecting quality management systems to various organizational settings, our book provides several interventions for researchers to continue to focus on advancing knowledge on culture centric quality systems emerging as high performing organizations.

## REFERENCES

Adler, N. (1997). *International Dimensions of Organizational Behavior.* Cincinnati, OH: South-Western.

Al Mehairi, H. and Zakaria, N. (2014). "Understanding organizational culture for effective knowledge sharing behaviors in the workplace," *Organizational Cultures: An International Journal*, Vol. 13, pp. 33–52.

Carroll, A.B. (1999). "Corporate social responsibility," *Business and Society*, Vol. 38, No. 3, pp. 268–295.

Crosby, P.B. (1995). *A History of Managing for Quality: The Evolution, Trends, and Future Directions of Managing for Quality.* Milwaukee, WI: ASQC Quality Press.

Dahlgaard, J. and Mi Dahlgaard-Park, S. (2006). "Lean production, six sigma quality, TQM and company culture," *The TQM Magazine*, Vol. 18, No. 3m, pp. 263–281.

Deming, E.W. (1986). *Out of the Crisis*. Cambridge, Massachusetts: The MIT Press.

Furrer, O., Liu, B.S.C. and Sudharshan, D. (2000). "The relationships between culture and service quality perceptions: Basis for cross-cultural market segmentation and resource allocation," *Journal of Service Research*, Vol. 2, No. 4, pp. 355–371.

Gambi, L., Boer, H., Gerolamo, M., Jørgensen, F. and Carpinetti, L. (2015). "The relationship between organizational culture and quality techniques, and its impact on operational performance," *International Journal of Operations & Production Management*, Vol. 35, No. 10, pp. 1460–1484.

Hall, E.T. (1976). *Beyond Culture*. New York, NY: Anchor Books.

Hofstede, G. (1980). *Culture's Consequences: International Differences in Work-related Values*. Beverly Hills, CA: Sage.

Juran, J.M. (Ed.) (1995). *A History of Managing for Quality*. Milwaukee, Wisconsin: ASQC Quality Press.

Kluckhohn, F.R. and Strodtbeck, F.L. (1961). *Variations in Value Orientations*. Evanston, IL: Row Peterson.

Kull, T.J. and Wacker, J.G. (2010). "Quality management effectiveness in Asia: The influence of culture," *Journal of Operations Management*, Vol. 28, pp. 223–239.

Lasrado, F. (2017). "Perceived benefits of national quality awards: A study of UAE's award winning organizations," *Measuring Business Excellence*, Vol. 21, No. 1, pp. 50–64.

Lasrado, F. and Uzbeck, C. (2017). "The excellence quest: A study of business excellence award-winning organizations in UAE," *Benchmarking: An International Journal*, Vol. 24, No. 3, pp. 716–734.

Lasrado, F. and Zakaria, N. (2019). *Internalizing a Culture of Business Excellence: Perspectives from Quality Professionals*. New York, NY: Routledge, Taylor & Francis Group.

Mannion, R. and Davies, H. (2018). "Understanding organisational culture for healthcare quality improvement," *BMJ*, Vol. 363, p. k4907.

Maull, R., Brown, P. and Cliffe, R. (2001). "Organizational culture and quality improvement," *International Journal of Operations & Production Management*, Vol. 21, No. 3, pp. 302–326.

Mohammad Mosadegh Rad, A. (2006). "The impact of organizational culture on the successful implementation of total quality management," *The TQM Magazine*, Vol. 18, No. 6, pp. 606–625.

Powell, W.W. (1985). *Getting into Print*. Chicago, IL: University of Chicago Press.

Prajogo, D. and McDermott, C. (2005). "The relationship between total quality management practices and organizational culture," *International Journal of Operations & Production Management*, Vol. 25, No. 11, pp. 1101–1122.

Schein, E.H. (2004). *Organizational Culture and Leadership* (3rd ed.), San Francisco, CA: Jossey-Bass.

Trompenaars, F. and Hampden-Turner, C. (2000). *Riding the Waves of Culture Understanding Cultural Diversity in Business*. Naperville, IL: Nicholas Brealey Publishing.

Willar, D., Trigunarsyah, B. and Coffey, V. (2016). "Organisational culture and quality management system implementation in Indonesian construction companies," *Engineering, Construction and Architectural Management*, Vol. 23, No. 2, pp. 114–133.

Wu, C. and Huarng, K. (2015). "Global entrepreneurship and innovation in management," *Journal of Business Research*, Vol. 68, No. 4, pp. 743–747.

Zakaria, N. (2017). "Emergent patterns of switching behaviors and intercultural communication styles of global virtual teams during distributed decision making," *Journal of International Management*, Vol. 23, No. 4, pp. 350–366.

Zakaria, N. (2019). *Making Sense of Culture: Cross-Cultural Expeditions and Management Practices of Self-Initiated Expatriates in the Foreign Workplace*. New York, NY: Routledge, Taylor & Francis Group.

# 2

## The Chicken or the Egg? On the Interplay between Culture and Quality Management Systems

*Roslina Ab Wahid and Nigel P. Grigg*

### CONTENTS

*"Which comes first—the chicken or the egg?"*

### INTRODUCTION

#### Culture and the Evolution of Quality Management Theory

The field of quality management has evolved over the twentieth and twenty-first centuries; from an era of mass production and inspection, through more preventive quality control including statistical methodologies, to the documentation of systems providing quality assurance, and finally the extension of quality management to the whole organization, or even the supply chain (Dale et al., 2016; Bounds et al., 1994; Kaye and Anderson, 1999; Saad and Siha, 2000). The final stage in this evolution has been known as total quality control (TQC) and total quality management (TQM), and now goes by many names including organizational excellence or performance excellence. The essential component element that is continuous improvement is increasingly tackled using methodologies such as Lean thinking, Six Sigma, Kaizen, and other variants.

It is also well reported that quality management, including quality control (QC) and continuous improvement (CI) flourished in Japan post-World War II under the teachings of gurus W. Edwards Deming, Joseph Juran, and Armand Feigenbaum (Garvin, 1988). The Japanese democratized QC and CI by utilizing quality circles and Kaizen teams, while Japanese engineers such as Taguchi, Imai, Kano, Kondo, and Ishikawa brought further statistical tools and methodologies to the arsenal. However, when attempts were made to re-import these methods and approaches to Western nations, they frequently proved unsuccessful (Hill, 1991; Bradley and Hill, 1983; Flynn, 1992). This hard lesson was an early indicator of the potential impact that national culture could have on managing quality. The lesson was that a more collectivist Asian nation— Japan—was able to assemble multidisciplinary teams to systematically and routinely solve problems and improve processes, while Western nations ran aground on the rocks of unionization, managerialism, apathy, and (to some extent) post-imperial arrogance in regard to their position in the developed world as traditional manufacturing nations. There is perhaps no stronger evidence of this perception at the time, than is provided by W. E. Deming's formulation of the "seven deadly diseases" of Western management (Deming, 1986).

Today, quality management theory and practice are arguably well established and defined and they have evolved relatively little since the 1980s. The fundamental concepts within quality management are sufficiently well captured by the seven quality management principles (QMPs) developed by ISO (2015), and in the Plan-Do-Check-Act (PDCA) cycle that has long been the "engine room" of quality improvement. These models are apparently universal, yet, it remains interesting to note that the PDCA cycle also encapsulates some of the dichotomy between Western and Eastern thinking. Japan favored and adopted the PDCA cycle as it was developed by Shewhart, while Deming—who is widely credited with its introduction to Japan—himself disliked the use of "check" and preferred to refer to the PDSA (Plan-Do-Study-Act) cycle (Moen and Norman, 2010; Imai, 1986). The current version of the international quality system standard ISO 9001 2015 uses PDCA as its underpinning improvement cycle, while the (US-based) Institute of Health Improvement whose method for improvement is widely used in international healthcare (IHI) advocates for the use of PDSA (Scoville and Little, 2014).

During the post-war period, the Toyota Motor Corporation developed the approach to automotive manufacture that would later become the (conceptual) "Toyota Way" (TW) and the (practical) "Toyota Production System" (TPS), both comprising the foundation of modern day Lean (Liker and Morgan, 2006). Lean (essentially encompassing the TPS and TW) is similarly based on the twin pillars and simple philosophy of continual improvement toward perfection (*Kai-zen*) and respect for people. In the late 1980s, the US countered with the Six Sigma improvement methodology, developed over a number of years by Motorola and GE (Harry, 1998). In contrast with Lean thinking's subtle continual incremental improvement "toward perfection," Six Sigma instead advocates for big, bold projects, large-scale bottom line improvements and the use of statistical methods. The methods almost seem to encapsulate the underlying culture of the two nations. Chiarini et al. (2018) compare lean with Zen Buddhism, with (among other things) its unending search for perfection. Six Sigma, on the other hand, is often associated with less subtle language, e.g., "aggressive" targets and goals (Harry, 1998; Hong and Goh, 2003; Schroeder et al., 2008) or "TQM on steroids" (Seddon, 2005).

The twentieth century also saw the gradual development of the ISO 9000 series of international standards for quality management systems. From post-war Allied Quality Assurance Procedures (AQAPs) grew BS5750, which became ISO 9000 in 1987 and has since evolved as a universal, international set of requirements for an effective quality management system. The lessons of quality history were that an international standard might not be universally accepted or effective; and yet the international growth and global penetration of ISO 9001 stands as testament to its universal acceptance, having recently exceeded one million international system certifications. ISO 9001 is also part conceptual model and part practical guidance. The seven major requirements clauses (4–10) form the compliance or contractual aspects of the standard, while the underlying philosophy is encapsulated within the seven QMPs and the PDCA cycle that underpins it and which provides an improvement cyclic structure to the clauses.

In this era of multinational corporations and global supply chains that span oceans and cross many national borders, organizations cannot afford to take for granted the importance of understanding the impact and influence of culture. Attempts to introduce corporate management models and methods may stumble on the rocks of organizational or national culture. In this chapter, we will examine the influence of culture on quality by using the Toyota Way and ISO 9000 as examples of universal management models that are partly oriented toward culture, and partly toward practice. We begin with a review of culture, and then focus on recent research conducted by the authors in New Zealand and Malaysian contexts, which serve to highlight the circular nature of the impact of culture on these management systems/models, and the impact of these systems/models on culture.

## LITERATURE REVIEW

### Prevailing Theories of National and Organizational Culture

Hofstede (1997) defines culture in terms of values, attitudes, and actions guiding the ethical behaviors of individuals within a group and nation. Global Leadership and Organizational Behavior Effectiveness (GLOBE) (Schein, 1997), a group that conducts research based on the work performed by Hofstede, defines culture as *"shared motives, values, beliefs, identities and the interpretation or meaning of significant events that result from common experiences of members of collectives that are transmitted across generations"* (Kats et al., 2010). Hofstede and GLOBE identify key values from which they developed what are referred to as "cultural dimensions" to define the culture of nations and organizations. The implication of their research suggests the importance for organizations to understand the impact culture has on employee and manager interactions as well as operating in a multicultural environment. The GLOBE framework in particular, provides an invaluable insight into understanding quality management across countries as it shows that some national cultures are more conducive to the implementation of quality management than others. Because national culture influences both organizational and quality culture, the knowledge will help managers better understand how to transfer best quality management practices from one country to another as the adoption of certain quality practices across different countries can follow distinctive patterns.

The types of organizational culture (such as bureaucratic, innovative, and supportive) can also impact quality management practices. As summarized by Ababneh (2010), bureaucratic subcultures are oriented toward rules and regulations, where employees are expected to perform tasks with a minimum of freedom and autonomy, and where coordination and communication are hierarchically based. Organizations with innovative subcultures value and nurture the creativity of people toward entrepreneurial ends. Such organizations accept risks more readily, and communication is generally more lateral. Those with supportive subcultures emphasize collaboration between people and groups. In his study undertaken in large hospitals, the three types of organizational culture were found to have a significant positive influence on quality improvement practices with innovative culture playing a stronger role in quality improvement. While bureaucratic actions enhance rather than hinder quality improvement practices (Ababneh, 2010).

## The Influence of Culture on Quality Management Systems

### *ISO 9000*

Schein (1997) defined organizational culture as "*a system of norms, shared values, concerns, and common beliefs that are understood and accepted by the members of an organisation.*" The underlying value systems influence people's decisions and their behaviors and this affects the way the organization operates. Organizational culture is also thought to affect people's beliefs and indirectly influences practices and performance. If an organization adopting a QMS is lacking in culture to support it, its employees may not stop mistakes or defects from happening that would lead to failure of the QMS. They might be too afraid, or not empowered to do so. Quality management practices like those prescribed within ISO 9001 need to be embedded in a supportive quality culture (e.g., Terziovski et al., 2003). An organizational culture that is supportive supports the effective implementation of QMSs as culture is viewed as the glue that binds together all of the key elements of QMSs and it may support or inhibit the implementation process and effectiveness. The hard aspects (e.g., tools, techniques, practices, and systems) cannot be implemented successfully without relevant value elements presented by behavioral and cultural aspects of quality management. Past research has found that TQM programs are more likely to succeed if the prevailing organizational culture is compatible with the values and basic assumptions proposed by the TQM discipline.

A quality culture is an organizational value system that results in an environment that is conducive to the establishment and continual improvement of quality. It consists of values, traditions, procedures, and expectations that promote quality (Evans and Lindsay, 2005). Although it has been implied that quality is created by a quality culture, the relationship between culture and quality management practices (e.g., ISO 9001) has not been adequately studied and there has been little empirical investigation on culture's influence on quality management. To understand quality culture, the concept of organizational culture must be understood. An organizational culture consists of its underlying values and traditions and it can be shaped, for example, by the business environment, organizational values, cultural role models, organizational rites and rituals, communication, slogans, and ceremonies.

In order to have a conducive environment for quality, one must understand the need for change and improvement. Therefore, there is a need to understand and manage change in moving toward this culture. According to Goetsch and Davis (2014), an organization with a culture that is conducive to quality has several characteristics such as:

- The behavior of its people matches its slogans.
- Actively seek and use inputs from customers to continually improve quality.
- Employees are involved, engaged, and empowered.
- Doing work in teams.
- Top management are committed and involved.
- Responsibility for quality is not delegated to staff by the top.
- Resources are sufficient where and when needed and for continuous improvement.
- Training and education are provided to employees to improve their knowledge and skills to improve quality continuously.
- Employees are viewed as internal customers.
- Suppliers are treated as partners.
- Emphasized on peak performance by people, processes, and products.

- Contribution to continual improvement of quality is the basis for reward and promotion of employees.

Therefore, an organization that has an embedded quality culture will be different in its approach with regard to management, problem-solving, and performance improvement as compared with one that has not. The organization with a quality culture will also be different in certain areas such as operating philosophy, objectives, attitude toward customers, and relationships with suppliers.

Some researchers have examined the impact that culture has on quality management, and close variants such a Business Excellence. Rode, Huang, and Flynn (2016) used GLOBE study dimensions to operationalize and therefore examine the influence of collectivism on individual organizational commitment HRM practices. They classified four countries as either high of low on collectivism. Comparing the effects of HRM practices "training," "teamwork," and "employee involvement in decision making" on organizational commitment across national cultures, they found significant differences for training and teamwork, and partial support for employee involvement in decision making.

Naor et al. (2008) analyzed data from manufacturing plants from six countries to investigate the relationships of organizational culture, infrastructure, and core quality management practices on manufacturing performance. They found that organizational culture has a stronger influence on infrastructure quality management practices than on core quality management practices, irrespective of whether the plants are located in Eastern or Western countries. Infrastructure quality management practices were in turn found to have a significant effect on manufacturing performance. The authors report that these findings emphasize *"the importance of accounting for culture when making decisions to implement quality management practices to achieve a performance advantage"* (Naor et al., 2008).

### The Toyota Way and the Toyota Production System

Ongoing research is being conducted by researchers within the Operations and Engineering Innovation Department of Massey University examining the impact of national culture on management models such as the Toyota Way, Toyota Production Systems, the PDCA cycle, and ISO 9001. A summary of the main findings to date follows.

Wagner, Mann, Grigg, and Mohammad (2017) examined the impact of national culture on TPS. TPS represents a fixed management model, whereby TPS and its underpinning philosophy, TW, are approaches adopted by all organizations under the Toyota umbrella, and TW effectively represents Toyota's organizational culture. If national culture does not impact significantly on TPS, then it would be expected that this universal model would need no local adaptation to be successful. However, these researchers (Wagner et al., 2017) compared Toyota logistics facilities in New Zealand and Spain, and found that it was considered necessary to introduce job rotation in the Spanish facility in order to overcome the issues of "in-group favoritism" and "social loafing," whereas this intervention was not required in New Zealand. One reason given is that the Spanish culture is more "collectivist" than that of New Zealand, and *"individuals in collectivistic societies are more likely to exhibit behaviours that favour other members of their real ingroup"* (Fischer and Derham, 2016 in Wagner et al., 2017).

Jayamaha, Wagner, and Grigg (2014) used empirical data from Toyota's annual, global 'Toyota Way Index' study, in which Toyota facilities were surveyed annually (via Gallup Corporation) to determine their degree of adherence to the TW organizational culture model. This research compared responses obtained from over 2000 Toyota employees engaged in logistics, sales, and marketing functions in 22 countries, against the national cultural dimensions developed by Hofstede, using covariance-based structural equation modeling. The study found a greater level of acceptance for "People Development," "Continuous Improvement," and "Operational Results" (subelements inclusive) in cultures exhibiting high uncertainty avoidance (UA) (e.g., Greece, Belize), than in cultures low on this dimension (e.g., Denmark, Iceland). However, the effects of UA (mean score differences) were found to be practically small, suggesting good transferability of TW principles across international boundaries (Jayamaha et al., 2017). The research further supported a hypothesis that individualistic cultures are more results-oriented in relation to process improvements than collectivistic cultures, although both individualistic and collectivist cultures were found to deploy the TW equally effectively—a finding that has practical implications (Jayamaha et al., 2014). Therefore, while small tweaks or modifications such as those identified by Wagner et al. (2016) are necessary because of cultural differences, the production system model appears equally effective for practical purposes across the different cultures. This finding is certainly borne out by Toyota's global performance over the past 80 years.

In research currently ongoing at Massey University in New Zealand, Pallawala, Jayamaha, and Grigg (2017a, 2017b) are examining the influence of Hofstede's cultural dimensions on the underpinning conceptual framework of ISO 9001, consisting of the PDCA improvement cycle, and the common management system structure described within *Annex L.* The research uses survey data from Australia/New Zealand, India /Sri Lanka, and Greece to develop structural equation models via PLS-SEM. Findings to date indicate no significant (or practical effect) of national culture on the PDCA cycle.

## THE INFLUENCE OF MANAGEMENT SYSTEMS ON CULTURE

There are two sides to the relationship between culture and quality. In the above studies, we reported the influence that culture has on management practices (including QM). However, under certain conditions, the management practice can in turn help shape the prevailing culture.

Total quality culture involves change and improvement for the organization and its people. Schein (1997) stressed that a quality culture involves developing shared learning of quality-related values as the organization develops capacity to survive in its environment. It consists of an organizational quality-based vision, mission, and goals, organizational structures (formal and informal), reward systems, technology and job design, and attention to important personnel issues (Terziovski et al., 2003). To create a quality culture, managing a change process like ISO 9001 implementation includes managing employees' attitudes toward change. If the reactions to change are not properly anticipated and managed, the change process will be needlessly painful and perhaps unsuccessful (Jick, 1993). Hence, a positive attitude toward change is a key to success in ISO 9001 implementation (Hind, 1996).

Ab Wahid (2019) conducted a study on sustaining an ISO 9001-based QMS in higher education and found that an organization can effectively use ISO 9000 certification as a means of promoting and facilitating a quality culture. This is in contrast with the long held anecdotal view that the development of a strong quality culture should precede ISO

9000 certification. However, it also shows that ISO certification can promote this culture and that the motivation for seeking certification would determine which comes first: the quality culture or ISO 9000 certification. Terziovski and Power (2007) developed a four-quadrant model for ISO-certified organizations to provide a framework for the analysis of client organizations in terms of quality culture and ISO 9000 benefits on a stratified basis. This stratification was based on the premise that organizations' quality culture goes through a process of maturing over time. The division was based on whether the quality culture of the organization was assessed as being strong or weak. It was found that organizations which seek ISO 9000 certification with a proactive approach driven by a continuous improvement strategy are more likely to derive significant business benefits as a result.

Ab Wahid et al. (2011) examined the ISO 9001 implementation and maintenance in service organizations and found that organizations implement ISO 9001 for various reasons. Some certified organizations implement it just for the sake of obtaining a certificate and therefore they do not recognize the potential of ISO 9001 as a foundation for continuous improvement and excellence. As a result, they fail to capitalize on the efforts required to achieve certification. Therefore, their learning from the implementation of ISO 9001, which can be considered as a tool of organizational development, is not sustainable. On the other hand, others seemed to have thrive and progress significantly beyond the standard as these organizations embrace the culture of continuous improvement. In the context of organizational learning, organizations which conceptualize ISO 9001 as a platform to business excellence through continuous improvement, ISO 9001 will provide them with a significant learning exercise (Ab Wahid, 2019). The following presents the implementation, influence, and impact of culture on quality systems at several higher learning organizations.

## Case Example: Quality Culture Development in a Large Malaysian University

In general, to be successful, organizations must have shared vision of a desired future state and proactive culture. Before it can be done, a university, for example, is expected to understand its organizational context as specified by Clause 4.1 of ISO 9001:2015. It must be able to identify risks and opportunities and have the willingness and capacity to learn and understand that all change involves learning.

Ab Wahid (2012) found that the main challenges faced by organizations in maintaining its ISO 9001 QMS are trying to introduce changes for improvement, and changing people's attitude and behavior. These two challenges must be overcome to motivate and obtain support and commitment from people in the organization. At one of the universities in Kenya, some of the challenges faced by the university in sustaining its QMS are in terms of inadequate people's involvement and commitment from some faculty and staff (Moturi and Mbithi, 2015). In Ireland, the quality management implementation process of one of the universities utilized a number of strategies to bring about cultural change; the strategies focused on information, systematic analysis, measurement, and internal audits.

Ab Wahid (2019) examined a large public university in Malaysia that underwent four phases of QMS: initiation; internalization; alignment; and improvement over the span of more than 20 years. Throughout the 20-year period, the culture of quality within the university evolved with the maturity of its QMS. A number of strategies were adopted to bring about cultural change to the university. The strategies included: building capacity through training of quality managers, internal auditors, academics, and staff; setting the objectives with key performance indicators and measures; having a yearly improvement project cycle; conducting integrated internal audits; and bestowing award and recognition to staff. During the *initiation phase*, there was not much change observed in terms of culture. Culture change is considered a central component of an effective QMS implementation. Although researchers observed that quality improvement in higher education rarely happens if it is imposed, the university during its *internalization phase*, had managed to embed some aspects of quality culture through various training and workshops on QMS related matters. Commitment from top management, academics, and staff was obtained once quality culture became embedded within the university. Once the strategies were deployed, top management of the university displayed their commitment by developing and communicating the university's vision, mission, goals, policy, and objectives university-wide. In an organization with many layers like the university, involvement and participation on a large scale can be a problem. Top management commitment to the culture and climate, shared trust, motivation, and support for the QMS, demonstrated through provision of the necessary resources is critical for the success of ISO 9001 implementation in the university.

Further, people at the university started working in teams to continuously improve the QMS and this improvement culture can be observed during the *alignment* and *improvement* phases of the QMS. Participation and involvement from academics and staff came in the form of their engagement in the quality system and its processes, where they are willing to participate in quality improvement and enhancement activities of the university.

For quality transformation to take place, the university found that relying on the hard dimensions of ISO 9001 such as training, management review, internal audits, and measurement of KPIs is not enough. The soft dimension such as communication and employee participation and teamwork are important to bring about cultural change. Good communication is a prerequisite for a meaningful and effective implementation and maintenance of ISO 9001 in an organization. Good communication will prevent miscommunication, misunderstanding, and poor morale from the staff and creates a sense of importance, urgency, and belonging to the university's overall quality system.

The study shows that a strong quality culture is critical to sustain the ISO 9001 implementation and culture affects the success of quality management practices. Without a strong quality culture, people will not be ready to commit and involve themselves fully in maintaining the QMS. During the course of implementation and maintenance of ISO 9001, top management behavior and the emergent culture must become consistent over time with the quality system philosophy or people will become cynical (Ab Wahid et al., 2011). In short, organizational culture should be compatible with the quality values.

---

## DISCUSSION

Based on these studies, the following model can be posited showing the interactive relationship between organizational culture and quality management models (see Figure 2.1). Drawing on systems theory, the model depicts the organization as existing within its environment. The environment can be widely interpreted, and might include a region, a country, or (for a multinational) several countries. For our purposes, let us assume the organization to be a single organizational entity operating in a single (homogenous) national cultural context. That organization may or may not be part of a wider organization or supply chain. The discontinuous boundary of the organization suggests that it is semi-permeable (like

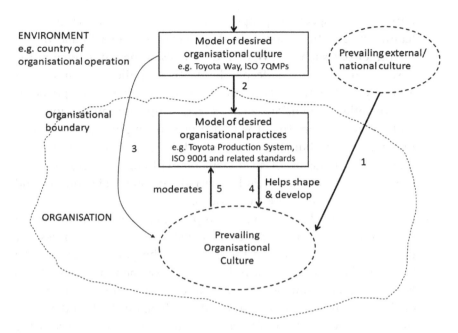

**FIGURE 2.1**
Conceptual model illustrating the relationships between national culture, organizational culture, and management models.

a cell wall), capable of both influencing, and being influenced by, its environment.

The following system elements and relationships are depicted in the model. The numbering below relates to the numbering of relationships between elements within Figure 2.1.

- The prevailing culture of the region or nation exerts a causal impact directly on organizational culture (arrow 1, e.g., Cray and Mallory, 1998; Low and Chapman, 2003). For example, in most cases (not all), a large proportion of the employees will live locally and emanate from the local culture. Exceptions may be those organizations that prefer to "import" their own workforces. The organizational culture will not influence the local culture sufficiently to merit illustration via a bi-directional arrow, although it can be realistically envisaged that many organizations will have some degree of impact on their local communities.
- Corporate Senior Management may desire a particular organizational culture to be in place. This might be a quality culture, lean thinking

philosophy, respect for people, anti-bullying, anti-discrimination, teamwork, etc. To achieve this, they may deploy a particular model or framework such as TW or ISO 7QMPs, aimed at achieving the desired culture at the deeper level. These philosophical models arguably exist for that very purpose, otherwise, what *is* their purpose? Clearly, other dimensions such as leadership, communication, and management commitment will also play an important role in this implementation, but that is not considered part of our (simplified) model. The inclusion of such elements will create a very complex model, as then we must include external and internal facilitators and barriers, which are many and various.

- To achieve the desired change, Top management also deploys a practice-based model (TPS or ISO 9001) to create the necessary behaviors and systems "on the ground." The philosophical model becomes the necessary cultural condition for the practice model to be effective. For example, TPS relies and builds upon the foundation of the TW, and ISO 9001 relies and builds upon the foundation of the seven QMPs. While the conceptual model may underpin the practice-based model, deployment is normally via the practice-based model. So an arrow (2) flows from cultural model to practice model, another (3) flows from cultural model directly to organizational culture, and another (4) flows from practice model to organizational culture.

- Organizational culture is shaped and impacted by the practice-based models, but it also impacts on the model requiring it to be fine-tuned in many cases. So there exists a two-way relationship (arrow 5) to account for local adaptations such as that discovered by Wagner et al. (2017).

---

## CONCLUSION

Research-based literature indicates that general organizational systems, such as quality systems, can be influenced by organizational culture and by national culture (acting through organizational culture). Conversely, organizational culture can be shaped by management models and practices such as ISO 9001 and its underpinning cultural prerequisites, such as the seven ISO Quality Management Principles and the PDCA cycle.

In the Malaysian university example presented herein, implementing ISO 9001 has effectively promoted and facilitated a quality culture which is in contrast with the long held anecdotal view that the development of a strong quality culture should precede ISO 9000 implementation and certification. This was due to the contrast between the quality management system approach and what the people in the university were accustomed to. So the culture change took some time to happen as the people needed time to overcome the past cultural influence and to embrace the new culture. The possibility of a mismatch between the quality system and the culture of the university was a risk that could reduce the effectiveness of ISO 9001. However, as ISO 9001 itself provides a set of requirements that can help standardize practice, it therefore alleviates the effect of culture on the effectiveness of a quality management system. Managers need to take into account the peculiarities of the culture they are dealing with, to make occasional fine-tuning adjustments to the practice models to ensure that strong cultural traits do not cause the desired organizational practices to be derailed.

In this chapter, we have presented a new model that illustrates the interactive, circular relationship between organizational culture and management models that aim to shape, but are also influenced by, that culture.

## REFERENCES

Ab Wahid, R. (2012) "Beyond certification: A proposed framework for ISO 9000 maintenance in service," *The TQM Journal*, Vol. 24, No. 6, pp. 556–568.

Ab Wahid, R. (2019) "Sustaining ISO 9001-based QMS in higher education: A reality?" *The TQM Journal*, doi:10.1108/TQM-12-2018-0185.

Ab Wahid, R., Corner, J. and Tan, P.L. (2011) "ISO 9000 maintenance in service organisations: Tales from two companies," *International Journal of Quality & Reliability Management*, Vol. 28, No. 7, pp. 735–757.

Ababneh, R.I. (2010) "The role of organizational culture on practising quality improvement in Jordanian public hospitals," *Leadership in Health Services*, Vol. 23, No. 3, pp. 244–259.

Bounds, G., Yorks, L., Adams, M. and Ranney, G. (1994) *Total Quality Management: Towards the Emerging Paradigm*, McGraw-Hill, NY .

Bradley, K. and Hill, S. (1983) "'After Japan': The quality circle transplant and productive efficiency," *British Journal of Industrial Relations*, Vol. 21, pp. 291–311.

Chiarini, A., Baccarani, C. and Mascherpa, V. (2018) "Lean production, Toyota Production System and Kaizen philosophy: A conceptual analysis from the perspective of Zen Buddhism," *The TQM Journal*, Vol. 30, No. 4, pp. 425–438.

Cray, D. and Mallory, G.R. (1998) *Making Sense of Managing Culture*, Thomson Business Press, London.

Dale, B.G., Van De Wiele, T. and Van Iwaarden, J. (2016) *Managing Quality*, 5th Ed., Wiley-Blackwell, U.K.

Edward, D.W.. (1986) *Out of the Crisis* , MIT Press, Cambridge, MA.

Evans, J.R. and Lindsay, W.M. (2005) *The Management and Control of Quality*, 5th Ed., International Thomson Publishing.

Fischer, R. and Derham, C. (2016) "Is in-group bias culture-dependent? A meta-analysis across 18 societies," *SpringerPlus*, Vol. 5, p. 70.

Flynn, B.B. (1992) "Managing for Quality in the US and in Japan," *Interfaces*, Vol. 22, No. 5, pp. 69–80.

Garvin, D. (1988) *Managing Quality*, Free Press, New York, NY.

Goetsch, D.L. and Davis, S. (2014) *Quality Management for Organizational Excellence: Introduction to Total Quality*, Pearson Education Limited Essex, England.

Harry, M. (1998) "Six Sigma – A breakthrough strategy for profitability," *Quality Progress*, Vol. 31, No. 5, pp. 60–64, Milwaukee, WI.

Hill, S. (1991) Why quality circles failed but Total Quality Management might succeed, *British Journal of Industrial Relations*, Vol. 29, No. 4, pp. 541–568.

Hind, M. (1996) "Are the cultures required to attain ISO 9000 and total quality management mutually exclusive?" *Training for Quality*, Vol. 4, No. 2.

Hofstede, G. (1997) *Cultures and Organisations: Software of the Mind*, McGraw-Hill, New York, NY.

Hong, G.Y. and Goh, T.N. (2003) "Six Sigma in software quality," *The TQM Magazine*, Vol. 15, No. 6, pp. 364–373.

Imai, M. (1986) *Kaizen: The Key to Japan's Competitive Success*, Random House, p. 60.

ISO. (2015) *Quality Management Principles*, International Organization for Standardization, Geneva, Switzerland, ISBN:978-92-67-10650-2.

ISO 9001:2015. (2015) *Quality Management Systems – Requirements*, International Organization for Standardization, Geneva, Switzerland.

Jayamaha, N.P., Grigg, N.P. and Pallawala, N.M. (2017) "The effect of uncertainty avoidance on lean implementation: A cross cultural empirical study involving Toyota," IEEE International Conference on Industrial Engineering and Engineering Management (IEEM), Singapore, pp. 436–440.

Jayamaha, N.P., Wagner, J.P. and Grigg, N.P. (2014) "The moderation effect of the cultural dimension 'Individualism/Collectivism' on Toyota Way deployment – A global study on Toyota facilities," IEEE *International Conference on Industrial Engineering and Engineering Management*, Malaysia, December 9–12.

Jick, T.D. (1993) *Managing Change: Cases & Concept*, Irwin, Boston, MA.

Joseph, C. Rodeand Xiaowen Huang and Barbara Flynn. (2016) "A cross-cultural examination of the relationships among human resource management practices and organisational commitment: An institutional collectivism perspective," *Human Resource Management Journal*, Vol. 26, No. 4, pp. 471–489.

Kats, M.M.S., Hetty Van Emmerik, I.J., Blenkinsopp, J. and Khapova, S.N. (2010) "Exploring the associations of culture with careers and the mediating role of HR practices: A conceptual model," *Career Development International*, Vol. 15, No. 4, pp. 401–418.

Kaye, M. and Anderson, R. (1999) "Continuous improvement: The ten essential criteria," *International Journal of Quality and Reliability Management*, Vol. 16, No. 5, pp. 485–506.

Liker, J.K. and Morgan, J.M. (2006) "The Toyota way in services: The case of lean product development," *Academy of Management Perspectives*, Vol. 20, No. 2.

Low, David and Chapman, Ross. (2003) "Organisational and national culture: A study of overlap and interaction in the literature," *International Journal of Employment Studies*, Vol. 11, No. 1, pp. 55–75, 21.

Moen, R.D. and Norman, C.L. (2010) "Circling back: Clearing up the myths about the Deming cycle and seeing how it keeps evolving," Quality Progress, November, pp. 22–28.

Moturi, C. and Mbithi, P. (2015)"ISO 9001:2008 implementation and impact on the University of Nairobi: A case study," *The TQM Journal*, Vol. 27, No. 6, pp. 752–760.

Naor, M., Goldstein, S.M., Linderman, K.W. and Schroeder, R.G. (2008) "The role of culture as driver of quality management and performance: Infrastructure versus core quality practices," *Decision Sciences*, Vol. 39, No. 4, pp. 671–701.

Pallawala, N.M., Jayamaha, N.P. and Grigg, N.P. (2017a) "Testing the validity of the ISO 9001:2015 process model in South Asian vis a vis Australasian manufacturing context," *17th* ANZAM Operations, Supply Chain *and* Services Management *Symposium*, Brisbane, Australia, July 13–14.

Pallawala, N.M., Jayamaha, N.P. and Grigg, N.P. (2017b) "Validating the theoretical underpinnings of the ISO 9001:2015 quality management system standard: A cross cultural perspective," *15th* ANZAM Operations, Supply Chain *and* Services Management *Symposium*, Queenstown, New Zealand, June 13–14.

Saad, G.H. and Siha, S. (2000) "Managing quality: Critical links and a contingency model," *International Journal of Operations and Production Management*, Vol. 20, No. 10, pp. 1146–1164.

Schein, E.H. (1997) *Organizational Culture and Leadership*, Jossey-Bass, San Francisco, CA.

Schroeder, R.G., Linderman, K., Liedtke, C. and Choo, A.S. (2008) "Six Sigma: Definition and underlying theory," *Journal of Operations Management*, Vol. 26, No. 4, pp. 536–554.

Scoville, R. and Little, K. (2014) *Comparing Lean and Quality Improvement*. IHI White Paper, Institute for Healthcare Improvement, Cambridge, MA (Available at ihi. org).

Seddon, J. (2005) *Freedom from Command and Control: A Better Way to Make the Work Work*, Productivity Press, New York, NY.

Terziovski, M. and Power, D. (2007) "Increasing ISO 9000 certification benefits: A continuous improvement approach," *International Journal of Quality & Reliability Management*, Vol. 24, No. 2, pp. 141–163.

Terziovski, M., Power, D. and Sohal, A.S. (2003) "The longitudinal effects of the ISO 9000 certification process on business performance," *European Journal of Operational Research*, Vol. 146, No. 3, May 1, pp. 580–595.

Wagner, J.P., Grigg, N.P., Mann, R.S. and Mohammad, M.M. (2017) "High task interdependence: Job rotation and other approaches for overcoming ingroup favoritism," *Journal of Manufacturing Technology Management*, Vol. 28, No. 4, pp. 485–505.

# 3

## Building Ethical Cultures in the Gulf Construction Sector: Implications on Corporations' Quality Management

*Froilan T. Malit, Jenny Knowles Morrison, and Kristian Alexander*

## CONTENTS

---

## INTRODUCTION

Organizational culture is "shared beliefs of an organization's members, hence the ethical culture of an organization would be reflected in the beliefs about the ethics of an organization which are shared by its members" (Key, 1999, p.217). These ethical cultural values, behaviors, and practices (i.e., integrity, fairness, honesty, transparency) are not only practiced but also promoted within the organization and beyond. In a globalized, multidiverse workforce, Key (1999, p.217) additionally suggests that "it is logical to conceptualize the ethics of different organizations as existing on a continuum bounded at one end by unethical companies and at the other, highly ethical companies." In the context of the Asia-Gulf migration corridor, these two types of ethical and unethical entities widely exist, whereby ethical multinational corporations (MNCs) often comply with national and international labor standards, while simultaneously emphasizing the overall rights and welfare of migrant workers. Conversely, unethical MNCs often violate both national and international labor standards utilizing various techniques to undermine the rights and welfare of migrant workers, thus undermining the overall quality of management within these organizations.

Furthermore, Gulf-based construction MNCs have increasingly received global attention due to unethical recruitment practices, which are perceived to have become integrated within both the organizations' and industries' culture.* These include, but are not limited to, the imposition of excessive recruitment/placement fees beyond the law, debt bondage, slave-like working or living conditions, non-payment of, or illegal deduction of salary (Jureidini, 2014; Segall and Labowitz, 2017; Human Rights Watch, 2006; Amnesty International, 2018; IOM, 2017). These types of unethical business practices support the creation of foundational elements, leading to the building of an unethical culture of recruitment, which has evolved into a region-wide ecosystem of unethical recruitment practices (CORE, 2016; Jureidini, 2016).

To an extent, individual Gulf-based MNCs have—either directly or indirectly—entrenched an entire regional corridor in inefficient and

---

* Unethical recruitment is defined as a "deception regarding employment terms and conditions, illegal or unethical placement fees charged to foreign contract workers, unexplained fees and costs, lack of transparency, and workplace practices such as passport retention and "runaway insurance" deposits" (UNODC, 2015: 21).

unethical business practices that have a significant impact on quality management and excellence, as well as on migrant rights and welfare. Examining the intricacies of these unethical cultures among construction MNCs operating within the Asia-Gulf migration corridor provides new questions about global ethical compliance levels, standards, and practices in the supply chain recruitment practices, as well as provides insights into the implications on long-term quality management and business competitiveness for academics, policymakers, and business leaders in the long run.

To put the issue of ethical culture and its impact on quality management and excellence into context, high-performing Gulf-based construction MNCs have faced social, economic, and legal threats from local, regional, and global stakeholders, including challenges from striking migrant construction workers. These forces have significantly undermined business operations, excellence, and reputations globally. The issues driving such actions are complex. In 2013, the *Financial Times* reported that UAE-based contractor, Arabtec confronted massive pressures from the "thousands of workers, demanding pay increases on their monthly salaries of $160–$200 ... refused to leave their accommodation—known locally as labor camps—on the outskirts of Dubai for a third day. The rampant inflation that accompanied Dubai's last construction frenzy prompted outbursts of labor unrest as workers demanded better pay and conditions" (Kerr, 2013). In 2013, the International Trade Union Confederation (ITUC) reported 1,239 deaths of migrant construction workers in Qatar, while others estimated close to 2,000 migrant construction workers in preparation for the World Cup 2022 (Stephenson, 2015). In 2010, Saudi-based construction MNC, Al-Arab Contracting Co faced major labor protests from more than 200 overseas Filipino migrant construction workers, who listed as their grievance "delayed salaries, illegal deductions, and non-payment of overtime" (Ferris-Lay, 2010). These labor cases reflect some outcomes of the unethical corporate practices in the origin countries' recruitment practices. Most significantly, they highlight the industry-wide failure of construction MNCs in the Gulf to execute contractual obligations to migrant construction workers, raising fundamental questions about the role of ethical culture within their global recruitment practices. Unpacking specific case exemplars provides new insights to these questions, which have implications for overall quality management, the achievement of organizational excellence, and industry performance on the whole.

This paper broadly examines the growing presence of unethical culture in the Asia-Gulf migration recruitment corridor and how it both: a) impacts the quality management of Gulf-based construction MNCs; and b) weakens their global market status and excellence in the long run. Using the concepts of globalization, ethical culture, and quality management perspectives, we argue that unethical culture in the Asia-Gulf migration recruitment corridor does not only impact the quality management of Gulf-based construction MNCs but also negatively weakens their global status and potential investment returns in the long run. The selected cases of construction MNCs in the Gulf countries, combined with secondary policy literature, further illuminate the multilevel drivers of unethical recruitment practices on quality management and consequences for innovation of construction Gulf-based MNCs in the long run.

We divide the paper into four sections. First, we contextualize the unethical culture in the Asia-Gulf migration conceptually by identifying and analyzing the market context, as well as exemplars of unethical culture within the global recruitment practices of Gulf-based construction MNCs. Second, we frame the complex linkages between globalization, ethical culture, and quality management to explain the effects of unethical culture on quality management and performance among high-performing MNCs. Third, we examine the specific drivers, as well as potential determinants necessary to enable construction MNCs to develop more ethical cultures to drive recruitment practices. Fourth, we investigate the implications of creating an ethical culture on quality management and excellence, while the concluding section highlights the future scenarios and impacts of unethical culture on the quality management, excellence, and performance of construction MNCs operating in the Gulf region.

## ETHICAL CULTURE AND LABOR UNDER GLOBALIZATION

Globalization is a deterritorialization process which "diminishes the necessity of a common shared territorial basis for social, economic, and political activities, processes, and relations" (Crane and Matten, 2010, p.19). In the era of intense competition and globalized market, the strategic survival of MNCs depends on their dynamic ability to enhance their competitive advantage in the global market and focus on important factors such as technological capability, product quality, adherence to standards, and access to a supply chain of human capital/labor in a globalized world. In order to achieve superior business performance and innovation, MNCs business operations have also increasingly transformed their operations from national to global levels. Such entities are often expected to address complex organizational responsibilities, specifically the ethical culture and climate as a critical feature of their global operational processes.* Globalization thus has not only critical implications for business ethics, but also raises fundamental questions about the complex and multilevel roles and functions of MNCs operating in multiple countries with varying laws, cultures, and accountability levels in a globalized world.

Ardichvili and Jondle (2009) further describes ethical cultures within business operations as:

> based on an alignment between formal structures, processes, policies, training and development programs, consistent value-based ethical behavior of top leadership, informal recognition of heroes, stories, and the use of rituals, metaphors and language that inspire organizational members to behave in a manner consistent with high ethical standards (p.415).

As MNC operations become more globalized and less fixed territorially, they are often confronted with complex and diverse conflicting ethical dilemmas. In particular, MNCs are expected to adopt more organizational ethical standards and culture in their internal and external business operations (Schein, 2010; Martin, 1992, 2002; Frost et al., 1991). Therefore, the ethics of different organizations not only builds critical global values and standards but are a vital driver in securing a global reputation and competitiveness in the long run. Although MNCs under globalization have, to a large extent, led to deterritorialization (i.e., subcontract or outsource) of their operations, and as such constructed a more "uniform culture," it also reveals the contradictory logic of globalization, as well as the governing social, economic, and cultural variations that often generate a complex ethical dilemma for MNCs operating in the host country

---

* In the UAE and other GCC countries, MNCs have strategically established their business operations in free zone companies due to flexible legal structures that enable them to achieve greater business competitiveness, constituting a large part of the country's diversified economic strategy. They also receive full benefits including but not limited to full foreign ownership of the business that has encouraged commercial values, foreign direct investment, entrepreneurialism, and higher employment rates (King, 2017).

(At-Twaijri and Al-Muhaiza, 1996). For example, Gulf-based construction MNCs may benefit from the "loopholes in legislation and weak enforcement [which] have perpetuated the misery of these site operatives. South Asian countries try to manage labor migration but avoid over-regulation [toward Gulf countries] because of much-needed remittances" (Abdul-Aziz et al., 2018, p.165). Thus, the varying comparative legal cultures between sending and receiving countries can influence the degree of global labor standard compliance and ethical practices across cultures.

While cultural variations across countries exist globally, the globalized nature of MCNs' operations also engenders legal dilemmas, as they escape the domestic sovereign control of their respective national governments through their economic transactions in new geographic locations. Although existing studies suggest that ethical culture has the transformative capacity to ethically guide organizations' individual and institutional complex operations (i.e., people, processes, operations) in a more globalized world (Key, 1999; Ardichvili and Jondle, 2009), MNCs face complex legal compliance dilemmas given the differential legal cultures and expectations across countries. Since the state government's power has been traditionally confined at the "national" level, there are significant changes across international borders in the legal framework in which MNCs must operate, thus potentially impacting their ethical decision-making process within their global business practices.

As Crane and Matten (2010) acknowledge, "business ethics largely begins where the law ends, then deterritorialization increases the demand for business ethics because deterritorialized economic activities are beyond the control of national (territorial) governments." Key (1999) argues that an organization's ethical culture can influence individual cognitive processes and provides clues to how people decide to act in ethical situations within organizations. Valentine et al. (2002, p.349) suggests that the organizational establishment and promotion of an ethical context "might enhance employees' workplace experiences. Companies should also consider adopting ethical policies that support principled conduct, punish unethical actions, and increase individual perceptions of an ethical company environment."

Ardichvili and Jondle (2009) further emphasize the "moral leadership" of leaders as a vital element in establishing the organizations' ethical climate and culture. They also highlight the strategic importance of addressing formal compliance requirements, identification of vital corporate values, and their alignment to the governing organizational culture and values.

Therefore, the growing deterritorialization of MNC operations against the backdrop of globalization does not only erode state government capacity to regulate their behaviors, but also raises fundamental questions about the moral and ethical responsibilities of MNCs to embody organizational ethical culture as a long-term operational, strategic, and dynamic approach of the organizations in a globalized environment.

Furthermore, as the economic transactions of MNCs become more deterritorialized and globalized, state governments often struggle to govern and control MNCs' dynamic business practices and operations across various geographic locations. The eroding capacity of state institutions has increased the call from international rights activist organizations to reinforce the expanding corporate accountability of MNCs operating in countries with extremely weak legal institutions and cultures (Farooqi et al., 2017). As MNCs globalize their business operations, their global corporate accountably also increases, as does their moral responsibility to uphold and comply with national and international laws. While upholding corporate accountability and ethical culture has positive implications within MNCs (Blome and Paulraj, 2013; Shafer and Simmons, 2011), Gulf Cooperation Council (GCC)-based MNCs have largely remained weak in enforcing certain corporate welfare responsibilities (i.e., mandatory training, health insurance, upskilling) related to migrant labor in the construction sector. This study examines the effects of unethical culture on quality management by analyzing the drivers, pressures, and implications of unethical culture on construction MNCs in the Gulf region.

## RESEARCH DESIGN

This exploratory case investigates the broader industry of construction MNCs in Gulf countries, highlighting how their global dependency on migrant foreign labor has not only challenged their ethical business practices and decision-making, but also illuminates multilevel struggles found between, and among, principal migration stakeholders operating in the Asia-Gulf migration corridor. While a growing body of policy and media publications have focused on the negative effects of unethical cultural practices among Gulf-based construction MNCs (see the Business and Human Rights Resource Centre), they often fail to empirically examine and unpack the complex market and state dynamics in which construction MNCs operate in a globalized market.

The selection and identification of information-rich cases of construction MNCs in the Gulf have been purposively sampled to theoretically illustrate how unethical culture can have negative contributions to the quality management and business competitiveness of Gulf-based construction MNCs in the long run (Palinkas et al., 2016; Creswell, 2009). Using public reports (i.e., news media and policy reports) related to the Gulf construction sector, we identified several Gulf-based construction MNCs that heavily recruit, source, and hire their migrant labor workers from South Asian countries, specifically India and Pakistan. These construction MNCs do not only principally rely on their transnational recruitment practices to continuously maintain their infrastructure development operations, but also have been linked to various national and regional disputes with migrant workers due to their weak national and regional compliance to fundamental national and international labor standards.

These Gulf-based construction MNCs are considered large in size, employing between 10,000 and 40,000 foreign workers (and in some cases more), depending on the projects. They also have massive infrastructure project developments and hold a common set of characteristics, specifically their weak compliance and enforcement of national and international labor laws, limited corporate social responsibility which has methodologically formed the basis for the case selection, and their heavy negative publicity related to unethical practices in migrant recruitment practices (Suri, 2011). The critical basis for selecting these Gulf-based construction MNCs mainly come from the actual unethical practices that have been heavily publicized in various local, regional, and global newspapers and reports. With such particularly rich convenience samples and cases of unethical practices, we therefore draw our empirical and theoretical analysis from these publicly recorded data and attempt to explain the overall impacts of unethical culture on the quality of management in the long run.

This case study attempts to fill in this gap by highlighting how globalization has posed unique and dynamic challenges to construction MNCs and governments. It has also illuminated how their deterritorialized migrant recruitment approach has manifested cultural, legal, and accountability issues linked to national and international labor standards, which are critical to developing long-term, highly ethical business standards in a globalized market.

## CONTEXTUALIZING THE UNETHICAL CULTURE IN THE CONSTRUCTION MNCs IN THE ASIA-GULF MIGRATION CORRIDOR

In the Asia-Gulf migration corridor, Gulf-based construction MNCs constitute a large share of the Gulf economy, contributing at least USD $130 billion in construction projects in 2017, compared with USD $100 billion in construction projects in 2016 (John, 2018). Figure 3.1 suggests that construction project rewards totaled USD $63 billion in 2017, which is 21% down from the USD $76 billion contracts signed in 2016 (Thompson, 2018). A regional business intelligence report, MEED, emphasizes that "the market is changing and, at the start of 2018, the outlook was improving rapidly for the Gulf construction industry" (Ibid, 2018, p.1). While the sudden economic decline in 2017 had direct negative impacts on construction MNCs, the projected government contract awards and projects indicate upward economic prospects for the construction sector in the Gulf. The rising oil prices in the Gulf region, along with new megaprojects in Saudi Arabia, Dubai, and Abu Dhabi linked to their Vision 2030 (Expo 2020 in Dubai) economic restructuring initiatives, and growing Gulf construction and transport investments could play an essential role in expanding economic opportunities for construction

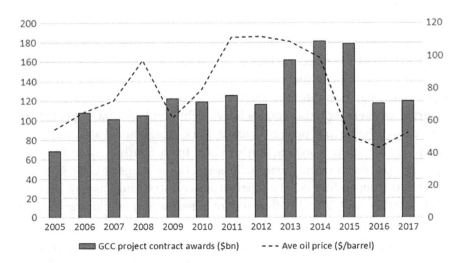

**FIGURE 3.1**
GCC project contract awards versus average oil price. Source: MEED Projects

MNCs.* The large mega infrastructure projects demand a complex form of recruitment processes and international collaboration with recruitment institutions in the Asian origin countries. These recruitment agencies often capitalize on migrant workers' vulnerabilities, producing an unethical nature of recruitment within the supply chain. Therefore, Gulf-based construction MNCs are key private sector actors in the Gulf economy with complex global corporate responsibilities and challenges in managing and governing large numbers of migrant construction workers, particularly those from Asian origin countries.

First, many Gulf-based companies do not pay for any recruitment costs, and often the agency/subagencies collect the payments from workers, creating an unethical culture of "contractual deception" in the initial migrant recruitment phase (Segall and Labowitz, 2017; Jureidini, 2017). The United Nations' *Global Compact on Safe, Orderly, and Regular Migration* (GCM) calls on migration stakeholders, specifically the private sector/ multinational corporations, to "facilitate fair and ethical recruitment and safeguard conditions [of migrant workers] that ensure decent work" (United Nations, 2018, p.13). In particular, the GCM further states:

> prohibits recruiters and employers from charging or shifting recruitment fees or related costs to migrant workers in order to prevent debt bondage, exploitation, and forced labor, including by establishing mandatory, enforceable mechanisms for effective regulation and monitoring of the recruitment industry.

By knowingly transacting with such agents/subagents, construction MNCs engage in unethical or illegal recruitment transactions, and commit industry code of conduct violations within their global supply chain operations. Furthermore, the recruitment cost is not only shifted to the migrant workers, but also creates heavy debt bondage that impacts their overall well-being and performance at work. Segall and Labowitz (2017) found that migrant construction workers from South Asia to the Gulf typically pay recruitment costs, on average, in the range of USD $400 and USD $700, depending on the destination country. Indians pay between USD $1,000 and USD $3,000 to secure construction employment in the

---

* Some reports, however, suggest a growing slowdown in the UAE construction sector, but with the hosting of Dubai Expo 2020, it could potentially lift the industry with little growth potential for the sector due to critical factors, including limited project activity, low house prices, and government fiscal restraint capping growth (Fitch Solutions, 2019).

Gulf, while others like Bangladeshis pay up to USD $5,200 to the agents or subagents (Starbird, 2017). Another study also indicates such high debt incurred in the recruitment process often leads to mental depression, thus influencing some construction workers to abscond from their employers or commit suicide (Verite, 2016). The heavy debt, often financed by selling material possessions (i.e., cows, jewelry, house), often becomes a critical daily financial pressure for the migrant working for high-performing construction MNCs in the Gulf, in tandem with obligations to their families in the origin countries.

Under International Labor Organization (ILO) conventions, employers are mandated under national Gulf laws and international conventions to pay for recruitment fees. However, the reality is that most construction MNCs often do not pay because recruitment agencies or subagents offer to shift all or part of the recruitment costs to prospective migrant construction workers, in order to secure a contract. In some cases, some MNCs mandate recruitment agencies or subagencies to maintain a zero recruitment cost for employers, thus shifting the recruitment costs fully to migrant construction workers. Such individual corporate actions create a widespread culture of unethical recruitment, in direct violation of Gulf labor laws and international conventions. Further, such actions highlight more structural legal gaps that empower construction MNCs to operate outside the boundaries of the governing law.

Second, the substandard living conditions (i.e., overcrowding) of migrant construction workers in some Gulf countries—offered and paid by construction MNCs—have also increasingly received an international spotlight. Multiple field reports highlight the squalid unsanitary living accommodations of migrant workers in these Gulf labor camps, which directly impact their overall health and living conditions (Segall and Labowitz, 2017; Jureidini, 2017). The high presence of contractual labor violations among construction MNCs has, in turn, influenced various transnational labor rights groups (i.e., ITUC, Amnesty International, Human Rights Watch) to directly force Gulf countries to address migrant construction workers' living conditions. In Qatar, Jureidini (2014) highlighted how the Qatari government legislatively mandated subcontracting companies linked to construction MNCs—specifically those operating under the Qatar Foundation system— to follow certain ethical guidelines and codes of conducts on how to deal with migrant workers' living, working, and recruitment conditions. In addition, global pressures from the international sports community also appear to have influenced the Qatari government to sign a technical working agreement between Qatar and the ILO to eradicate problems surrounding the migrant labor living and working conditions in Qatar and across the Gulf. Some critiques, however, highlight that such labor market reforms in Qatar's use of the labor supply chain in origin countries were mainly derived from the political "pressures" from the World Cup, and may only (or may not) act as a temporary political response to global criticisms from the international community. Therefore, there is a need to codify case specific experiences into a national or regional best practice case, which is also an essential step in determining state commitment toward migrant labor and quality management in the long run.

Third, the working conditions of migrant construction workers are another crucial factor that often creates an exploitative culture in construction MNCs in Gulf countries. In fact, the long working hours and mobility restrictions embedded in the Gulf countries' *Kafala* Sponsorship Program were often highlighted to be a major factor for the ongoing labor and human rights exploitations faced by migrant workers working in construction MNCs in Gulf countries. Some argue that the failure to establish a minimum wage for migrant workers does not only violate international labor violations but also systematically generates a culture of labor market exploitation and bondage in the Gulf labor markets. While some Gulf countries like Qatar have introduced new minimum wage laws and abolished exit permits (written employer permission required by workers prior to traveling outside the country), others like the UAE have strongly liberalized the internal mobility laws in the labor market by eliminating labor bans (e.g., six months or one year) and enabling migrant workers, in general, to move easily to another employer. Gulf countries committed to such labor market reforms do not only slowly address the exploitative culture within construction MNCs operations, but also help enhance the overall working conditions and raise the collective consciousness of migrant construction workers regionally. These particular state efforts are essentially important to demonstrate attention to an ethical culture in the long run. With the unethical and illegal practices surrounding MNCs operations in the Asia-Gulf migration corridor, the following section attempts to explain the drivers of unethical culture rooted in the unethical business practices identified in the Gulf-based construction industry, and their implications on quality management and business competitiveness in the long run.

## DRIVERS OF UNETHICAL CULTURE IN THE ASIA-GULF MIGRATION CORRIDOR INDUSTRY

In the Gulf countries, three factors, including the lack of sovereign rights, weak enforcement and capacities of some Gulf states to enforce labor laws, and strong domestic resistance to reforms, have appeared to generate an exploitative space for construction MNCs to operate in the Asia-Gulf migration corridor.

First, the lack of sovereign rights among the Gulf countries to interfere in the growing unethical and illegal recruitment practices make it difficult to holistically monitor and govern the labor recruitment process in the labor-sending countries. This constraining factor enables construction MNCs to legally exploit such sovereign state limitations. In fact, these sovereign limitations call for stronger bilateral negotiations with sending countries. While the Colombo Process and Abu Dhabi Dialogue (ADD) have diplomatically attempted to address ways to control recruitment problems in the Gulf-Asia construction sector, there are, however, still no concrete bilateral or corridor-specific mandates or solutions, except for some pilot schemes. These include an ongoing ADD Pilot Project on Skills Recognition and Qualification Framework that attempts to understand the unethical and illegal recruitment practices, as well as the potential of mutual skills recognition and qualification frameworks to enhance workers' mobility, wages, and skills in the long run. This state sovereign limitation thus empowers Gulf-based construction MNCs to make unethical cultural practices uncontrollable and difficult.

Second, the lack of enforcement capacities of some Gulf states to implement their governing Gulf national labor laws within their own national labor markets—pertaining to recruitment regulations — has also been highlighted as a potential explanation for the continuing rise of recruitment violations in the construction sector (Jones, 2014; Jureidini, 2017). While certain labor legislation exists that specifically deals with the recruitment nature of construction work, the level of prosecutorial enforcement is allegedly weak due to the limited number of inspectors relative to the construction firms operating in the Gulf countries (Abdul-Aziz et al., 2018). Migrant construction workers, to an extent, often do not report the large excessive recruitment fees paid to local courts in the Gulf due to a fear of retaliation (i.e., deportation, threats, sanctions) from recruitment agencies or construction MNCs, thus furthering difficulties in utilizing existing legislative frameworks to make construction MNCs accountable for illegal or unethical practices (Jureidini, 2017; Segall and Labowitz, 2017; Human Rights Watch, 2006). This particular legal limitation thus makes it difficult to assess the accountability, transparency, and performance of some Gulf states in addressing various migrant labor issues in the construction MNC sector. This weak legal enforcement further reinforces unethical business practices that often affect not only state responsibility, but also the ethical and corporate responsibilities of Gulf-based construction MNCs in the long run.

Finally, the strong domestic resistance to reform in the Gulf countries' *Kafala* Sponsorship Program, combined with the weak enforcement of governing labor laws, has also created an enabling environment for construction MNCs to thrive in a highly unethical and exploitative recruitment environment in the sending countries (Abdul-Aziz et al., 2018; Jureidini, 2017). While some Gulf countries like the UAE use various economic rewards to incentivize firms to comply with national labor laws, the absence of a strong legal penalty system and prosecutions, along with the "transnational corruption culture" deeply rooted in the fee-charging system in origin and destination countries, exacerbate the migrant recruitment problems. It also guarantees a cheap, exploitable source of labor for construction MNCs in the Gulf countries and beyond (Jureidini, 2017). The construction MNCs' international recruitment operations and behaviors are not only conditioned by the Gulf and sending countries' regulatory enforcement levels, but also contribute to a thriving capitalist environment that exploits migrant workers and their families in the origin countries. In short, the embedded culture of corruption within the global labor recruitment practices, linked to Gulf-based construction MNCs, further deepens the unethical culture. This particular case can have negative implications on their quality management, performance, and competitiveness in the long run.

## MOVING TOWARD ETHICAL RECRUITMENT IN THE ASIA-GULF MIGRATION CORRIDOR

Using the selected public cases related to unethical cultural practices among construction MNCs in the Gulf, the following section highlights some of the complex and multilevel pressure points that could influence

Gulf-based construction MNCs to adopt more ethical cultural practices within their global labor recruitment practices in the Asia-Gulf migration corridor.

## Political Pressures: The Qatar World Cup 2022 Experience

Since securing the winning bid for the World Cup 2022, transnational rights groups have increasingly mobilized to force some Gulf countries, like Qatar, to respect global labor and human rights norms toward their treatment of migrant construction workers. The consistent global reporting from global rights groups (i.e., Amnesty International and Human Rights Watch) and media (i.e., *New York Times*, *The Guardian*), along with their proactive migration dialogues and roundtables in various migration consultative dialogues (both regionally and globally), have generated critical pressures. This has, in particular, generated critical pressures for Qatar to introduce new labor reforms (i.e., a minimum wage, mobility laws, domestic work) in accordance with international labor standards. Ongoing sociopolitical pressures may have potentially been a vital factor for the Qatari government to consider opening an ILO office in Doha and signing technical cooperation in order to address labor issues across various sectors. The "naming" and "shaming" strategies by transnational rights groups may have also triggered Qatar and the Gulf states to engage with some international organizations. The FIFA World Cup (2018) acknowledged their ongoing efforts to address construction workers' rights in Qatar:

> Since our last report, FIFA has stepped up its efforts to work in collaboration with the Local Organizing Committee (LOC) and other parties to the Memorandum of Understanding (MOU) supporting the decent work monitoring system. The Board recognizes the improved cooperation at the operational level between FIFA and the LOC and Building and Wood Workers' International (BWI) in particular; however, there is yet to be any formal public communication on jointly agreed results of the system (Business and Human Rights, 2018, p.2).

Thus, the political pressures of transnational rights groups acted not only as an essential global pressure to directly influence Gulf states' labor legislation, but also indirectly by influencing the construction MNC behavior. This represents a vital step in upholding the global rights and welfare of migrant construction workers in the Gulf countries.

## Legal Pressures: Global Civil Society Rights Advocacy's Legal Mechanisms

Global civil society groups like the ITUC and Migrant Rights have also played an essential role in deepening the ongoing global political and legal pressures on the Gulf countries. The ITUC, for example, consistently filed international complaints against Qatar, the UAE, and other Gulf countries for failing to address their migrant rights issues and initiated various labor rights campaigns to protect the rights and welfare of migrant construction workers. ILO has, in particular, also sanctioned Qatar by threatening to set up an ILO commission on an inquiry into alleged exploitation in the 2022 World Cup. However, the ILO immediately terminated the complaint after Qatar drastically passed major labor market reforms (Nebehay, 2017). Qatar, in turn, agreed to establish a technical working group with the ILO to bilaterally address migrant labor issues in the country.

The legal pressures (i.e., lawsuits) and public shaming at the international level may have become, to a large extent, a foundation for other international rights groups and academic institutions to further launch global labor rights campaigns to directly pressure the Gulf states. In fact, the international complaints and other cases simply legitimized rights groups' power to critique both the Gulf states and construction MNCs for not upholding national and international laws pertaining to migrant worker issues in the Gulf countries. This has also influenced the implementation of corporate codes of conduct to ensure the rights and welfare of migrant construction workers in the Gulf countries.

Global migration rights activists have also strategically exerted international political pressure on construction MNCs. The unethical and illegal recruitment practices of construction MNCs, in a similar fashion, collectively pressures Gulf governments and has had critical impacts on their global reputational image, perceptions, publicity, and status that could directly threaten their long-term return on investments and global investor relationships (ILO, 2016, 2017; Amnesty International, 2015). For instance, in 2013, the *Financial Times* reported that the UAE-based contractor, Arabtec, confronted massive pressures from the

> thousands of workers, demanding pay increases on their monthly salaries of $160–$200 ... refused to leave their accommodation—known locally as labor camps—on the outskirts of Dubai for a third day. The rampant inflation that accompanied Dubai's last construction frenzy prompted

outbursts of labor unrest as workers demanded better pay and conditions (Kerr, 2013, p.1).

Migrant deaths and workplace dangers are also significant challenges impacting construction MCNs' overall operations in the Gulf countries. In 2013, the ITUC reported 1,239 deaths of migrant construction workers in Qatar, while others estimated close to 2,000 migrant construction workers died in preparation for the World Cup 2022 (Stephenson, 2015).

In 2010, Saudi-based construction MNC, Al-Arab Contracting Co, faced major labor protests from more than 200 overseas Filipino migrant construction workers for complaints about "delayed salaries, illegal deductions, and non-payment of overtime" (Ferris-Lay, 2015, p.1). While these striking labor cases have clearly mirrored some of the corporate governance failures of Gulf-based construction MNCs, they further reinforce critical questions about the roles and impacts of unethical culture (i.e., "global shaming") on their corporate image, status, and competitiveness in the long run (Zhu and Chang, 2012; AliKhasabeh et al., 2014). Thus, the development of a collective voice through integration of global civil rights advocacy groups in the global labor recruitment discourse is not only an essential component of revitalizing an ethical culture in the Gulf construction industry, but also an influential area to exert stronger legal and public pressure for Gulf-based construction MNCs to uphold both international standards and corporate social responsibilities.

## Social Media Pressures

Virtual social media pressures, in some cases, can be another determining factor to influence construction MNCs in their effort to uphold and establish a fairer and equitable recruitment process system for their global recruitment operations in the Asia-Gulf migration corridor. While most international media pressures come from the West (UK, US, and other European countries), ongoing global social pressures and media reporting (e.g., fueled via Facebook, Twitter, etc.) have become a vital daily conduit for different transnational rights groups to bring forward various labor and human rights issues in the Gulf countries. For instance, Americans for Democracy and Human Rights in Bahrain, a Washington-based NGO which aims to "foster awareness of and support for human rights in

Bahrain and the Middle East," constantly supports the end of "#kafala" via Twitter (ADHRB, 2018).

Other labor and human rights groups, including Migrant-Rights. org, have also launched multiple social media campaigns to educate the broader public about the labor and human rights violations faced by migrant construction workers in the GCC region. These transnational activists often call for change in labor practices in Qatar, the UAE, and other GCC countries, indirectly targeting construction MNCs for their failure to uphold national and international laws pertaining to labor rights and welfare of migrant construction workers. In essence, the industry-specific social media pressures directed toward Gulf-based construction MNCs is not only becoming an emerging tool in enforcing ethical culture and standards within the construction business, but also a necessary mechanism to ensure strong global private sector compliance and state responsibility in the long run.

## Creating Diplomatic Space for Action: The Power of Regional Diplomacy Dialogues

Regional consultative dialogues can also be a vital diplomatic space to enable construction MNCs to consider fair and equitable migration recruitment models in the long run. In the context of the Asia-Gulf migration corridor, regional consultative dialogues on the management of overseas employment and contractual labor for countries of origins in Asia (the Colombo Process) and in the Gulf states (the Abu Dhabi Dialogue) have strongly recognized the need to promote fair and ethical recruitment as vital cornerstones of regional labor migration policies (Jones, 2014; Abu Dhabi Dialogue, 2016). The direct level state negotiation between Asian sending and Gulf receiving countries, specifically both during senior officials and ministerial level meetings, can collaboratively and strategically enable governments to develop regional policy solutions and initiatives (i.e., bilateral/multilateral pilot projects, commission studies) to better understand the unethical or illegal recruitment problems in the Gulf, and devise new approaches to influence construction MNCs to utilize a more fair and ethical recruitment approach in the sending countries.

Regional consultative dialogues can also further function as safe diplomatic spaces for Asian and Gulf senior officials to develop state networks or connections to design more corridor-specific approaches to eliminate illegal and unethical recruitment practices. Asian and Gulf countries, for example, jointly explore these common regional problems on recruitment through commissioned studies with international organizations and field migration experts, such as multicountry corridor pilot studies in order to develop more responsive, innovative policies to counter these unethical, illegal recruitment practices. By engaging construction MNCs, Gulf states would be able to reinforce and promote the economic benefits of a fair and ethical culture in the global recruitment of migrant labor, while developing incentives to strategically curb construction MNCs' behavior in the Asia-Gulf migration corridor.

## Efforts in Building Ethical Culture in the Gulf Construction Sector

Ethical culture can have direct or indirect transformative implications on the long-term quality management, global reputation, and business competitiveness of Gulf-based construction companies in the long run. In order to achieve effective total quality management and performance, Gulf-based construction MNCs need to constructively deal with the legal, cultural, and policy shortcomings, as well as their degree of national and international compliance, with existing global labor standards and corporate codes of conduct. First, construction MNCs need to provide more fair and equitable compensation in order to achieve excellence in performance and competitiveness in the long run. Given the strong criticisms toward construction MNCs' compensation issues (i.e., delayed salary, non-payment), it is vital that construction MNCs uphold living wage standards that correspond to the rising cost of living in the host country. This positive, ethical response has not only the capability to reinforce construction MNCs' corporate responsibility, but also to develop the need for a bolder ethical approach to the government labor market, specifically to enhance the general welfare of migrant construction workers.

Second, a more comprehensive strategic engagement with global rights advocacy groups or corporate social responsibility (CSR) entities (i.e., company initiatives to improve worker welfare) to improve the recruitment practices within the global supply chain may play an important role in improving the overall accountability, performance, and transparency of construction Gulf-based MNCs. This type of engagement will not only foster inter-collaboration and partnerships between the private sector and third-party actors in improving the general welfare of migrant construction workers (part of CSR business practice), but also enhance the quality management and performance of corporate businesses toward migrant construction labor, the community, and beyond. Such acts can certainly produce a positive corporate image and community engagement, but also can create valuable investment returns, partnerships, and better quality management practices in the long run.

Lastly, sectoral partnership with labor-sending and receiving countries can also contribute to corporate excellence and better quality management in the long run. In fact, Gulf-based construction MNCs have the untapped potential to contribute to policy engagement and collaboration for governments in order to better develop regulations and market incentives to encourage positive, compliant behavior with host county rules and regulations. The collective voices of industry/sectoral actors toward governments can help better identify critical and emerging issues (i.e., rights and welfare of migrants, living/accommodation issues, wage, and upskilling concerns) that are vital in improving not only the business efficiency of construction Gulf-based MNCs, but also their overall relationships with the community, the government, and other industry sectors (i.e., suppliers, CSR partners).

## The Future of Gulf Migration and the Construction Sector in Foreign Policy Contexts

Construction MNCs operating in the Gulf countries are vital to state national interests, given their core strategic functions within the long-term socio-economic development of the country, specifically in infrastructure development. The unfair and unethical recruitment practices across the Asia-Gulf migration corridor have not only forced migration stakeholders to directly pressure Gulf states to introduce stricter labor reforms, but have also influenced them to increasingly view labor migration as a foreign policy issue, impacting their national interests and image abroad. As an essential element of foreign policy interests, consultative dialogues can impact state perceptions toward regulating and incentivizing MNC operations to comply with national and international labor standards, which are vital to building a long-term ethical culture in the Asia-Gulf migration corridor.

As Gulf states embark on modernizing their infrastructures, construction MNCs will continue to play a critical role in the regional labor market, and thus face ongoing international criticisms in relation to their compliance level and business practices in the field of migrant labor recruitment. There are two potential scenarios that could significantly change the ethical culture dynamics of construction MNCs in the Gulf countries.

First, although minor labor policy reforms have already been introduced, the Gulf states may preserve the established status quo by allowing construction MNCs to operate and function with their existing migrant labor recruitment practices. This would mean that construction MNCs would, by and large, not carry the recruitment fees. This would indirectly empower agents/subagents to shift fees or excessively charge migrant workers recruitment costs for deployment. While some construction MNCs in the Gulf countries may benefit economically due to the cheap labor accessible in Asia, their global image, status, and corporate social responsibility reputation may be impacted in the long run. The global shaming and reporting of a minority of human rights advocates, including the Business and Human Resource Center, Institute for Business and Human Rights, and other transnational rights groups, for example, would further highlight the lack of government transparency (i.e., contract bidding, regulatory frameworks) in the Gulf countries. However, in reality, while the Gulf countries have been under the spotlight, it has had little effect on their image, as the vast majority of Gulf-based expatriates (i.e., CEOs, construction managers, and contractors) in the Gulf-based construction sector are more strategically focused on securing high paying, comfortable employment. Thus, the economic benefits of unethical culture in the Gulf construction sector largely trump certain cases of unethical behavior. However, if the level and quality of coordination and initiatives between the Asian labor-sending and Gulf receiving countries remain asymmetrical and weak, then the ongoing unfair and unethical business practices and the labor abuses in the origin countries will inevitably thrive and survive in the long run. In other words, the manner in which interests of Asian and GCC states diverge or converge can play a vital role in shaping how construction MNCs might functionally uphold ethical culture in their recruitment practices, as well as their treatment of migrant labor in the supply chain source in South Asia.

Second, the Gulf states may alternatively enforce stronger existing labor and criminal laws and regulations to curb unfair and unethical labor recruitment malpractices. At the same time, developing new bilateral projects or commission studies which aim to understand the causes and implications of labor violations and abuses in the labor market recruitment sector can better enable both Asian and Gulf states to bilaterally develop migration corridor-specific solutions in the long run. For example, the UAE-commissioned IOM study in 2014 was a government-initiated project that provided in-depth narratives and perspectives on the unfair and unethical recruitment practices from Kerala, India, and Nepal to the UAE. The study further reinforces the complex difficulty of addressing unethical/illegal recruitment practices, as well as the vital state-led discussions between sending and receiving countries necessary to eliminate unethical or illegal recruitment practices in the Asia-Gulf migration corridor.

Furthermore, Gulf states may also continue to place significant investments in academic and policy-based migration and labor market studies, while increasing dialogues on synergizing migration systems, linking digital technologies between sending and receiving countries, collaborating in recruitment systems (e-migrate in India as an example), and facilitating certification programs and qualification programs. Such initiatives might potentially eliminate the role of "bad" recruitment agencies and subagencies, while increasing long-term institutional transparency. This type of government-led investment and scenario will provide a vital foundation to better engage with construction MCNs. However, for the Gulf private sector, such actions also form a vital space for bilateral or regional collaborative policy leadership and engagement in developing new regulatory measures, incentives, and approaches in enforcing national and international labor legislation. As such, enhancing the promotion of an ethical culture as a vital dimension of long-term productivity and performance is of critical value in achieving strong quality management for construction MNCs in the long run.

## CONCLUSIONS

This paper has examined the complex role of ethical culture on the business practices of construction MNCs operating in the Asia-Gulf migration corridor and its implications on quality management. While the current status quo enables construction MNCs in the Gulf to operate at almost zero recruitment cost, the problem is that such unethical and illegal labor recruitment practices often have significant direct impacts on migrant construction workers. Such critical consequences include, but are not limited to, high debt bondage, excessive recruitment fees, and contract deception. Each of these activities constitute the unethical culture in which construction MNCs engage in and recruit from in order to complete their mega development projects in the Gulf countries.

Although these particular unethical and illegal business practices often result in higher profitability for some construction MNCs due to zero recruitment costs, they also have the strongest capacity to construct a negative image and long-term reputational damage to the construction MNCs' global reputation in the Gulf countries and beyond. Although ongoing state-led pilot projects are underway to address the culture of unethical/illegal recruitment by governments in the Asia-Gulf migration corridor, the regional and global perception and attitudes toward construction MNCs' "ethical practice" remains a vital concern for all stakeholders. The long-term political commitment from the Asian sending and Gulf receiving states are essential to increase construction MNCs' national and international labor compliance, as well as upholding a more ethical culture in the global labor market economy. With varying legal, political, and cultural compliance and variations, Asian labor-sending countries have more sovereign responsibilities to enforce stronger national and international labor standards in the origin countries. Such actions can curb unethical business practices or behaviors, while simultaneously upholding stronger labor protection for the rights and welfare of migrant construction workers migrating to the Gulf countries in the long run.

## REFERENCES

Abdul-Aziz, A.R., Olanrewaju, A. and Ahmed, A. (2018). "South Asian migrants and the construction sector of the Gulf," *South Asian Migration in the Gulf*. Springer.

Abu Dhabi Dialogue. (2016). *Research on the Labour Recruitment Industry Between the United Arab Emirates, Kerala (India), and Nepal.* Retrieved from http://abudhabi dialogue.org.ae/sites/default/files/document-library/Research%20on%20Labour %20Recruitment%20Industry%20between%20UAE%20Kerala%20and%20Nepal_ Final%20Report.pdf.

Ali-Khasasbeh, E., Harada, Y., Osman, A., Al-Dalayeen, B., et al. (2014). "The impact of business ethics in the competitive advantage (in the cellular communications companies operating in Jordan)," *European Scientific Journal* 10(10): 1857–7881.

Americans for Democracy and Human Rights in Bahrain (ADBHRB). (2018). Retrieved from https://twitter.com/ADHRB?lang=en.

Amnesty International. (2018). *Amnesty International Report 2017/2018: The State of the World's Human Rights.* Retrieved from https://www.amnesty.org/download/Do cuments/POL1067002018ENGLISH.PDF.

Ardichvili, A.A. and Jondle, D. (2009). "Ethical business cultures: A literature review and implications for HRD," *Human Resource Development Review* 8(2): 223–244.

At-Twaijri, M. and Al-Muhaiza, I. (1996). "Hofstede's cultural dimensions in the GCC countries: An empirical investigation," *International Journal of Value-Based Management* 2(9): 121–131.

Blome, C. and Paulraj, A. (2013). "Ethical climate and purchasing social responsibility: A benevolence focus," *Journal of Business Ethics* 3(116): 567–585.

Business and Human Rights. (2018. ). *Update Statement from the FIFA Human Rights Advisory Board.* Retrieved from https://www.business-humanrights.org/sites/de fault/files/documents/AB%20Update%20Statement_May%202018_Final.pdf.

CORE Coalition. (2016). *Beyond Compliance: Effective Reporting Under the Modern Slavery Act.* Retrieved from https://corporate-responsibility.org/wp-content/up loads/2016/03/CSO_TISC_guidance_final_digitalversion_16.03.16.pdf.

Crane, A. and Matten, D. (2010). *Business Ethics: Managing Corporate Citizenship and Sustainability in the Age of Globalization.* Oxford: Oxford University Press.

Creswell, J.W. (2009). *Research Design: Qualitative, Quantitative and Mixed Methods Approaches.* 3rd ed. Thousand Oaks, CA: Sage.

Ferris-Lay, C. (2010) "Workers strike in Saudi labor law protest," *Arabian Business.* Retrieved from https://www.arabianbusiness.com/workers-strike-in-saudi-labo ur-law-protest-8792.html.

Fitch Solutions. (2019). *UAE Construction Growth to Slow Following Pre-Expo Boost.* Retrieved from https://www.fitchsolutions.com/infrastructure-project-finance/uae -construction-growth-slow-following-pre-expo-boost-12-03-2019.

Frost, P., Moore, L., Louis, M., Lundberg, C. and Martin, J. (1991). *Reframing Organizational Culture.* Newbury Park, CA: Sage.

Harsh Suri (2011). "Purposeful sampling in qualitative research synthesis," *Qualitative Research Journal* 11(2): 63–75, doi:10.3316/QRJ1102063. https://www.emeraldinsigh t.com/doi/pdfplus/10.3316/QRJ1102063.

Human Rights Watch. (2006). *Building Towers, Cheating Workers: Exploitation of Migrant Construction Workers in the United Arab Emirates.* Retrieved from https ://www.hrw.org/report/2006/11/11/building-towers-cheating-workers/exploitat ion-migrant-construction-workers-united.

International Organization for Migration (IOM). (2017). *Research on the Labour Recruitment Industry in the United Arab Emirates, Kerala (India), and Nepal.* Retrieved from https://www.iom.int/research-labour-recruitment-industry-uni ted-arab-emirates-kerala-india-and-nepal.

John, I. (2018) "UAE remains no.1 in GCC construction," Khaleej Times. Retrieved from https://www.khaleejtimes.com/business/local//uae-remains-no1-in-gcc-for-con struction.

Jones, K. (2014). *Recruitment Monitoring and Migrant Welfare Assistance: What Works?* International Organization for Migration. Retrieved from https://www.iom.int/ sites/default/files/migrated_files/What-We-Do/docs/Recruitment-Monitoring-B ook.pdf.

Jureidini, R. (2014). *Migrant Labour Recruitment to Qatar.* Retrieved from http://www .qscience.com/userimages/ContentEditor/1404811243939/Migrant_Labour_Re cruitment_to_Qatar_Web_Final.pdf.

Jureidini, R. (2016). "Ways forward in recruitment of low-skilled migrant workers in the Asia-Arab states corridor," ILO White Paper. Retrieved from https://www.ilo.org/ wcmsp5/groups/public/---arabstates/---ro-beirut/documents/publication/wcms_ 519913.pdf.

Kerr, S. (2013). "Construction workers strike in Dubai as labor tensions rise," Financial Times. Retrieved from https://www.ft.com/content/af0ed09e-c15f-11e2-b93b-0014 4feab7de.

Key, S. (1999). "Organizational ethical culture: Real or imagined?" *Journal of Business Ethics* 20(3): 217–225.

King, D. "Free zones, a cornerstone of UAE success," Gulf NewsRetrieved from https:// gulfnews.com/business/property/free-zones-a-cornerstone-of-uae-success-1.2074 856.

Kluckhohn, C. (1951). "The study of culture," in D. Lerner and H.D. Lasswell (eds.), *The Policy Sciences*. Stanford, CA: Stanford University Press.

Martin, J. (1992). *Cultures in Organizations: Three Perspectives*. Cary, NC, USA: Oxford University Press.

Martin, J. (2002). *Organizational Culture. Mapping the Terrain*. Thousand Oaks, CA: Sage.

Nebehay, S. (2017). "ILO closes workers' complaint against World Cup host Qatar," Reuters. Retrieved from https://www.reuters.com/article/us-qatar-rights/ilo-clo ses-workers-complaint-against-world-cup-host-qatar-idUSKBN1D81EX.

Palinkas, L., Horwitz, S., Green, C., Wisdom, J., Duan, N. and Hoagwood, K. (2016). "Purposeful sampling for qualitative data collection and analysis in mixed method implementation research," *Administration and Policy in Mental Health* 42(5): 533–544.

Schein, E.H. (2010) *Organizational Culture and Leadership*. 4th ed. Hoboken, NJ: Jossey-Bass.

Segall, D. and Labowitz, S. (2017). *Making Workers Pay: Recruitment of the Migrant Labor Force in the Gulf Construction Industry*. NYU Center for Business and Ethics. Retrieved from https://bhr.stern.nyu.edu/statement/2017/4/6/center-report-finds-migrant-workers-bear-the-cost-burden-of-their-own-recruitment.

Shafer, W. and Simmons, R. (2011). "Effects of organizational ethical culture on the ethical decisions of tax practitioners in mainland China," *Accounting, Auditing & Accountability* 5(24): 647–668.

Stephenson, W. (2015) "Have 1,200 World Cup workers really died in Qatar?" *BBC News*. Retrieved from https://www.bbc.com/news/magazine-33019838.

Thompson, R. (2018). "GCC construction market outlook 2018," *MEED Middle East Business Intelligence*. Retrieved from https://www.meed.com/gcc-construction-in frastructure-transport-projects/.

United Nations. (2018). *Global Compact for Safe, Orderly and Regular Migration (Final Draft)*. Retrieved from https://www.un.org/pga/72/wp-content/uploads/sites/51/2 018/07/migration.pdf.

United Nations Office on Drugs and Crime (2015). *The Role of Recruitment Fees and Abusive and Fraudulent Recruitment Practices of Recruitment Agencies in Trafficking in Persons*. Retrieved from https://www.unodc.org/documents/human-trafficking/ 2015/15-05035_ebook-_Recruitment_Fees.Agencies.pdf.

Valentine, S., Godkin, L. and Lucero, M. (2002). "Ethical context, organizational commitment, and person-organization fit," *Journal of Business Ethics* 4(41): 349–460.

# 4

# Developing a Culture of Quality: Tailoring Strategies with All Stakeholders to Assure Student Learning

*Venkata Yanamandram*

## CONTENTS

## INTRODUCTION

Quality assurance through assurance of learning takes an ongoing development approach that involves the capturing, monitoring, and evaluating of data specific to student achievement of specific course learning (degree) outcomes (CLOs) (Krneta et al., 2012). The need to demonstrate outcomes is driven by a range of pressures that has placed increased emphasis on quality assurance and accountability. For example, the Australian Qualifications Framework (AQF) committed higher education providers to "new quality assurance arrangements involving the development of standards and implementation of a transparent process for assuring the quality of learning outcomes across all providers of higher education" (Commonwealth of Australia, 2009, p.60). Subsequently, the Tertiary Education Quality and Standards Agency (TEQSA) that evaluates the performance of providers against the Higher Education Standards Framework has sought to confirm that "the specified learning outcomes are consistent with the AQF level of higher education qualification offered and the student achievement of the course learning outcomes is credibly assessed" (HESF, 2015). Further, for business schools, the Association to Advance Collegiate Schools of Business (AACSB), one of the largest accreditation agencies for business schools worldwide, requires its member institutions to have a systematic and ongoing process to assess student learning.

The assurance of learning (AOL) process consists of making institutional expectations on course (program) learning outcomes explicit; setting high standards for learning quality and assessment; gathering, analyzing, and interpreting data systematically to determine how well performance matches those expectations and standards; and using the resulting performance information to continuously improve courses (AACSB, 2013). Therefore, assurance of learning is gaining recognition as "an emerging means of informing quality assurance in tertiary education through developing systems and processes for capturing and monitoring direct measures of learning achievement as related to generic cross-disciplinary attributes and program specific learning" (Kinash et al., 2012, p.3).

Despite the demonstrated value of assurance of learning, many schools still struggle in making the necessary changes to implement effective assurance of learning processes, resulting in an unintended creation of a culture of compliance rather than one of improvement (Gray, Smart, and Bennett, 2017). Jones et al. (2009) argue that mounting daily pressures and operational demands often mean that initiatives for improving the quality of academic courses become a low priority among other time demands.

In the higher education context, the literature points to the significance of effective leadership when implementing institutional change strategies to assure student learning outcomes. For example, both Krause et al. (2014) and Lawson et al. (2013) advocate a collegial leadership approach that provides the opportunity to highlight challenges, share strategies and exemplars, and develop support mechanisms including professional development, resources, streamlined technology, and coaching. They emphasize the importance of academic teaching staff acting as change agents, and program leaders taking a critical role. Fullan and Scott (2009) advocate a coordinated "top-down, bottom-up" approach that is systematic and empowering and builds leadership capacity. Lawson et al. (2013) provide further support that it is essential to include both a "top-down" approach to ensure executive buy-in and a "bottom-up" approach to ensure grassroots support.

What is not clear, though, is how mid-level leaders—when assigned a complex project aimed at creating new capabilities that span several activities—use tools and methodology to determine how to get different types of stakeholders to change their behaviors, routines, and activities. This is especially true when institutional executives specify a fuzzy vision, and mid-level leaders are tasked with implementing it. Nickerson (2014) notes that neither of the current fundamental approaches to leading change—compliance or commitment—alone would likely work if leading change from the middle of the organization, because mid-level leaders would have neither a substantial level of authority to make decisions and structure measurement and reward systems nor would they be able to empower enough stakeholders. Nickerson (2014) advocates that the likelihood of successfully leading change increases if a mid-level leader intuitively explores, identifies, and categorizes stakeholders into different but highly related groups, and tailors strategies to each stakeholder group important to the success of the project.

This chapter describes a change effort from the perspective of a Director of Assurance of Learning—a mid-level leader (hereinafter referred to as MLL) in the faculty of a large transnational university that operates across multiple locations. The value of the work however, lies not simply in his approach to strategic and persistent stakeholder engagement, iterative development of relevant and user-friendly information management infrastructure, and continued building of capacity in academic and professional colleagues, but in his leadership ability to work cooperatively to bring these three elements together in complex and dynamic interaction, enabling and embedding continuous transformation of teaching and learning governance and practice within the faculty. The chapter finishes with a set of recommendations integrating key steps of an organizational change management process with a best practice undertaken within the Master of Business Administration (MBA) program.

## LEADERSHIP APPROACHES

### Context

In the early implementation phase of AOL, key stakeholders co-constructed the AOL design and piloted activities by carefully selecting relevant data sources for evaluation. For example, on completion of the faculty's self-assessment report on the state of curricula management and assurance of learning to address a key requirement sought by AACSB, the MLL was nominated to conduct a pilot of assurance of learning with a postgraduate program. The MLL's role as the Program Director included making judgements about students' ability to demonstrate selected course learning outcomes (CLOs) as well as the management of the curricula. The MLL chaired a Working Party that recommended a plan of action to improve student results, simplify the wording of the CLOs, and revise the curriculum map. It also included the provision of assistance in drafting an AOL procedure, drafting the terms of reference for the AOL subcommittee, and a rollout schedule for the next four years, which was reviewed by the Working Party before seeking approval at the Faculty Education Committee (FEC). The pilot project was deemed successful by the senior executive of the faculty. As Chair of the AOL subcommittee, the MLL was tasked with championing AOL for all of the faculty's programs, across multiple campuses, which included responsibility for monitoring collection of learning assessment data and assuring its use in the continuous review of the programs. These activities focused on evaluations that aimed to analyze and improve the AOL process using the knowledge gained to change structures and modify activities as well as the specific interventions and outcomes of learning that they generated, thus identifying the use of evaluation to support decisions for the improvement of courses.

## Gaining Consent from the Executive: Strategic and Persistent Stakeholder Engagement

The MLL achieved consent from this stakeholder group (Executive) that included associate deans and heads of schools by applying *Listen-Link-Leverage-Lead* approaches (Fullan and Scott, 2009) to explore the sources and nuances of the AOL project timing and objectives, discover the stakeholder landscape, investigate their roles and support, and coordinate ongoing communications to encourage useful responses. For example, when the MLL actively learned during the early implementation phase that the set of practices and the sequencing associated with evaluation of the AOL process and key responsibilities of staff involved in the process were not well developed, he engaged in multiple dialogues with the Executive to develop a clear set of procedures and linked it with what most of the Executive said was most relevant and feasible. The MLL believed that stakeholders from all levels within the faculty needed to develop a shared meaning and a sense of "ownership" over the AOL process, so he, along with the faculty teaching and learning consultant, engaged in a process that was both consultative and adaptive. This involved building and maintaining relationships and facilitating collaboration and cooperation for collective action. A representative comment is as follows:

> *Venkat built a deep and trusting relationship with our School's discipline leaders, school manager, program directors and postgraduate advisors by demonstrating good character, goodwill and good ability. He judiciously explored challenges before offering suggestions to address some of our staff's resistance. His ability to manage upward and downward is excellent; he achieved this by communication with all stakeholders. Venkat showed that he cared for the stakeholders, and thoughtfully laid the groundwork for achieving success.*

## Curriculum Mapping Practices

The alignment of the curriculum with CLOs is an initial step in the curriculum design. AACSB advocates that there should be clear evidence that classroom activities, including assessment of students' learning directly support student achievement of learning outcomes at the course (program) level. Business schools typically use a matrix approach—known as curriculum mapping—where the academics responsible for teaching examine how CLOs are introduced, further developed, and assured throughout the degree and identify possible overload and gaps (Sumsion and Goodfellow, 2004). Lawson et al. (2013) recommend that this stage is conducted rigorously to ensure that CLOs are embedded into relevant subjects and that assessment tasks are suitable for collecting AOL data. Further, they advocate three key considerations for effective curriculum mapping practice: (1) *tool*—an instrument that allows aggregation and visualization of the course; (2) *process*—the way in which the tool is used by teaching and support staff; and (3) *purpose*—the reason for adopting curriculum mapping.

A key insight that was discovered when leading discussions among the academic program directors (APDs) and key members of each course team is that the existing curriculum maps did not adequately demonstrate how students learning was progressively developed throughout each course and how student attainment of each learning outcome was ascertained. In some instances, although the AQF criteria for the relevant level were often mentioned (Knowledge, Skills, and Application of Knowledge and Skills), the effective integration of these into developmental approaches in the classroom was somewhat tenuous, as has been previously documented in the literature (Taylor et al., 2009; Barrie, Hughes, and Smith, 2009). A probable cause for the initial lack of alignment, as Barrie (2004) reports, is that academics do not commonly understand the graduate attributes, with responsibility for teaching and development. Another cause for the lack of alignment was that the template developed around the AQF implementation phase did not identify and provide explicit, visual, and transparent information on the integration of subjects, and the progression of learning, throughout the course. While curriculum mapping cannot in and of itself ensure that a shared understanding is developed, the process highlights the need to develop information knowledge infrastructure, including how and where the CLOs will be taught and developed, which are necessary first steps to developing a shared understanding. The development of trust and commitment among team members to enable the knowledge infrastructure development is discussed next.

### Supporting Team Members and Managing Information Infrastructure

The traditional "buy-in" approach, as in "I need your buy-in to get my project done" often undermines commitment, as it implies that a leader wants his/her team to accept the leader's decision and that they were not important enough to be part of the team that makes the decision

(Nickerson, 2014). In contrast, building trust and supporting team members implies that the team is involved in the decision making from beginning to end, focusing not just on the outcome to which a leader and his/her team is committing, but on the process by which the leader will build capabilities (Nickerson, 2014).

The MLL built trust and commitment from staff who worked with him, but did not report to him, by comprehensively formulating a challenge, verifying the formulation before deciding how to approach a solution, developing alternative solution approaches, verifying the solution approach before planning implementation, and designing and executing the implementation plan. The MLL used a model of community of practice to draw other faculty members into the activity of AOL and developed a shared language and understanding around the process. For example, using the trigger question, "why does the enactment of curriculum differ from its documentation?" the conversations that ensued helped the team to refine and formulate the challenge. The MLL concomitantly engaged with other stakeholders to verify the information uncovered, the assumptions made, symptoms identified, root causes deduced, and end-user needs fully determined. Such an exercise enabled the MLL's team to verify that he had not missed any critical details, fully captured the faculty Executive's initial vision, and switched from an approach that merely validated the MLL's authority to an approach that emphasized building commitment. The outcomes of the open and honest feedback provided from stakeholder engagement highlighted in the previous section and team building were:

- The AOL rollout schedule coincided with other decision-making cycles, namely determination of subjects to be offered in each session as well as the sequencing of subjects.
- The team expanded the current curriculum mapping template by taking a "whole of program" approach to identify the progression of learning throughout the course.

The MLL also took steps to avoid reducing that commitment. By reiteratively evaluating the design of curriculum mapping and its practice, the team became more capable of accounting for symptoms of any further challenges in curriculum mapping. Recognizing this capability, the MLL engaged with experts within the university and explored alternative solution approaches, and then secured support from a relevant associate dean for the design and development of an online curriculum mapping system. The team took ownership and reached a final solution through a process of seeking meaningful feedback to address any inadequacies in the solution approach, interactions, and new ideas, and by comparing alternatives, brainstorming, and further thinking. The final solution—an innovative online system—is capable of interacting with various databases to create new subjects and amend CLOs at the course level as well as having other features that show the relationship between course and subjects at the time of building the curriculum map and its approval process. By team members owning the problem, solution, and implementation, the MLL successfully led a project through their commitment to it. A representative comments is as follows:

> *The AOL Team's collegiality allowed them to incorporate our concerns, collective experience, and expertise in their development of an innovative online system that we use to build the curriculum map and its approval process.*

Additionally, the engagement in a community of practice to build the online system has improved selected members of the AOL team's own capability that has informed the enhancement of the university's course and subject management system. For example, the development of the curriculum mapping system in EQUELLA included the design of business rules to ensure it meets regulatory and policy requirements. It involved working with IT specialists and facilitating workshops with faculty users and other university stakeholders to ascertain their feedback and get "user buy-in." Since its introduction in 2017, one of the members of the AOL team has continued to make further enhancements to the functionality of the EQUELLA curriculum mapping system, including improvements to the user functionality and the development of automated reporting.

> [The colleague's] *insightful contribution on the design of business rules has informed us to make further enhancements to the user functionality and the development of automated reports in the course and subject management system (COSMOS) that the University is building.*

## Development of Rubrics

The use of assessment rubrics in collecting data on students' capability, and subsequently analyzing student performance in relation to each CLO has been identified as a key step in the AOL process (Yorke, 1998; AACSB,

2013). Rubrics include evaluative criteria, often in matrix form, which include quality definitions for those criteria at particular levels aligned with assessment outcomes and a scoring strategy, and are intended to make expectations to students transparent (Mansilla, Duraisingh, Wolfe, and Haynes, 2009). In order to reduce the problems associated with the use of rubrics in assessment (O'Donovan, Price, and Rust, 2004), the MLL and his team (AOL team) followed a progressive approach that initially consisted of providing academics a standardized set of rubrics based on the VALUE rubric design network (AAC&U, 2015) that are broad, discipline-neutral descriptions of selected essential learning outcomes. Some of the academics adapted to the specific context in which they used, while others adopted the ones we provided. In order to assist students and academics to more readily understand and clarify the criteria outlined in each assessment rubric, the AOL team used a social constructivist approach of communicating the meaning of assessment criteria, supported by short four to five minute digital stories to be shown in class. The specific rubric digital story can be uploaded into a subject's Moodle site for students to access at will. Subsequently, many academic colleagues involved in teaching a course learning outcome developed a clear appreciation of the criteria and standards in each rubric, which in turn, enabled them to work with students to develop the standards in each rubric. To further provide teaching and learning strategies and support, the AOL team developed a Teaching and Learning Toolkit. This tool recommends many teaching and learning strategies, rubrics, and the digital stories that explain the criteria within each rubric and other links. Representative comments are:

> *The AOL process resulted in a relatable set of feedback mechanisms that have improved clarity of expectations for students. This is evidenced by an increased quality of response to assessment criteria and an improved level of coherence in overall submissions.*

> *The teaching and learning resources in the online Toolkit led by Jan provides great support to staff ... The engaging in-class learning experience was complemented by in-class discussion of assessment standards, strong assessment support and feedback.*

Drawing on continuous data analysis and stakeholder feedback from the many iterations of AOL data collection in all courses, the AOL team continued to refine and expand the Faculty Procedure for Assurance of Learning. Key changes included explicitly articulating the requisite sequence of the AOL process to enable the collection, analysis, and reporting of assessment information at a course level; refining faculty staff roles, responsibilities, and their workflows in relation to AOL; delineating a process for amendments to assessments; and incorporating AOL information in the Course Review Report template. Further, the AOL team detailed how course review recommendations needed to address closing the loop actions arising from AOL meeting decisions. Several other operating assumptions were important to the ultimate successful establishment of the AOL process. Perhaps the most critical was the fact the course review and assurance of learning processes were not decoupled, but rather integrated. The policy of the university specified that thorough course review and strategic planning should occur on a five-year rotating basis. This culture, which valued teaching and learning, was a good foundation for the faculty to integrate AACSB AOL standard. A representative comment was:

> *Starting from a slim base, the AOL Team produced a comprehensive policy and a detailed set of procedures. More importantly, they successfully engaged the academics and there is universal acceptance of the ideas.*

### Engagement with End-Users: Building Capacity in Colleagues

Although the "buy-in" approach is problematic for team members, the approach suggested here for end-users (academic colleagues) is appropriate. This is consistent with Martell (2005), who reinforces the need both to "anoint a champion" (p.220) and to obtain buy-in from faculty as well as to increase awareness and socialization in order to secure a critical mass. The MLL generated sufficient perceived value for both the academic colleagues that ultimately implement AOL in their programs and professional staff that support AOL, and gained their support by applying three key alternative strategic alternatives: inviting them to co-construct practices; engaging them in psychosocial and relational mentoring; and marketing the value of involvement in the AOL process.

## Co-Construct Practices

Academic staff responsible for assuring multiple CLOs in capstone subjects have benefited from the redesign of AOL output though co-construction practices. They have progressively migrated from using separate Excel-based marking templates to an integrated one, which itself underwent iterative evaluations, to more recent efforts to migrate to an online environment to increase marking efficiency while ensuring data accuracy, allowing a more in-depth process for analyzing results, reporting, and improvement purposes. By jointly seeking support via internal grant schemes for educational design, programming, and Moodle development, the MLL has led academics to claim co-ownership of the problem and be committed to the solution and its implementation.

## Psychosocial and Relational Mentoring

Mentoring is deliberate and tailored to the unique context and developmental experience of a faculty member and is one of the most essential and enduring roles for the higher education faculty member. Johnson (2016) advocates that the application of psychosocial and relational mentor functions such as modeling, coaching, advising, encouragement, support, counseling, and collegiality help mentees master professional skills that are associated with gains in both confidence and professional identity. He adds that mentoring enhances the relational skills and attitudes to build other high-quality relationships, leading to institution affirming behaviors. Mullen (2005) notes that mentoring can be informal, where arrangements occur spontaneously and not overly structured or managed.

According to Social Learning Theory, models are an essential source for learning new behaviors and for accomplishing planned behavioral change in organizational settings, for example, when employees learn new behaviors by observing another individual that performs the behavior (Sims and Manz, 1982). They advocate that leaders recognize the potential efficacy of modeling-based training situations for employee development and provide evidence of its effectiveness in training those in leadership roles. In meetings with the Academic Program Directors (APDs), the MLL demonstrated collaborative and creative problem-solving facilitation techniques to model an appropriate leadership style the APDs might employ in progressing AOL procedure. This involved using solution-focused questioning techniques, for example, "how can we ensure we provide sufficient teaching and learning activities to develop reflective writing skills across the course, before asking students to demonstrate that skill?" These discussions, followed by APDs' participation in reflective discussion groups that we led, enabled APDs to devise their own solutions.

> *As a new staff member, I have benefited from collegiate discussions with the AOL Team about the imperative importance of assurance of learning and its relationship to facilitating personalised student learning experiences. The coherent, transparent and consistent communication about AOL has ensured that both students, and I as their teacher/facilitator, understand how the subject fits within the wider MBA ecosystem. I have witnessed students develop a clearer understanding of the interrelationship between their learning intentions, assessment expectations and learning outcomes of the MBA program that I teach into.*

> *Venkat's role modelling of academic program leadership behaviour resulted in a high level of learning that has enabled me to create action plans to progressively develop student learning outcomes in the course.*

Joyce and Showers (2002) show how coaching facilitated the transfer of training and the development of organizational norms of collegiality and experimentation. They found that coaching appeared to contribute to the transfer of training in many ways, where coached academics practiced new strategies more often and with greater skill than uncoached academics with identical initial training; they adapted the strategies more appropriately to their own goals and contexts than uncoached academics who tended to practice observed or demonstrated lessons; they retained and increased their skill over time; and they demonstrated a clearer understanding of the purposes and use of the new strategies. The MLL and his team mentored the APDs and subject coordinators as they engaged in the process of gathering, analyzing, and reporting on AOL data. In turn, APDs and their teaching teams developed the capacity to evaluate AOL data and formed their own working parties. The continually refined *information management infrastructure* became critical support resources in this process. As the APDs became more proficient, the AOL team functioned as coaches, being called upon to provide advice on policy matters, relevant teaching and learning strategies, assessment design, and any persistent problems with student performance. The AOL team also engaged with academic staff required to evaluate AOL output by scaffolding the interpretation of student cohort's AOL performance data and creation of narratives with both qualitative and quantitative evidence, and suggesting interventions to be implemented in the program/subject as an outcome of the data, before submitting AOL documentation for the subcommittee's consideration in meetings.

*Venkat has coached me in the mechanics of AOL activities providing sugges-tions and advice on the efficient segmentation of student cohorts, completion of AOL documentation, and value of maintaining a professional record of interventions and outcomes. His leadership in post AOL activity discussion has encouraged cross functional and multi-disciplinary collaboration in a way that ensures people like me are able to draw on expertise we may not otherwise have access to. For example, looking at qualitative and quantita-tive data and experiences across different departments to show the impact/ similarities/differences of AOL activity on students e.g., changes in the num-ber of students who meet or exceed expectations and individual teacher eval-uation by students.*

The AOL team's provision of an active "just-in-time and just-for-me" learning method stimulated academic staff to realize the perceived benefits that they were not fully aware of themselves, thus allowing them to improve their experience and perform the activity better. The outcome was that academic staff have been better prepared when asked in the subcommittee meeting to discuss key issues and successful in incorporating appropriate teaching and learning activities to address deficiencies in student performance relating to each LO. The MLL's development of a "why don't we" not a "why don't you" culture has thus facilitated him to gain buy-in from users of AOL.

## Market the Value of AOL

The MLL led other evaluation practices and marketed their value. Highlights of his practices and outcomes are: (1) presenting in school meetings about the real purpose for, and the uses of, the evaluation, and publicizing how the faculty used student performance information for continuous improvements; (2) conducting customized workshops aimed at staff development activities in particular areas of practice, for example, tabling the report at a meeting to evaluate its implication; (3) identifying and disseminating exemplary reports of student assessments and subject coordinators' AOL evaluation, and advising inexperienced evaluators on how best to develop and use them; (4) holding people who agreed to undertake an action in a previous meeting to account for the next one and follow through; and (5) producing a faculty intranet site that explains how AOL is carried out, including 'do-it-yourself' guides and documentation on the rubrics used, data gathered, results analyzed, and actions conducted following a review of AOL data, which have assisted in improving the teaching practices of subject coordinators.

### Seeking Support from Other Types of Stakeholders

According to Nikerson (2014), this category of stakeholders consists of those individuals who control needed resources, provide requisite approvals, and guidance and other forms of assistance, but over whom the leader has no authority. The MLL engaged with such a stakeholder group to shape their perception and support of the AOL project by involving them in the problem formulation and solution, gaining their buy-in, engaging in instrumental exchanges, and occasionally gaining their agreement to achieve what Nickerson calls as "Allow in." For example, when workload issues of academic colleagues involved in undertaking AOL activities were brought up in a FEC meeting by a member who was also part of the Faculty Workloads Committee, the MLL engaged with stakeholders that resulted in that committee member and MLL successfully formulating the challenge. The MLL then negotiated a solution for academic colleagues with a key member of the faculty Executive.

The MLL also engaged with opinion leaders on matters concerning quality assurance practices. For example, the MLL engaged with the accreditation manager, whose input, perceptions, and feedback on curriculum mapping tools, the AOL report template, and the Closing the Loop template and meeting minutes, enabled the filtering, interpreting, and evaluating of information better in a reiterative manner, and rendered evidence in ways that academic staff could "read" them.

Offshore, the MLL had purposeful interactions with stakeholders to build, maintain, and repair social relationships. For example, before leading the implementation of AOL at an offshore campus, the MLL drew on his knowledge of systems and processes and professional connections to respond to the challenges faced by those educators when seeking approvals for ethics applications onshore, and subsequently delivered workshops and tools at offshore that laid the foundation for the collaboration necessary for AOL implementation and AACSB requirements. The MLL enabled the AOL team to adapt the AOL process when implementing AOL at offshore campuses, and ensured the offshore programs met Principles of Equivalence by aligning offshore CLOs with that of onshore to resolve roadblocks to undertaking AOL activities for those programs offshore.

*I have had the opportunity to work closely with Venkata Yanamandram as part of the AOL processes being led by Dr Yanamandram as partial fulfilment for AACSB documentation. We were very successful in achieving the stated objectives of AOL and a large part of this success can be credited to Dr Yanamandram's ability to build collaborative relationships with the Faculty team here at UOWD. Given that the Assurance of learning project is a change journey, it was necessary for colleagues to buy into this process, while continuing to enable the students to achieve the learning outcomes. I would like to take this opportunity to acknowledge Dr Yanamandram's excellent efforts towards enabling the Faculty colleagues to understand the purpose behind AOL, and leading them to achieve the collective goals through being a constant source of support in an informed, empathic and able manner. It is not always easy to run projects of this nature successfully across transnational contexts, but Dr Yanamandram's openness and willingness to constantly provide the necessary learning opportunities was a significant driver for building a shared understanding and commitment, leading to successful completion of the AOL project, each semester. He embodies both the attitude and skill necessary to lead a change project of this magnitude, and through this process building communities of practice and contributing to goals of scholarship of teaching and learning.*

### Continuous Improvement: Enhancing Teacher Pedagogical Practices

*Embed Governance*

A significant outcome of the MLL's leadership of the three sets of interconnected activities—strategic and persistent stakeholder engagement, iterative development of relevant and user-friendly information management infrastructure, and continued building of capacity in academic and professional colleagues—for the Faculty of Business is how the AOL process has become embedded in the governance of courses (degrees) as a continuous improvement process that enables focused conversations on various teaching, assessment, and other practices. Creating change requires, in Kotter's (2007) words, putting together a powerful coalition. The coalition—The Assurance of Learning (AOL) Subcommittee of the Faculty Education Committee (FEC)—is powerful in terms of titles, information and expertise, reputations, and relationships. The committee chaired by the MLL (Director, Assurance of Learning) comprises the full range of key stakeholders designated for AOL data collection and review, namely, Associate Dean (Education), Faculty Education Consultant, a representative of the university's Learning, Teaching and Curriculum Unit, and the relevant heads of schools, discipline leaders, school managers, academic program directors, and coordinators of the subjects designated for AOL data collection. The Teaching and Learning Coordinator prepares all reports for discussion, takes minutes, and organizes storage of all data and creates a record of actions. The structure of the AOL subcommittee was very important in creating this social change, as it came together and developed a shared commitment to excellent performance. The core members of the subcommittee monitored collection of student cohort "assessment outcome" data, evaluated the effectiveness of interventions, and assured its use in continuous review of courses. Over a three-year period, 31 meetings have been conducted in which the members evaluated, debated, and collectively reflected on over 700 AOL reports.

> *As an external member of the AOL Sub-committee, I have experienced the AOL process being instrumental in identifying gaps in teaching and learning practices, offering engaging student-focused resources and producing better learning.*

## Close the Loop

Closing the loop (CTL)—the development and implementation of curricular changes that are driven by the data collected during the assurance of learning process to improve student learning at both the subject and course levels—is recognized as the final step in assurance of learning (Rexeisen and Garrison, 2013). The raison d'être for having an AOL process is to create an environment of continuous improvement, where internal and external stakeholders can be guaranteed that students are learning a well-defined set of knowledge and skills (Rexeisen and Garrison, 2013). *Therefore, the CTL stage is critical because it represents the tangible actions that are taken to improve student learning.* Today, every course within the faculty has completed several iterations of AOL data collection, with the analysis of data in each iteration triggering improvements to teaching, learning, and assessment practices. More importantly are the *Closing the Loop* AOL subcommittee meetings for each course where the outcomes of the AOL meetings, data analysis, and discussion result in an action plan for improvement. The power of these meetings is evident in the rich discussions that cover responsive teaching and learning innovations, identification of potential changes in the structure and design of curriculum, and development of strategies for building students' skills across the degree. For example, in 2016, 25% of the student cohort demonstrated little evidence of utilizing feedback in their reflections, leading to poor design of their improvement plans. Following the AOL subcommittee's recommendations, the MBA teaching team introduced learning interventions in earlier subjects of the course in 2017, resulting in 84% achieving satisfactory results in the *Reflection* CLO. Both qualitative and quantitative AOL data informed the MBA course review that ultimately led to the development of a learner-centered curriculum to develop students' personal effectiveness as responsible leaders with a heightened self-awareness.

*The collaborative refinement of the Reflection rubric ensured everyone teaching on the MBA developed a shared understanding of reflection. This resulted in consistent feedback to students so that they can use feedback from one subject in later subjects. The standards-based curriculum design, leveraged by AOL process, has made the program more cohesive in MBA.*

*I stand confident today on how to critically reflect on responsible leadership incorporating personal ideas, practices, learning, feedback and feedforward.*

In order to share with the wider university community, the faculty's philosophy of continuous improvement and inspiring the sharing of good practices, the faculty has defined a number of ways to disseminate the improvement actions for implementation and achievements. The approval process and responsibility for implementation of improvement activities varies with the nature of improvement activities. Changes to curriculum mapping or assessment tasks are initiated by the subject coordinator, discussed with APD, HOS, and the discipline leader, and approved by the Faculty Education Committee and implemented by the subject coordinator. APDs complete with the support from the director and assurance of learning CTL reports, describing how AOL data were used to close the loop, including progress against action items at the course level. APDs incorporate the portfolio of evidence arising from participating in AOL activities when undertaking course reviews. The Assurance of Learning Subcommittee provides an annual update on the AOL implementation process to associate deans.

The quality of narratives prepared for the AOL reports and suggested action items documented in the minutes of AOL meetings demonstrate that faculty staff, leveraged by the MLL's leadership, now have a better understanding of how their teaching, learning and assessments impact on the achievement of outcomes.

> *I have adjusted my original impression of AOL of being quality control for assessments to fully embracing the philosophy of AOL, with a strong belief that it improves the quality of my teaching and student learning. A large part of this belief has been driven by working with Venkat. Students have clarity on how learning outcomes are assessed objectively, transparently and fairly.*

> *The AOL Team have been instrumental in bringing about a paradigmatic shift in the attitudes of stakeholders and taking a whole-of-course approach. The end result has seen continuing professional development in teaching and learning that would not have otherwise occurred.*

## RECOMMENDATIONS AND CONCLUSION

This chapter provided insights into the method and tools used by the MLL to get stakeholders up and down as well as across the organization to change their behaviors, routines, and activities regarding assuring student learning. The dynamic interaction between the various sets of activities—stakeholder engagement, information management infrastructure, and capacity building of colleagues—created the conditions for continuous improvement through the AOL process. While the MLL served as a catalyst for change during the assurance of learning process, a more widespread successful implementation is more likely to be achieved with a faculty-directed process, focusing on improving student learning and performance and not just meeting the accreditation requirements, thus propagating a culture of assessment.

In managing the link between an organization's culture and performance, it is prudent to define both culture and a culture of assessment, before providing a set of recommendations. Schein (1992, p.12) defines culture as

> a pattern of shared basic assumptions—invented, discovered, or developed by a given group as it learns to cope with its problems of external

adaptation and internal integration—that have worked well enough to be considered valid, and therefore, to be taught to new members as the correct way to perceive, think and feel in relation to those problems.

Applying this line of thinking to creating a culture of assessment would mean that assurance of learning is widely and clearly understood. It is a shared belief in a systematic process for continuous improvement by using, and not just collecting, AOL data to improve student practice and performance; relying on open communication; extensive faculty development; faculty ownership of the process; permission to fail but not to stall; and experimentation (Eder, 2005; Gray, 2010; Lane et al., 2014). Creating a culture of assessment presents a challenge for those working in academia as the focus shifts on the quality of a course (degree program) rather than merely the quality of its parts (subjects or units of study).

Nash et al. (2016) report on Lawson's (2015) adapted Kotter model of creating a change management culture, contextualized for assurance of learning, which is the basis of the recommendations proposed here.

## Executive Support and Governance

In the world of assessment and accreditation, universities may promote assurance of learning through a variety of mechanisms to help establish a sense of urgency and form a powerful guiding coalition. These include creating Assurance of Learning committees; having both Associate Dean (International) and Associate Dean (Education) taking overarching leadership; adopting mission statements reflecting assessment; creating policies and procedures involving assurance of learning with having a clear responsibility process that tracks recommended and actual actions around AOL data; giving discipline teams responsibility for assurance of learning; and having program directors require their respective teaching teams to attend quality assurance and alignment sessions. However, with people not necessarily acting on things they do not believe, the key to moving actions from enacted to espoused values, according to Schein's (1990) organizational culture framework, is to signal the importance of the associated activities by explicitly acknowledging and rewarding staff effort. Such activities could include making a place for assurance of learning in staff development (e.g., Career Development Record interviews) and referencing it in other important documents such as probation and promotion, and school teaching and learning plans. Gray, Smart, and Bennett (2017, pp.256–257) observe that

> an analysis of artefacts and espoused values with regard to assessment can expose whether there is a difference between the espoused value of assessment activities and the enacted values that are actually experienced within an institution...For universities to demonstrate that assessment is what the majority of people value and believe, learning assurance must be an espoused value. Evaluating the formal, documented procedures...that explicitly articulate rewards is one way of determining how faculty members feel and what an organisational values.

## Develop and Communicate a Strategy

A critical function of the guiding coalition is the importance of clarifying the direction of change. In the context of assurance of learning, it includes a commitment to provide a good evidential support identifying the areas of strength and any areas needing improvement related to graduates (Gray, Smart, and Bennett, 2017), while providing a scaffolded learning experience to develop students throughout their degree program, thus, not merely assurance at an exit point, but a continual process to support students to achieve the expectations of a degree program (Lawson, 2015). Training and professional development of staff are key. The activities could include providing increased support for academics in designing subjects and programs leading to improvements not just at subject level, but also at program level; support of teaching and learning consultants and designers; delivering workshops where staff develop assessment tasks as an outcome; having discipline groups meetings with curriculum designers engaging in discussions; delivering workshops to share views on what seems to work and what does not; and offering teaching grants, both internal and external.

## Empower Others to Act on the Vision

The next step of the guiding coalition is to empower broad-based action by actively working with the rest of the faculty and schools. These activities could include involving assurance of learning champions, program directors, subject coordinators, administrative person to feedback the results, and supporting them through mentoring and coaching, ensuring that every stakeholder does their part by using evidence to create quality as part of a systematic process.

## Create Short-Terms Wins, Consolidate Improvements, and Institutionalize New Approaches

In this step, academics occupying leadership positions should ensure to define and engineer visible performance improvements. The key is to start with something simple, for example, ensuring that academics within a course (degree program) team have a shared understanding of where in the curriculum, key concepts, skills, and attributes articulated in the program learning outcomes are developed and ultimately assessed at the level expected of a graduate. The subject coordinators should then ensure that the enacted curriculum mirrors the intended or mapped curriculum, and if does not, following discussion of the analysis of assurance of learning data at a relevant assessment committee, make appropriate changes within subjects (units), and disseminate that information within the relevant program team. Academics contributing to those improvements should be recognized and rewarded. Once assurance of learning data has been collected for all learning outcomes within a course, a closing of the loop meeting could be held to discuss and implement broader changes to the course. Other mechanisms to consolidate improvements could include using the increased credibility from early wins to change systems, structures, and policies undermining the mission; hiring, promoting, and developing academics who can implement the mission; and reinvigorating the change process with new projects and change agents. Finally, it is important that assurance of learning processes are embedded within broader institutionalized mechanisms such as program design and program review policy and procedures, as well as relevant codes of practices, so that the changes are consistent with social norms and shared values.

In concluding this chapter, while there is not a one-size-fits-all approach to creating a culture of assurance of learning, following the MLL's approach within a broader Lawson and Kotter model may help lay the foundation for building an effective approach to assuring student learning. To change assessment from a compliance mentality to one of assuring student learning and continuous improvement, both espoused and enacted values should reflect its importance in critical documents, processes, and practices.

---

## ACKNOWLEDGMENT

The author thanks Dr. Jan Turbill, Faculty Education Consultant, for her helpful comments on an earlier version of the chapter.

## REFERENCES

Association to Advance Collegiate Schools of Business (AACSB). (2013. ). AACSB assurance of learning standards: An interpretation. White Paper No. 3.

Association of American Colleges and Universities (AAC&U). (2015). *VALUE Rubrics*. Retrieved from https://www.aacu.org/value-rubrics/

Barrie, S.C. (2004) A research-based approach to generic graduate attributes policy, *Higher Education Research and Development*, 23(3), 261–275.

Barrie, S., Hughes, C. and Smith, C. (2009). *The National Graduate Attributes Project: Integration and Assessment of Graduate Attributes in Curriculum*. Retrieved from Australian Learning & Teaching Council website: http://www.altc.edu.au/resource-national-graduate-attributesproject-sydney-2009

Commonwealth of Australia. (2009). *Transforming Australia's Higher Education System*. Canberra, Australia: Attorney-General's Department.

Eder, D.J. (2005) A culture of assessment. In K. Martell and T. Calderon (eds.), *Assessment of Student Learning in Business Schools: Best Practices Each Step of the Way* (Vols. 1, No. 1, pp. 51–65). Tallahassee, FL: Association for Institutional Research.

Fullan, M. and Scott, G. (2009). *Turnaround Leadership for Higher Education*. San Francisco, CA: Jossey-Bass.

Gray, P.J. (2010). Assessment that transforms an institution. In G.L. Kramer and R.L. Swing (eds.), *Higher Education Assessments: Leadership Matters* (pp. 179–212). Lanham, MD: Rowman & Littlefield, Inc.

Gray, D.M., Smart, K.L. and Bennett, M.M. (2017). Examining espoused and enacted values in AACSB assurance of learning, *Journal of Education for Business*, 92(5), 255–261.

Johnson, W. (2016). *On Being a Mentor: A Guide for Higher Education Faculty*, 2nd edition. New York: Routledge.

Johnson, W.B. (2006) *On Being a Mentor: A Guide for Higher Education Faculty*. Mahwah, NJ, USA: Erlbaum.

Jones, S., Ladyshewsky, R., Oliver, B. and Flavell, H. (2009). *Leadership Foundation for Higher Education. Leading Courses: Academic Leadership for Course Coordinators*. Australian Learning and Teaching Council Ltd., Creative Commons.

Joyce, B. and Showers, B. (2002). *Designing Training and Peer Coaching: Our Needs for Learning Student Achievement Through Staff Development*, 3rd edition. Alexandria, VA: Association for Supervision and Curriculum Development.

Kinash, S., Mathew, T., Lawson, R., Herbert, J., French, E., Taylor, T., Hall, C., Fallshaw, E. and Summers, J. (2012) Australian higher education evaluation through assurance of learning, *8th International Conference on Evaluation for Practice: Evaluation as a Tool for Research, Learning and Making Things Better*, June, Pori, Finland.

Kotter, J.P. (2007). Leading change: Why transformation efforts fail, *Harvard Business Review*, 85(1), 96–103.

Krause, K., Scott, G., Aubin, K., Alexander, H., Angelo, T., Campbell, S., Carroll, M., Deane E., Nulty, D., Pattison, P., Probert, B., Sachs, J., Solomonides, I. and Vaughan, S. (2014). *Assuring Final Year Subject and Program Achievement Standards Through Inter-University Peer Review and Moderation*. Canberra: Australian Government Office of Learning and Teaching. Retrieved from http://tinyurl.com/p9r2f84

Krneta, R., Milosevic, D., Bozovic, M. and Mitrovic, A. (2012). Self-evaluation of distance learning study program as a part of internal quality assurance, *International Journal of Emerging Technologies in Learning*, 7(1), 14–20.

Lane, M.R., Lane, P.L., Rich, J. & Wheeling, B. (2014) Improving assessment: Creating a culture of assessment with a change management approach, *Journal of Case Studies in Accreditation and Assessment*, 4, 1–11.

Lawson, R.. (2015). *Assuring Learning; Leadership*. Retrieved from http://www.assuringl earning.com/leadership

Lawson, R., Taylor, T., Herbert, J., Fallshaw, E., French, E., Hall, C., Kinash, S. and Summers, J. (2013). *Hunters and Gatherers: Strategies for Curriculum Mapping and Data Collection for Assuring Learning*. Final Report, Office for Learning and Teaching, Department of Industry, Innovation, Science, Research and Tertiary Education, Sydney, Australian Government.

Mansilla, V.B., Duraisingh, E.D., Wolfe, C.R. and Haynes, C. (2009) Targeted assessment rubric: An empirically grounded rubric for interdisciplinary writing, *The Journal of Higher Education*, 80, 334–353.

Martell, K. (2005). Overcoming faculty resistance to assessment. In K. Martell and T. Calderon (eds.), *Assessment of Student Learning in Business Schools: Best Practices Each Step of the Way* (Vol. 1, No. 2, 210–226). Tallahassee, FL: Association for Institutional Research.

Mullen, C.A. (2005). *Mentorship Primer*. New York: Peter Lang.

Nash, R., Lawson, R., Williams, A., Kelder, J., Scheepers, M. and Taylor, T. (2016) Surveys unite to provide current status of Assurance of Learning in Higher Education. In M. Davis and A. Goody (eds.), *Research and Development in Higher Education: The Shape of Higher Education* (Vol. 39, pp. 235–247). Australia: Fremantle, July 4–7.

Nickerson, J. (2014). *Leading Change from the Middle: A Practical Guide to Building Extraordinary Capabilities (Innovations in Leadership)*. Washington, DC: Brookings Institutional Press.

O'Donovan, B., Price, M. and Rust, C. (2004). Know what I mean? Enhancing student understanding of assessment standards and criteria, *Teaching in Higher Education*, 9(3), 325–335.

Rexeisen, R.J. and Garrison, M.J. (2013). Closing the loop in assurance of learning programs: Current practices and future challenges, *Journal of Education for Business*, 88(5), 280–285.

Schein, E.H. (1990). Organizational culture, *American Psychologist*, 45, 109–119.

Sims, H.P. and Manz, C.C. (1982). Social learning theory: The roles of modeling in the exercise of leadership, *Journal of Organizational Behavior Management*, 3–4, 55–63.

Sumsion, J. and Goodfellow, J. (2004) Identifying generic skills through curriculum mapping: A critical evaluation, *Higher Education Research & Development*, 23(3), 329–346.

Taylor, T., Thompson, D., Clements, L., Simpson, L., Paltridge, A., Fletcher, M. and Rohde, F. (2009). *Facilitating Staff and Student Engagement with Graduate Attribute Development, Assessment and Standards in Business Faculties.* Retrieved from Australian Learning & Teaching Council website: http://www.altc.edu.au/resourc e-facilitating-staff-student-uts-2009

The Higher Education Standards Framework. (2015). *Learning Outcomes and Assessment.* Retrieved from https://www.legislation.gov.au/Details/F2015L01639

Yorke, M. (1998). Assessing capability. In J. Stephenson and M. Yorke (eds.), *Capability and Quality in Higher Education* (pp. 174–191). London: Kogan Page.

# 5

## Combining Coaching and Mentoring to Support Gender Inclusion in Quality Management-Focused Organizations in the UAE Private Sector

*Meredith Henthorn and Jenny Knowles Morrison*

## CONTENTS

In this chapter, we argue that quality management-focused organizations can use coaching and mentoring to enable gender inclusion in culturally diverse and male-dominated environments such as the United Arab Emirates (UAE) private sector. We focus on the UAE private sector, given its emphasis on quality, the vast cultural diversity of the workforce, and the presence of cultural barriers that negatively impact women's careers. Our chapter presents a framework that combines specific coaching and mentoring practices that can be implemented within male-dominated workplaces to achieve the behavior and cultural changes necessary to enable gender inclusion and women's career advancement. Given that the coaching and mentoring practices described in the scholarly literature are Western in origin, we describe three specific modifications to make coaching and mentoring more culturally appropriate for use in collectivist and high power distance cultures, such as the UAE. In addition to benefiting practice by providing guidance to organizations, our research adds to five areas of limited scholarship: (1) gender inclusion within the quality management (QM) profession; (2) gender inclusion in the Middle East region; (3) utilizing mentoring and coaching to promote gender inclusion; (4) combining mentoring and coaching within organizations; and (5) the cultural adaptation of mentoring and coaching practices for use in non-Western cultures.

> The Middle East, Africa, and Asia still suffer from women-in-authority issues, which limits [women's] ability to serve in quality management roles.
>
> **Quality Management Journal Editorial Board Member, 2019**
> **(Foster, 2019, p.66)**

## INTRODUCTION

In this chapter, we argue that mentoring and coaching can assist quality management-focused organizations in the United Arab Emirates (UAE) in achieving gender inclusion. The framework we advance extends research concerning national culture, mentoring, and coaching, as well as QM practice. This chapter provides guidance to organizations in the form of a framework that combines specific uses of mentoring and coaching to foster women's inclusion in male-dominated workplaces. As mentoring and coaching are Western in origin, we modify mentoring and coaching practices for the collectivist and high power distance culture of the UAE through three recommendations: (1) emphasize the future-oriented, developmental aspects of mentoring and coaching; (2) offer group mentoring; and (3) provide interactive skill-building training and process guidance to proactively support all involved in mentoring and coaching.

In addition to benefiting practice by providing guidance to organizations, our research adds to five areas of limited scholarship: (1) gender inclusion within the QM profession; (2) gender inclusion in the Middle East region; (3) utilizing mentoring and coaching to promote gender inclusion; (4) combining mentoring and coaching within organizations; and (5) the cultural adaptation of mentoring and coaching practices for use in non-Western cultures.

Mentoring has been critical to the advancement of most managers and leaders, particularly women (Abalkhail & Allan, 2015; Eagly & Carli, 2007; Gray, Lee, & Totta, 1995; Metz, 2009). Organizations have used mentoring and coaching to reduce stereotyping and bias for the purposes of engendering a climate of gender inclusion to benefit women's careers (Chao, 2007; Dobbin, Schrage, & Kalev, 2015; Gray et al., 1995; Nair & Vohra, 2017; Metz, 2009). Specific to the Middle East context, mentoring and coaching have been identified as promising employee and organization development practices, and women leaders in the region have expressed interest in using mentoring and coaching to facilitate career advancement and create gender inclusive organization cultures (Al-Nasser & Behery, 2015; Waxin & Bateman, 2016; Dunlop, Schreiber, & El Attar, 2015). However, mentoring and coaching are under-researched and not widely practiced in the Middle East (Al-Nasser & Behery, 2015; Palmer & Arnold, 2013; Waxin & Bateman, 2016).

We define mentoring and coaching as follows:

- Mentoring is a dyadic, relationship-based process through which a mentor, who is an experienced employee, provides career-related guidance and support to a mentee, who is a less experienced employee (Kram, 1985).
- Coaching is a helping relationship with a developmental focus played out in conversations that stimulate the person or group being coached to greater awareness, deeper and broader thought, and wiser decisions and actions (Riddle, Hoole, & Gullette, 2015, p.xvii).

Mentoring and coaching have been identified as valuable forms of learning and knowledge transfer within organizations engaged in QM (Ahmad & Daghfous, 2010; Gillies, 2015), yet the potential of mentoring and coaching to enhance QM practice has been under-researched (Gutierrez-Gutierrez, Barrales-Molina, & Kaynak, 2018). In this chapter, we argue that QM-focused organizations can combine coaching and mentoring to enable gender inclusion and strengthen leadership and management practices.

We focus this chapter on the UAE, given significant QM utilization within businesses (Dubai Quality Group, n.d.), the vast cultural diversity within the private sector workforce (Beyond Qatar Business Magazine, 2014; Gulf Research Center, 2015; Hodgson & Hanson, 2014), and the presence of cultural barriers that negatively impact women's careers, such as preventing them from being considered for management roles (Al Marzouqi & Forster, 2011; Al-Asfour, Tlaiss, Khan, & Rajasekar, 2017; Deloitte, 2016; Dunlop et al., 2015; Farrell, 2008; Foster, 2019; Hutchings, Metcalfe, & Cooper, 2010; Metcalfe, 2006; Tlaiss, 2013). While women are increasingly joining the UAE private sector, many workplaces remain male-dominated and women's presence in leadership is limited (al-Kazi, 2008; Al Marzouqi & Forster, 2011; GrantThorton, 2018; Kemp, 2015; Khoja & Thomas, 2017; Madsen, 2010; Suliman, 2006). While studies have described the disadvantages faced by women in male-dominated industries, limited scholarly research has provided guidance to organizations and leaders for using mentoring and coaching to mitigate these disadvantages, especially in the Middle East.

A further reason for focusing this chapter on the UAE is the fact that a national talent shortage may force businesses to become more inclusive (Korn Ferry, 2018). Women in the UAE are a highly educated and underutilized pool of talent who are increasingly successful in competing for knowledge economy jobs and thus could alleviate talent shortage concerns (Gallant & Pounder, 2008; Madsen, 2010). In support of women joining the private sector, the UAE government has stressed women should be empowered to contribute to the nation through employment in the private sector, yet the scholarly literature contains limited guidance for adapting organizational cultures and practices so that women are welcomed and their work contributions valued (Al Marzouqi & Forster, 2011).

This chapter begins by elaborating the case for gender inclusion in QM. Second, we provide an overview of the conventional mentoring and coaching literature. Third, we review the QM literature focused on mentoring and coaching. Fourth, we discuss cultural adaptations that

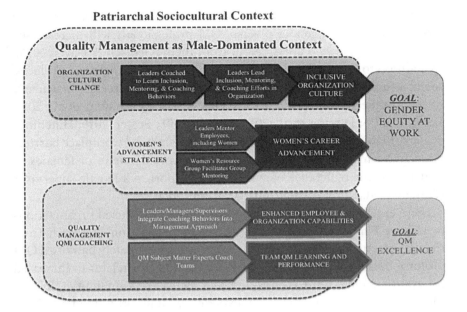

**FIGURE 5.1**
Using coaching and mentoring to promote gender equity and quality management excellence.

may be appropriate for mentoring and coaching programs implemented in UAE organizations. Fifth, we present our framework for mentoring and coaching in QM-focused organizations in the UAE private sector. Last, we discuss directions for future research. In Figure 5.1, we provide a visual overview of the concepts and processes discussed in this chapter.

## THE CASE FOR GENDER INCLUSION WITHIN QUALITY MANAGEMENT

Male-dominated industries, which are common settings for QM work, can pose significant barriers to women's career advancement (Burcher, Lee, & Waddell, 2008; CQI, 2018; Giffi, Huelsman, Rodriguez, & McClelland, 2017). Male-dominated organizations typically provide limited support for women's distinctive career needs and have fewer women in leadership positions to serve as role models and mentors (Bierema, 2016; Caleo & Heilman, 2013; Eagly & Carli, 2007; Germain, Herzog, & Hamilton, 2012; Hutchings et al., 2010; Ibarra, Ely, & Kolb, 2013; Metz & Kulik, 2014; Özdemir

& Albayrak, 2015; Panina, 2016). At the same time, as workplaces become more culturally and gender diverse, QM professionals will increasingly engage with those who are different from them (Geotsch & Davis, 2015). In addition to the challenges women face in male-dominated workplaces, sociocultural forces can negatively impact women's careers, particularly in the Middle East (Al Marzouqi & Forster, 2011; Al-Asfour et al., 2017; Deloitte, 2016; Dunlop et al., 2015; Farrell, 2008; Foster, 2019; Hutchings et al., 2010; Metcalfe, 2006; Tlaiss, 2013). Sociocultural workplace barriers faced by women in the region include unfavorable views of females as leaders and the reluctance of some men to report to a female supervisor (Dunlop et al., 2015; Farrell, 2008; Metcalfe, 2006).

There are compelling economic reasons for QM-focused organizations to remove barriers to women's workplace participation. Research from the manufacturing industry, which employs approximately half of all QM professionals (ASQ, 2018), shows gender diversity correlates to increased innovation, higher returns on equity, and increased profitability (Noland, Moran, & Kotschwar, 2016). As experiences and skills tend to differ between men and women, gender inclusive teams have the potential to be more innovative and productive (Greenwood, Carnahan, & Huang, 2018; Ostry, Alvarez, Espinoza, & Papageorgiou, 2018; Wasserman, Gallegos, & Ferdman, 2008). In addition, inclusive organizations are better able to recruit and retain talent (Bierema, 2016). For example, an important criterion for early career women deciding which male-dominated employer to join is how well employers treat the early career women they already employ (Jagsi, Griffith, DeCastro, & Ubel, 2014). Gender inclusion may help organizations realize employee potential and improve performance.

To provide recommendations to guide organizations in developing their own inclusion strategies, we introduce Nishii's (2013) three dimensions of inclusive organization climates. First, organizational employment and diversity practices should focus on eliminating bias (Nishii, 2013). Second, diversity should be valued and respected, with diverse individuals welcomed and included by others. Third, diverse individuals and diverse perspectives should be actively sought out and integrated into organizational decision-making (Nishii, 2013). Extending this framework to promote women's inclusion within male-dominated contexts would likely include: eliminating practices that unfairly discriminate against women; enacting strategies that promote equity; actively soliciting women's perspectives; valuing women's contributions; and integrating women into all levels of organizational decision-making and leadership.

In the next section, we discuss how organizations and leaders can utilize mentoring and coaching to foster such practices.

## MENTORING AND COACHING ENABLE INCLUSION

In this section, we explain the rationale for combining coaching and mentoring to guide gender inclusion efforts, including why coaching may be particularly useful in mitigating patriarchy's detrimental influence on women's careers. We argue that coaching, as an individualized, interactive, and iterative form of learning and skill building, is an appropriate development technique for realizing the behavior changes necessary to achieve gender inclusion (Jackson & Cox, 2018). We also argue that if all top leaders authentically participate in coaching to learn inclusion behaviors, the cumulative effect will be a more inclusive organizational climate (Riddle et al., 2015). By working with a professional coach, leaders learn to effectively coach and mentor across gender and culture. The goal of the coaching is for leaders to become comfortable integrating coaching behaviors into their management work and gain confidence in their ability to serve as effective mentors, especially to female employees. This is particularly important in patriarchal societies and organizations, where men hold a majority of leadership positions and structural factors may limit women's influence in important matters (Glick & Fiske, 1997; Mostafa, 2005).

We argue that coaching leaders about gender inclusion is essential to the success of mentoring programs intended to advance women's careers in patriarchal organizations. This is based on the assumption that leaders may not possess the knowledge and skills necessary to be inclusive mentors and coaches, along with evidence that leadership participation is critical to the success of organizational mentoring and inclusion efforts (Allen, Finkelstein, & Poteet, 2009; Booysen, 2014; Dawson, Thomas, & Goren, 2013; Dobbin et al., 2015; Gray et al., 1995; Stokes & Merrick, 2016; Tabbron, Macaulay, & Cook, 1997). In other words, mentoring alone is not enough to advance women's careers in patriarchal organizations. For women's mentoring programs to succeed, leaders must ensure the organization climate is conducive to women's career advancement. In addition, leaders must actively engage in mentoring to signal their support of women's advancement. In an example from a male-dominated bank, leaders fostered dialogue about diversity and mentored women, activities that reduced gender bias and enabled women to fairly compete for available leadership roles within the bank (Gray et al., 1995; Metz, 2009). Leadership participation in inclusion and mentoring efforts is important because leaders influence perceptions of cultural norms and acceptable behavior (Lankau & Scandura, 2007).

Through working with an external coach, leaders learn about obstacles that hinder women's advancement, such as stereotype-based discrimination (Heilman & Eagly, 2008; Hoobler, Masterson, Nkomo, & Michel, 2018; Schein, 1973, 1975). Stereotype-based discrimination occurs when women are unfairly viewed as being less managerial than men, often resulting in hiring, evaluation, and promotion decisions that are biased against women (Eagly, 1987; Eagly & Diekman, 2005; Hoyt, 2012; Rudman, 2005). A leader works with his or her coach to develop strategies to mitigate discrimination and promote inclusion. Depending on the leader's position in the organization, leadership activities might include helping define and communicate the organization's inclusion strategy; making explicit the connections between inclusion and organization values; fostering dialogue about diversity; role modeling inclusive behaviors; and promoting accountability for inclusion (Chrobot-Mason, Ruderman, & Nishii, 2013; Ferdman, 2014; Gotsis & Grimani, 2016).

While the focus of this chapter is the culturally appropriate use of coaching and mentoring for gender inclusion, with the desired outcome being equity of opportunity for women in male-dominated environments, men should not be excluded from access to mentoring and coaching. In inclusive organizations, all employees, including men, should have access to development opportunities. Inclusive organizations value and engage employees of all identities and facilitate understanding and collaboration across differences (Booysen, 2014; Ely & Thomas, 2001; Nishii, 2013), with inclusion occurring when all individuals and groups are supported (Syed & Ozbilgin, 2009). Later in this chapter, we will discuss how organizations can equitably provide mentoring and coaching to all employees.

## MENTORING AND COACHING ASSIST WOMEN'S CAREER ADVANCEMENT

As mentoring and coaching are adaptable forms of learning and development, they can be customized for specific organizational uses, such as promoting gender inclusion, and modified for application in different cultural contexts (Chao, 2007; Clutterbuck, 2007; Clutterbuck & Ragins, 2002; Clutterbuck, Kochan, Lunsford, Dominguez, Haddock-Miller, 2017; Megginson, Clutterbuck, Garvey, Stokes, & Garrett-Harris, 2006; Murrell & Blake-Beard, 2017; Murrell, Crosby, & Ely, 1999; Passmore, 2013). Because mentoring and coaching are personalized and are interactive forms of learning and development that are carried out over time, they have the potential to be more effective than training in accomplishing behavior change though consistent reinforcement (Bright & Megginson, 2017; Ulanovsky & Perez, 2017).

Formal, organization-sponsored mentoring programs are beneficial to women in male-dominated organizations, as women may have particularly limited organization networks through which to recruit an effective mentor on their own (Blancero & Cotton-Nessler, 2017). Therefore, an important element of our framework is the establishment of a formal, organization-sponsored mentoring program through which all employees, including women, can be matched to a capable mentor and provided with mentoring training, resources, and process support. Formal mentoring programs equalize access to networking and career support for underrepresented employees. Formal programs are also particularly beneficial for newly hired employees (Blancero & Cotton-Nessler, 2017).

## MENTORING AND COACHING

Mentoring and coaching are both relationship-based, developmental activities (Rock & Garavan, 2006). Multiple similarities can be observed between the practices of mentoring and coaching. As these similarities can cause confusion, we point out the following prominent distinctions. Coaching is typically focused on improving performance within a relatively short time frame, while mentoring is career-focused and thus concerned with both short-term and long-term career matters. In sum, coaching focuses on improving short-term job performance, while mentoring focuses on supporting the mentee's current and future professional development needs (Beattie et al., 2014; Ellinger & Kim, 2014; Garvey, Stokes, & Megginson, 2018; Gray, Garvey, & Lane, 2016; McDonald & Hite, 2016; Rock & Garavan, 2006; Sturges, 2012).

## Mentoring

Mentoring is a relationship-based process through which a mentor, who is an experienced employee, provides career-related guidance and support to a mentee, who is a less experienced employee (Kram, 1985). The main purpose of mentoring is to facilitate the mentee's career development. Mentoring takes the form of a series of dialogue sessions over an extended period of time. The contents of the discussions are mostly driven by the mentee, as the focus is addressing the gap between the mentee's present-day competencies and those necessary to achieve the mentee's career goals. The role of the mentor is to provide the mentee with two different forms of support: (1) psychosocial support and (2) career-related support (Eby, Rhodes, & Allen, 2010). Psychosocial support includes providing emotional and social support, role modeling, and counseling. Career support includes coaching, championing, and sponsoring the mentee (Kram, 1985; O'Neill, 2002). For example, to provide career support, a mentor would leverage his or her knowledge as a subject matter expert and organizational insider to suggest developmental strategies that would benefit the mentee (Kram, 1985).

There are multiple benefits associated with mentoring for mentees, mentors, and organizations. Mentees receive more promotions and report higher job satisfaction and self-efficacy than those who are not mentored (Allen et al., 2009; Hegstad, 1999). Through mentoring, mentors improve their leadership skills and increase their organizational influence (Hegstad, 1999; Lockwood, Evans, & Eby, 2010; Ramaswami & Dreher, 2010). Organizations that encourage mentoring benefit from enhanced organizational attraction, commitment, and retention of employees (Allen, Eby, Poteet, Lentz, & Lima, 2004; Allen et al., 2009). In addition, mentoring fosters networking and knowledge sharing among employees, helps new employees learn organization norms, and assists employees in adjusting to organizational changes (Allen et al., 2009; Kram & Hall, 1989; Scandura & Siegal, 1995). Learning how to effectively mentor is a form of leadership development and organizations may purposely arrange mentor-mentee pairings to support succession plans (Allen et al., 2009).

It is typical to characterize mentoring relationships as either formal or informal. Informal mentoring relationships are arranged by the mentee without employer involvement. In contrast, a formal mentoring relationship occurs within the context of an organization-sponsored mentoring program. An organization-sponsored program facilitates the matching of mentees and mentors and provides process guidance to increase mentoring effectiveness (Giscombe, 2007). Formal, organization-facilitated mentoring programs are purposely implemented for the benefit of both employees and the organization (Hegstad, 1999). Resources provided to mentors and mentees often include training as well as templates for developing a mentee's career plan, a mentoring agreement, and a mentoring action plan (Allen et al., 2009). Careful matching of mentors and mentees is important, as what the mentee gains from the mentoring relationship is dependent on the career experiences and abilities of the mentor (Lockwood et al., 2010).

Unfortunately, there are numerous shortcomings in the mentoring literature that limit our chapter. Burke and McKeen (1997) critiqued mentoring research as lacking an integrated research model or framework (Bozeman & Feeney, 2007). Bozeman and Feeney's (2007, p.721) summarized the literature's shortcomings, "Despite the publications of hundreds of studies of mentoring, many of the findings are less useful than one might hope because fundamental, conceptual, and theoretical issues have been skirted. Findings are abundant but explanations are not." The strategies, practices, and behaviors associated with mentoring, including how mentoring facilitates learning, are not well understood (Bozeman & Feeney, 2007). Even less is known about mentoring and coaching across cultures (Abbott & Rosinksi, 2007; Zhuang, Wu, & Wen, 2013; Salomaa, 2015).

## Mentoring Women

Mentoring can benefit all employees, particularly women (Abalkhail & Allan, 2015; Eagly & Carli, 2007; Gray, Lee, & Totta, 1995; Metz, 2009). Mentoring's potentially greater benefit to women is not attributable to deficiencies among women; instead, the heightened benefit is the result of women gaining access to equitable development opportunities and networking opportunities (de Vries, 2011; Giscombe, 2007). Mentoring is particularly useful to women because it provides access to career counsel from influential leaders, which may otherwise by difficult for women to obtain in male-dominated organizations (Giscombe, 2007).

Recent mentoring research advises the utility of having more than one mentor (Murphy et al., 2017; Shen & Kram, 2011). Having multiple mentors may be especially relevant for women for two reasons. First, in patriarchal cultures, distinct career needs arise from women's substantial family responsibilities (Blake-Beard et al., 2017). Second, men and women mentors tend to provide different forms of mentoring support. Male mentors typically provide access to instrumental social networks that can lead to career advancement opportunities, while female mentors provide coping support for navigating gender bias and balancing home and work commitments (Eagly & Carli, 2007; Murphy, Gibson, & Kram, 2017). Given the benefits of having access to a male mentor, later in this chapter we provide a recommendation for how organizations might offer cross-gender mentoring in a culturally appropriate way.

## Coaching

While mentoring is typically focused on career development, coaching is used to address a variety of learning and performance concerns. Riddle et al. (2015, p.xvii) describe coaching as practiced in organizations as follows:

> Coaching is a helping relationship with a developmental focus played out in conversations that stimulate the person or group being coached to greater awareness, deeper and broader thought, and wiser decisions and actions. The conversations are developmental because they always have in mind the improvement of the person's perceiving, thinking, and reflecting, as well as the solution to the concern at hand. It is a helping relationship because the benefit is clearly focused on the value to the person being coached and her leadership responsibilities. Coaching conversations are an important means by which experiences are turned into learning.

For purposes of this chapter, we address two types of coaching practiced within organizations. To differentiate between the two, we borrow portions of the International Coach Federation's (ICF) coaching continuum, as shown in Figure 5.2. First, there are external coaches who are contracted by an organization to coach an employee, typically a leader, on a particular

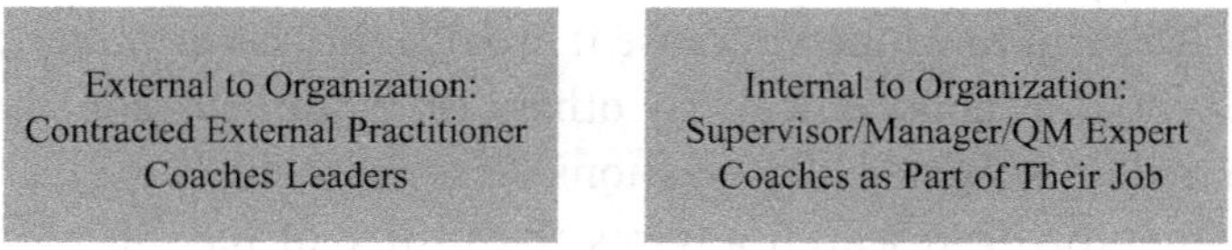

| External to Organization: Contracted External Practitioner Coaches Leaders | Internal to Organization: Supervisor/Manager/QM Expert Coaches as Part of Their Job |
|---|---|

**FIGURE 5.2**
Coaching external and internal to the organization. (Adapted from ICF, 2016.)

topic. Second, there are employees, such as managers and supervisors, who engage in coaching as part of their work. In Figure 5.1, the left box represents external coach practitioners, while the right box represents managers and supervisors who are employees who utilize coaching behaviors as part of their work (ICF, 2016).

Our framework recommends one specific use of external coaching and two specific uses of internal coaching. First, our framework utilizes external coaches to help leaders develop three skill sets: (1) gender and cultural inclusion; (2) mentoring; and (3) coaching. More specifically, leaders will be coached to become more inclusive leaders, to learn how lead or support organizational inclusion efforts, to become effective mentors within their organization's formal mentoring program, and to employ coaching behaviors in their leadership and management work. We suggest external coaches work individually with all executive and senior leaders for these purposes.

As noted in the paragraph above, through working with external coaches, leaders learn how to use coaching behaviors in their work. More specifically, the intention is for leaders to learn basic coaching techniques that can be used to enhance the learning and performance of direct reports, and possibly other employees with whom the leader interacts. The coaching behaviors leaders learn to implement in their work are less sophisticated than the coaching processes used by professional coaches. When leaders, managers, or supervisors use coaching behaviors in their work with employees, this can be referred to as managerial coaching. Managerial coaching is one of two specific uses of internal coaching in our framework. The second use of internal coaching in our framework is QM-specific. In this use, QM subject matter experts implement coaching behaviors to facilitating QM learning and performance, particularly with teams who have QM responsibilities.

To transition from external to internal coaching, we suggest managers and supervisors be provided guidance for how to integrate coaching behavior into their work with employees. The executive and senior leaders who are coached by external coaches can help the managers in their chain of command learn coaching behaviors. Other forms of support such as training or self-study materials could be offered. Alternatively, if resources allow, organizations can arrange for all those who have supervisory authority to work with external coaches.

Recommending that leaders, managers, and supervisors engage in coaching behaviors aligns with the QM literature's suggestion that coaching

| Empowering Coaching Behaviors | Facilitating Coaching Behaviors |
|---|---|
| • Instead of giving directions or answers, ask questions that support others in thinking through issues and problem solving<br><br>• Transfer ownership and accountability to employees<br><br>• Serve as a resource to employees and assist in removing obstacles | • Provide feedback<br>• Solicit feedback<br>• Talk through problems together<br>• Promote workplace learning<br>• Communicate expectations<br>• Help by reframing and providing alternative perspectives<br>• Make use of analogies, scenarios, and examples<br>• Help others develop skills to become facilitators of learning |

**FIGURE 5.3**
Behavioral taxonomy of coaching by managers. (Adapted from Ellinger et al., 2014.)

behaviors can be effective for promoting QM learning and performance. However, a shortcoming of the QM literature is that it provides limited guidance to those wishing to use coaching behaviors in their work; therefore, we fill this gap by describing how managerial coaching is presented in the organizational coaching literature. Managerial coaches serve as facilitators of on-the-job learning and development for employees, while also supporting and encouraging effective employee performance (Ellinger, Beattie, & Hamlin, 2014). Specific activities involved in managerial coaching include cultivating a learning environment, providing care and support to employees, promoting open communication and feedback, and securing resources (Hamlin, Ellinger, & Beattie, 2006). As depicted in Figure 5.3, these behaviors can be grouped into two clusters: (1) behaviors that empower direct reports and (2) behaviors that facilitate effective processes and outcomes.

Our purpose in the above section was to provide an overview of mentoring and coaching in organizations. Having this foundation is useful for addressing how to best employ mentoring and coaching to support gender inclusion and QM activities. Specific to gender, while it has been established that mentoring can be especially beneficial to women, gender's relevance to coaching remains understudied. For example, no studies have investigated the role of gender or cultural diversity in managerial coaching, and some scholar-practitioners have suggested that the mentoring literature's discussion of diversity should be used to inform managerial coaching practice (Hunt & Weintraub, 2017). Next, we review the QM literature to describe uses of mentoring and coaching specific to QM.

## QUALITY MANAGEMENT LITERATURE'S DISCUSSION OF MENTORING AND COACHING

In this section, we discuss the QM literature's coverage of mentoring and coaching. QM can be defined as "a holistic management philosophy that strives for continuous improvement in all functions of an organization" (Kaynak, 2003, p.406). As some QM publications use the terms mentoring and coaching interchangeably, we do not distinguish between mentoring and coaching in this section.

QM publications typically positioned mentoring and coaching as behaviors for supervisors or other experienced employees to use in one of two ways: (1) as a preferred orientation to supervision intended to empower employees rather than "boss" (Goetsch & Davis, 2015, p.147) them (Caldwell, 1993), or (2) as a technique to facilitate learning and improve QM performance (Ahmad & Daghfous, 2010; Anthony, Gijo, Kumar, & Ghadge, 2016; Berian et al., 2017; Bourg, Stolzfus, McManus, & Fry, 2010; Eitzen & Cunningham, 2009; Gillies, 2015; Goetsch & Davis, 2015; Henderson & McAdam, 2000; Lasrado, 2016; Lasrado & Pereira, 2018; Lin & Wu, 2005; Melan, 1998; Ndihokubwayo et al., 2016; Perrone et al. 2016a; Perrone et al., 2016b; Pollock & Mott; 2015; Psychogios, Atanasovski, & Tsironis, 2012; Ross, 2019; Rother & Aulinger, 2017; Rother, 2018; Thiagaragan, Zairi, & Dale, 2001; Waterbury, 2015). In addition to the QM-specific uses, several QM publications described mentoring as an activity that enhanced learning, career development, and organization effectiveness, which are typical uses of mentoring within a variety of organizations (Conklin, 2016; Goetsch & Davis, 2015; Kovach, 2017; Smith, 2011; Tabbron et al., 1997).

We observed that the publications provided limited guidance for how to engage in mentoring and coaching, with noted exceptions (Rother; 2018; Rother & Aulinger; 2017; Pollock & Mott; 2015; Ross, 2019; Conklin, 2016; Kovach, 2017). Relatedly, few of the publications referenced scholarly mentoring and coaching literature. We noticed gender and inclusion were infrequently discussed in the QM literature (Goetsch & Davis, 2015; Rochetti, 2016; Lanza, 1997; Wilkof & Schneer, 1995; Hyter, 2004; Hopen, 2004), apart from the acknowledgement that as workplaces become more culturally and gender diverse, QM professionals are increasingly working across differences (Geotsch & Davis, 2015; Lasrado, 2018). Next, we discuss cultural adaptations of mentoring and coaching appropriate for the UAE.

## MENTORING AND COACHING CONSIDERATIONS IN THE UAE

The UAE is a demographically diverse country with one of the world's highest ratios of expatriates to nationals (Hodgson & Hanson, 2014). As shown in Table 5.1, UAE nationals make up only about 11% of the country's population, thereby constituting a minority in their own country (Hodgson & Hanson, 2014; Metcalfe & Murfin, 2011). In contrast, nearly half of the UAE population is made up of expatriates from South Asia. In addition, the UAE hosts significant populations of expatriates originating from other Middle Eastern countries.

Given the extensive cultural diversity within UAE workplaces, cross-cultural training will likely be of benefit (Zakaria, 2000), particularly for those engaged in cross-cultural mentoring and coaching practice. Organizations interested in cross-cultural training may wish to consult Brislin and Yoshida's (1994) four-part framework, which can be customized to address specific organization needs. Cross-cultural training should provide guidance on cross-gender interactions.

## CULTURALLY ADAPTING MENTORING AND COACHING FOR USE IN THE UAE

In this section, we discuss how mentoring and coaching might be adapted for use in the cultural context of the UAE. Culture is critical to address in workplaces as culturally diverse as those of the UAE private sector. In particular, we focus on two cultural phenomenon: (1) collectivism

**TABLE 5.1**

Nationalities with Highest Percentage of UAE Residents

| India | 27% | Egypt | 4% | Palestine | 2% |
|---|---|---|---|---|---|
| Pakistan | 13% | Nepal | 3% | South Africa | 1% |
| UAE national (Emirati) | 11% | China | 2% | Lebanon | 1% |
| Bangladesh | 7% | Sri Lanka | 3% | UK | 1% |
| Philippines | 5% | Jordan | 2% | Ethiopia | 1% |
| Iran | 5% | Afghanistan | 2% | Other | 10% |

*Note.* Percentages rounded to whole numbers.
Beyond Qatar Business Magazine, 2014; Gulf Research Center, 2015.

and (2) power distance, as these have been identified as relevant to cross-cultural mentoring and coaching success (Apospori, Nikandrou, & Panayotopoulou, 2006; Clutterbuck, 2007). Of the limited studies of Middle Eastern culture, several have utilized Hofstede's (1997) national culture survey. As Hofstede's UAE profile (Hofstede Insights, n.d.) is one of few sources of UAE-specific cultural data, we use it as a general reference for this section.

Culture strongly influences individual behavior and gender roles with the result being cultural gender norms are often replicated within organizations (Blancero & Cotton-Nessler, 2017; Mostafa, 2005). Arab cultures and South Asian cultures, which are the origin cultures of most expatriates working in the UAE, are patriarchal and pose barriers to women's career advancement (Al Marzouqi & Forster, 2011; Al-Asfour et al., 2017; Budhwar, Saini, & Bhatnagar, 2005; Deloitte, 2016; Dunlop et al., 2015; Farrell, 2008; Foster, 2019; Haynes & Ghosh, 2012; Hutchings et al., 2010; Metcalfe, 2006; Mostafa, 2005; Nair & Vohra, 2017; Smetana, Chakraborty, & Banerjee-Batist, 2018; Tlaiss, 2013). In a patriarchal culture, men retain structural control over economic, political, and religious institutions (Glick & Fiske, 1997; Mostafa, 2005). In patriarchal organizations, men fill top leadership positions and retain decision-making authority, thereby limiting women's opportunities for career advancement (Haynes & Ghosh, 2012).

## Collectivism and Individualism

Emirati and South Asian cultures are collectivist (Hofstede Insights, n.d.). In collectivist cultures, the needs of a group are often prioritized over the needs of individual members (Blancero & Cotton-Nessler, 2017; Hofstede, 1997). Members of collectivist cultures construe identity as interdependent with group memberships, with typical affiliations including family, work, and nation. Collectivists tend to be motivated by group norms and duties (Triandis, 1995). Collectivistic behaviors may vary subtly across nations, regions, and demographic categories (Triandis, 1995). For Emirati women in particular, collectivism within organizations may present barriers, as there may be few other Emirati women employed in the same organization with whom to form a supportive in-group.

Human resource development practices in collectivistic cultures are influenced by the concept of face, which can be described as a need to maintain respectability and social status (Ho, 1976; Leung & Cohen,

2011; Palmer & Arnold, 2013). An example of preserving face would be providing feedback on an individual's work performance that is more positive than warranted (Palmer & Arnold, 2013). Giving positive feedback preserves harmony, avoids casting doubt on one's in-group, and maintains face for all involved (Feghali, 1997). In the Middle East, offering criticism and directly pointing out weaknesses is typically avoided so face can be maintained (Palmer & Arnold, 2013).

## Power Distance

Power distance reflects the degree to which a society endorses hierarchical authority and status privileges (Blake-Beard et al., 2017; Carl, Gupta, & Javidan, 2004; Hofstede, 1997). Emirati and South Asian cultures are high power distance cultures (Hofstede Insights, n.d.). In high power distance cultures, authority is concentrated at the top of organizational hierarchies (Carl et al., 2004; Hofstede, 1997; Hofstede Insights, n.d.). In high power distance organizations, communication is typically more formal, there are multiple layers of management, and employees may have limited influence over organizational processes. Those with less status must demonstrate respect and deference to those with higher status (Blancero & Cotton-Nessler, 2017). However, some scholars suggest Islamic teachings that require employers to provide meaningful knowledge and skill development opportunities to all employees regardless of level or rank may soften power distance in Islamic-dominant workplaces (Hassi, 2012).

Researchers suggest status-conscious, hierarchical communication norms may hinder mentoring, as reciprocity and candor are considered important for successful mentoring in the West (Apospori et al., 2006; Blake-Beard, 2009). Power and status differences inherent in social and organization systems are important to recognize when mentoring women. In high power distance organizations, those lower in the organization hierarchy must defer to those above them. If men hold most high-level positions, women will routinely be deferring to men. Adding to the likelihood that women are in a lower status position relative to men, in patriarchal societies, the need for women to show deference to men is heighted (Ramaswami, Huang, & Dreher, 2014). Last, being a mentee often requires deferring to a mentor, as mentors typically possess more status and power than mentees (Kalbfleisch, 2007). Therefore, female mentees in high power distance, patriarchal organizations may benefit from alternative forms of mentoring support designed to minimize power difference, such as group mentoring with other women.

## Recommended Cultural Adaptations

Based on the preceding discussion of cultural influences, we make three recommendations for implementing mentoring and coaching in UAE organizations: (1) emphasize the future-oriented, developmental aspects of mentoring and coaching; (2) offer group mentoring; and (3) provide training and support to all involved in mentoring and coaching to mitigate potential challenges. In collectivistic cultures, mentoring should be purposed as a developmental, future-oriented activity, with an emphasis on building knowledge and skills for career advancement. Likewise with coaching, the tone should be positive and activities should focus on enabling future performance rather than addressing weaknesses in current performance (Palmer & Arnold, 2013). To appeal to the desire for status in high power distance cultures, learning to mentor can be positioned as a component of an organization's leadership development strategy, thereby encouraging participation by managers and supervisors (Allen et al., 2009).

Our second recommendation is mentoring programs in collectivistic cultures should encourage various mentoring formats, particularly group formats. Group activities are typically preferred in collectivistic cultures (Gelfand et al., 2004). In addition, group mentoring may lessen social challenges posed by cross-cultural and cross-gender mentoring (Kim & Egan, 2011), such as when cultural norms call for avoiding closed-door conversations between a man and a woman. Group mentoring can also be used to reduce the many layers of power distance women mentees must contend with in high power distance, patriarchal organizations.

Third, a number of potential challenges that may occur in the course of mentoring and coaching can be proactively covered in training to prepare participants for issues they may encounter in practice. For example, training could address the possibility of tension occurring between an employee's mentor and supervisor, given the supervisor may perceive his or her responsibility for employee development is undermined by the guidance provided to an employee by a mentor. Training should incorporate interactive demonstrations by skilled mentors and coaches and provide participants opportunities to practice new behaviors in ways that limit the potential for embarrassment, such as practicing in small groups.

Given the importance of saving face combined with the more prescribed and reserved communication norms of collectivist, high power distance societies (Rugh, 2007), training should provide carefully worded sample scripts designed for use in potentially challenging situations. Training should include creating awareness that power distance can hinder communication and should provide strategies for enhancing communication frequency and candor (Blake-Beard, 2009; Blancero & Cotton-Nessler, 2017). Power distance also has implications for the pace and ownership of mentoring processes. In the West, mentees are usually responsible for taking the lead in arranging mentoring meetings and setting the pace of mentoring activities. However, given the relative lack of familiarity with mentoring and the high power distance culture of the UAE, organizations should provide guidelines that help mentors and mentees share control and responsibility of mentoring activities.

## COMBINED MENTORING AND COACHING FRAMEWORK

In this section, we present our mentoring and coaching framework, which is intended to help organizations become more gender inclusive while improving QM learning and performance. Our framework is informed by: (1) UAE-specific cultural considerations; (2) insights from the QM literature; and (3) the scholarly mentoring and coaching literature.

Earlier we discussed how combining coaching and mentoring may be particularly useful in mitigating patriarchy's detrimental influence on women's careers. We described how inclusive organization cultures and inclusive leadership are critical for the success of women's career advancement (Dobbin et al., 2015). We discussed how male-dominated organizations have used mentoring and coaching to reduce stereotyping and bias and create a climate of inclusion conducive to women's career advancement (Gray et al., 1995; Metz, 2009). We revealed that gender and inclusion are infrequently discussed in the QM literature (Goetsch & Davis, 2015; Rochetti, 2016; Lanza, 1997; Wilkof & Schneer, 1995; Hyter, 2004; Hopen, 2004), despite QM professionals working in increasingly diverse workplaces (Geotsch & Davis, 2015; Lasrado, 2018). We also described the QM literature's interest in employing coaching to facilitate

QM learning and performance. These learnings from the literature inform our framework.

Recent mentoring and coaching scholarship has avoided making overly prescriptive recommendations, instead encouraging organizations to customize activities to their specific set of needs (Megginson et al., 2006; Riddle, 2015). Mentoring and coaching are of greater benefit to organizations when used in ways that complement existing employee development practices (Riddle et al., 2015), and organizations that purposefully align mentoring and coaching activities may see benefits (Riddle, 2015). Therefore, we have chosen to provide a framework that can be modified by organizations to fit their particular needs.

Our combined mentoring and coaching framework is depicted in Figure 5.4. While the five coaching and mentoring practices—depicted as the small circles numbered one through five—that comprise our framework are intended to be implemented as a comprehensive whole, the framework can be divided into two sections, as shown in the background of the framework and are labeled as (a) coaching and mentoring promote inclusion and (b) coaching improves QM. The top portion of our framework labeled coaching and mentoring promotes inclusion, and consists of circles two, three, and four, which is primarily concerned with promoting inclusion. The bottom portion of our framework labeled coaching improves QM and consists

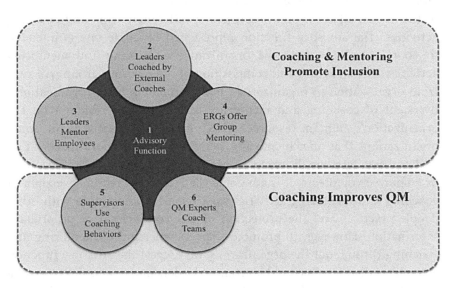

**FIGURE 5.4**
Combined coaching and mentoring framework.

of circles five and six, which is primarily concerned with enhancing QM learning and performance. To guide, support, and coordinate mentoring and coaching activities, we suggest organizations establish an advisory function. This function is represented by circle one, the large circle in the background that connects all mentoring and coaching activities.

In total, our framework supports three uses of coaching and two uses of mentoring. The three specific uses of coaching are: (1) external coaches work individually with executive and senior leaders to develop leaders' skills in inclusion, mentoring, and coaching; (2) those with supervisory authority learn to use coaching behaviors with their direct reports to enhance learning and performance; and (3) QM subject matter experts implement coaching behaviors with teams to facilitate QM learning and performance. Our two recommended uses of mentoring are: (1) a formal mentoring program open to participation by all employees; and (2) group-format mentoring arranged by employee resource groups (ERGs).

―――――――――――

## ADVISORY FUNCTION

In Figure 5.4, the advisory committee is represented by circle one, a large circle in the background of the framework that supports and connects each of the five small circles that represent specific mentoring and coaching activities. The advisory function represented by circle one is intended to coordinate and guide the organization's coaching and mentoring activities. The structure and composition of the advisory group will vary from organization to organization. For example, in large organizations, oversight of coaching and mentoring activities often resides with the organization's human resources (HR) group. Alternatively, in small organizations that offer mentoring, activities may be coordinated on an ad hoc basis by a small group comprised of leaders, HR professionals, or employee volunteers. It is advisable the HR group retains oversight of coaching and mentoring activities for reasons of integration with other people practices and the protection of any confidential or proprietary information. However, to promote shared ownership of mentoring and coaching throughout the organization, we suggest the advisory function assemble a distinct stakeholder group of leaders and employees to serve a consultative function. Leaders who are active in ERGs would make ideal stakeholders.

In addition to adapting mentoring and coaching activities to specific organization needs, the advisory function would likely facilitate the mentor-mentee matching process, pilot test various aspects of mentoring and coaching initiatives, and evaluate the impact and effectiveness of activities. In matching mentors and mentees, compatibility in values and goals can be particularly important (Lockwood et al., 2010; Perchiazzi, 2017; Ragins, 2002). For example, mentees who aspire to senior leadership roles should be matched with mentors who hold similar positions. While evaluation of such programs is organization-specific, Kirkpatrick and Kirkpatrick's (2016) four levels of measurement (i.e., reaction, learning, behavior, and results) has been used to evaluate mentoring and coaching activities in organizations (Allen et al., 2009; Berg & Karlsen, 2012).

## LEADERS COACHED BY EXTERNAL COACHES

Our framework utilizes external coaches to help leaders develop three skill sets: (1) gender and cultural inclusion; (2) mentoring; and (3) coaching. This use of external coaching is represented by circle two in Figure 5.4. We suggest an external coach work individually with top organization leaders, employing a learning and development coaching approach (Jackson & Cox, 2018). Leaders will be coached to become more inclusive leaders, to learn how lead or support organizational inclusion efforts, to become effective mentors within their organization's formal mentoring program, and to employ coaching behaviors in their leadership and management work. In sum, the external coach will assist leaders in learning how to advocate for gender inclusion and become proficient practitioners of inclusive mentoring and coaching. If all top leaders authentically participate in coaching to learn inclusion behaviors, the cumulative effect will be a more inclusive organizational climate (Riddle et al., 2015).

As gender inclusion is not a priority for many businesses in the Gulf region (Deloitte, 2016), UAE business leaders, who are typically men, may not know how to lead organization inclusion efforts and assist women in advancing their careers. In addition to a lack of familiarity with gender inclusion, mentoring and coaching are uncommon in the region (Al-Nasser & Behery, 2015; Palmer & Arnold, 2013; Waxin & Bateman, 2016), thus leaders may need to be privately coached to learn how to inclusively mentor and coach others in their organizations. Coaching by an expert external coach is a face-saving way for leaders to develop new competencies and practice new behaviors. Leaders will use the skills they develop to mentor others and integrate coaching behaviors into their management work.

## LEADERS MENTOR EMPLOYEES

In Figure 5.4, leaders mentoring employees is represented by circle three. The mentoring portion of our framework is a formal approach in which the organization facilitates the matching of mentees and mentors and provides process guidance and training to increase mentoring effectiveness (Giscombe, 2007). Mentoring relationships as typically practiced in Western contexts involve one mentor and one mentee. However, a common organization constraint is having too few mentors available to pair with mentees, therefore, mentors may be asked to mentor multiple individuals. While the degree of personalization afforded by individual mentoring is ideal in individualist cultures and presumably also useful in collectivist cultures, group mentoring could be a viable alternative when there are few available mentors. A challenge in implementing group mentoring is research on the topic is limited (Huizing, 2012).

In the culturally diverse context of the UAE, it is likely many mentoring relationships will be cross-cultural. A possible benefit associated with cross-cultural mentoring is the strengthening of employees' intercultural competencies. For example, an expatriate mentor of an Emirati mentee may gain insights into Emirati culture, while also learning about his or her own cross-cultural strengths and weaknesses. Intercultural mentoring may have additional benefits for the organization, such as increasing cross-cultural trust and knowledge sharing (Al-Alawi, Al-Marzooqi, & Mohammed, 2007; Perchiazzi, 2017).

## EMPLOYEE RESOURCE GROUPS
## FACILITATE GROUP MENTORING

In Figure 5.4, circle four represents group mentoring arranged by ERGs. ERGs, also referred to affinity groups, are voluntary, organization-sanctioned groups that support employees who are underrepresented or have specific workplace needs. For example, it is common for organizations to sponsor separate ERGs for women, newly hired employees, disabled employees, racial and ethnic minorities, and other underrepresented or disadvantaged groups. ERGs typically arrange mentoring, networking, and other forms of professional development for members (Nugent, Dinolfo, & Giscombe, 2013). In male-dominated environments, a women's ERG may be particularly beneficial for helping women gain access to professional development opportunities.

We suggest leaders of ERGs work with the organization's advisory group to coordinate group mentoring opportunities for underrepresented employees or employees with distinct needs. Group mentoring involves at least one mentor and at least two mentees; however, mentoring groups with two mentors and as many as five or six mentees are not uncommon. Group mentoring is most appropriate when multiple mentees have similar development needs (Kim & Egan, 2011), as would typically be the case for members of the same ERG. Group mentoring may also help provide access to mentors of the same gender or race, which can help mentees overcome identity-specific challenges. For example, female mentors can help female mentees develop strategies to balance career and family responsibilities (Eagly & Carli, 2007; Murphy, Gibson, & Kram, 2017).

If there are no Emirati women presently employed within a particular workplace, group mentoring can be used to provide career and social support to early career Emirati women who join the company. For example, two experienced females, preferably at least one who is Muslim, can be paired as mentors to a group of early career Emirati women mentees. A different scenario would involve pairing a female mentor and a male mentor to work with a group of female mentees, which would provide culturally appropriate access to male mentorship. However, participating in cross-gender mentoring should always be at the discretion of mentees and mentors.

The purpose of ERG mentoring is to ensure employees with distinct needs have the opportunity to receive appropriate and supportive mentoring. A member of an ERG would be eligible to participate in ERG mentoring in addition to the organization's formal mentoring program. ERG engagement in mentoring programs helps ensure the career development needs of underrepresented employees are adequately addressed, thus supporting equity of opportunities within organizations.

## SUPERVISORS USE COACHING BEHAVIORS

Coaching by a manager or supervisor is represented by circle five in our framework. All those with supervisory authority will be supported in learning basic coaching techniques that can be used to enhance the learning and performance of direct reports. A coaching form of management involves cultivating a learning environment, providing care and support to team members, promoting open communication and feedback, and securing resources for the team (Hamlin et al., 2006). To engage in coaching, supervisors should employ listening, questioning, reframing, and advising (Ellinger, 1997; Ellinger & Bostrom, 2002; Ellinger, Ellinger, & Keller, 2005; Ellinger et al., 2014). Coaching is described as a preferred orientation to supervision intended to empower employees rather than "boss" them (Goetsch & Davis, 2015, p.147). Replacing authoritarian and directive supervisory behaviors with coaching behaviors should enhance organization capabilities and performance. Unfortunately, the QM literature provides limited guidance to supervisors wishing to implement coaching and inclusion within organizations. Organizations should provide training or other forms of development to help supervisors learn how to adapt coaching behaviors to effectively engage across differences.

## QUALITY MANAGEMENT EXPERTS COACH TEAMS

Coaching of teams by QM experts is represented by circle six. To support QM learning, employees with significant quality experience should be trained to serve as team QM coaches. Similar to master black belts, QM coaches act as subject matter experts, providing technical and process assistance and developing the QM knowledge of teams throughout the organization (Fleig-Palmer & Schoorman, 2011; Hagen, 2010). More specifically, through listening, indirect questioning, problem reframing, and advising, QM coaches facilitate and empower teams to take ownership of problem identification and solution development (Ellinger, 1997; Ellinger & Bostrom, 2002; Ellinger et al., 2005; Ellinger et al., 2014). As with all others who engage in coaching, QM experts should be provided with gender and cultural inclusion learning resources. Ideally in collectivist, high power distance cultures, QM practice should be anticipatory and proactive, thus avoiding a deficiency-based approach rooted in mistake identification and correction.

## CONCLUSION

In this chapter, we discussed how mentoring and coaching can be combined in organizations to promote gender inclusion. We suggested adaptations to organization-facilitated mentoring and coaching programs appropriate for the UAE cultural context. We described applications of mentoring and coaching useful to advancing QM practice. As practice is significantly hindered by limited empirical research, we suggest three directions for future research:

- First, given the limited data on women's participation in QM both globally and in the UAE, empirical studies should be conducted to understand women's career experiences in QM. Al Marzouqi and Forster's (2011) study of Emirati women working in information technology occupations could serve as a model for studying the careers of women QM professionals.
- Second, to advance the practice of coaching in QM, we recommend researchers conduct qualitative studies to better understand how coaching improves QM learning and process outcomes. Interview research can more accurately capture the complexities and idiosyncrasies of mentoring and coaching than survey research (Shen & Kram, 2011).
- Third, there are few publications focused on either mentoring or coaching in the Middle East, so we encourage researchers to conduct empirical studies that would benefit practice in the region. In particular, studies should seek to fill the gap in how leaders can help their organizations become more gender inclusive through coaching (Gotsis & Grimani, 2016).

In closing, we intend our framework will help organizations foster meaningful collaboration across differences, an outcome of inclusive mentoring as practiced by IBM (Murrell, Forte-Trammell, & Bing, 2009, pp.104–105):

> Formal mentoring initiatives … must … be about supporting and understanding the unique experience diverse employee segments face when confronting challenging organizational cultures that may have historically been unsupportive of diversity and inclusion. … Thus an inclusive mentoring approach means connecting people not only across dimensions of difference but also connecting people who engage in meaningful and collaborative relationships within these differences.

## REFERENCES

Abalkhail, J. M., & Allan, B. (2015). Women's career advancement: mentoring and networking in Saudi Arabia and the UK. *Human Resource Development International, 18*(2), 153–168. doi:10.1080/13678868.2015.1026548

Abbott, G., & Rosinski, P. (2007). Global coaching and evidence based coaching: Multiple perspectives operating in a process of pragmatic humanism. *International Journal of Evidence Based Coaching and Mentoring, 5*(1), 58–77.

Ahmad, N., & Daghfous, A. (2010). Knowledge sharing through inter-organizational knowledge networks: Challenges and opportunities in the United Arab Emirates. *European Business Review, 22*(2), 53–174. doi:10.1108/09555341011023506

Al-Alawi, A. I., Al-Marzooqi, N. Y., & Mohammed, F. M. (2007). Organizational culture and knowledge sharing: Critical success factors. *Journal of Knowledge Management, 11*(2), 22–42. doi:10.1108/13673270710738898

Al-Asfour, A., Tlaiss, H., Khan, S., & Rajasekar, J. (2017). Saudi women's work challenges and barriers to career advancement. *Career Development International, 22*(2), 184–199. doi:10.1108/CDI-11-2016-0200

al-Kazi, L.A. (2008). Gulf societies: Coexistence of tradition and modernity. In A. Alsharekh, & R. Springborg (Eds.), *Popular culture and political identity in the Arab Gulf states* (pp. 171–179). London, UK: SAQI.

Allen, T. D., Eby, L. T., Poteet, M. L., Lentz, E., & Lima, L. (2004). Career benefits associated with mentoring for protégés: A meta-analysis. *Journal of Applied Psychology, 89*, 127–136.

Allen, T. D., Finkelstein, L. M., & Poteet, M. L. (2009). *Designing workplace mentoring programs: An evidence-based approach.* West Sussex, UK: Wiley-Blackwell.

Al Marzouqi, A. H., & Forster, N. (2011). An exploratory study of the under-representation of Emirate women in the United Arab Emirates' information technology sector. *Equality, Diversity and Inclusion: An International Journal, 30*(7), 544–562. doi:10.1108/02610151111167016

Al-Nasser, A., & Behery, M. (2015). Examining the relationship between organizational coaching and workplace counterproductive behaviours in the United Arab Emirates. *International Journal of Organizational Analysis, 23*(3), 378–403. doi:10.1108/IJOA-08-2014-0793

Anthony, J., Gijo, E. V., Kumar, V., & Ghadge, A. (2016). A multiple case study analysis of Six Sigma practices in Indian manufacturing companies. *International

*Journal of Quality & Reliability Management, 33*(8), 1138–1149. doi:10.1108/
IJQRM-10-2014-0157

Apospori, E., Nikandrou, I., & Panayotopoulou, L. (2006). Mentoring and women's career advancement in Greece. *Human Resource Development International, 9*(4), 509–527. doi:10.1080/13678860601032627

ASQ. (2018). *Top of your game: 2018 salary survey.* Milwaukee, WI: ASQ.

Baugh, S. G., & Fagenson-Eland, E. A. (2007). Formal mentoring programs: A "poor cousin" to informal relationships? In B. Ragins, & K. Kram (Eds.), *The handbook of mentoring at work: Theory, research, and practice* (pp. 249–272). Thousand Oaks, CA: Sage.

Beattie, R. S., Kim, S., Hagen, M. S., Egan, T. M., Ellinger, A. D., & Hamlin, R. G. (2014). Managerial coaching: A review of the empirical literature and development of a model to guide future practice. *Advances in Developing Human Resources, 16*(2), 184–201. doi:10.1177/1523422313520476

Berian, J. R., Thomas, J. M., Minami, C. A., Farrell, P. R., O'Leary, K. J., Williams, M.V., ... and Johnson, J. K. (2017). Evaluation of a novel mentor program to improve surgical care for U.S. hospitals. *International Journal for Quality in Health Care, 29*(2), 234–242. doi:10.1093/intqhc/mzx005

Berg, M. E., & Karlsen, J. T. (2012). An evaluation of management training and coaching. *Journal of Workplace Learning, 24*(3), 177–199. doi:10.1108/13665621211209267

Beyond Qatar Business Magazine. (2014). *UAE resident nationalities.* Retrieved from http://www.bq-magazine.com/

Bierema, L. (2016). Women's leadership: Troubling notions of the "ideal" (male) leader. *Advances in Developing Human Resources, 18*(2), 119–136.

Blake-Beard, S. (2009). Mentoring as a bridge to understanding cultural difference. *Adult Learning, 20*(1), 15.

Blake-Beard, S., Kram, K. E., & Murrell, A. J. (2017). Preface: Mentoring and diversity – Challenges and promises. In A. Murrell, & S. Blake-Beard (Eds.), *Mentoring diverse leaders: Creating change for people, processes, and paradigms* (pp. xvii–xxvi). New York: Routledge.

Blancero, D. M., & Cotton-Nessler, N. C. (2017). Mentoring Latinos: An examination of cultural values through the lens of relational cultural theory. In A. Murrell, & S. Blake-Beard (Eds.), *Mentoring diverse leaders: Creating change for people, processes, and paradigms* (pp. 44–64). New York, U.S.: Routledge.

Booysen, L. A. (2014). The development of inclusive leadership practice and processes. In B. Ferdman, & B. Deane (Eds.), *Diversity at work: The practice of inclusion* (pp. 296–329). San Francisco, CA, U.S.: Wiley.

Bourg, J., Stoltzfus, W., McManus, S., & Fry, P. J. (2010). Proactive coaching for employee development and improved business results. *Total Quality Management & Business Excellence, 21*(10), 1005–1016. doi:10.1080/14783363.2010.487705

Bozeman, B., & Feeney, M. (2007). Toward a useful theory of mentoring: A conceptual analysis and critique. *Administration and Society, 39*(6), 719–739. doi:10.1177/0095399707304119

Bright, T., & Megginson, D. (2017). A multi-country mentoring program across Eurasia with Anadolu Efes. In D. Clutterbuck, F. Kochan, L. Lunsford, N. Dominguez, & J. Haddock-Millar (Eds.), *The Sage handbook of mentoring* (pp. 587–589). London, UK: Sage.

Brislin, R., & Yoshida, T. (1994). *Intercultural communication training: An introduction.* Thousand Oaks, CA: Sage.

Budhwar, P., Saini, D., & Bhatnagar, J. (2005). Women in management in the new economic environment: The case of India. *Asia Pacific Business Review, 11*(2), 179–193.

Burcher, P. G., Lee, G. L., & Waddell, D. (2008). The challenges for quality managers in Britain and Australia. *The TQM Journal, 20*(1), 45–58. doi:10.1108/09544780810842893

Burke, R. J., & McKeen, C. A. (1997). Benefits of mentoring relationships among managerial and professional women: A cautionary tale. *Journal of Vocational Behavior, 51*(1), 43–57.

Caldwell, C. (1993). Mentoring: The evolving role of senior leaders in a TQM environment. *Quality Management in Health Care, 1*(2), 13–21.

Caleo, S., & Heilman, M. E. (2013). Gender stereotypes and their implications for women's career progress. In S. Vinnicombe, R. Burke, S. Blake-Beard, & L. Moore (Eds.), *Handbook of research on promoting women's careers* (pp. 143–161). Northampton, MA: Edgar Elgar.

Carl, D., Gupta, V., & Javidan, M. (2004). Power distance. In R. House, P. Hanges, M. Javidan, P. Dorfman, & V. Gupta (Eds.), *Culture, leadership, and organizations: The GLOBE study of 62 societies* (pp. 513–563). Thousand Oaks, CA: Sage.

Chao, G. T. (2007). Mentoring and organizational socialization: Networks for work adjustment. In B. Ragins, & K. Kram (Eds.), *The handbook of mentoring at work: Theory, research, and practice* (pp. 179–196). Thousand Oaks, CA: Sage.

Chrobot-Mason, D., Ruderman, M. N., & Nishii, L. H. (2013). Leadership in a diverse workplace. In Q. Roberson (Ed.), *The Oxford handbook of diversity and work* (pp. 315–340). New York: Oxford University Press.

Clutterbuck, D. (2007). An international perspective on mentoring. In B. Ragins, & K. Kram (Eds.), *The handbook of mentoring at work: Theory, research, and practice* (pp. 633–655). Thousand Oaks, CA: Sage.

Clutterbuck, D., & Ragins, B. R. (Eds.) (2002). *Mentoring and diversity: An international perspective.* Oxford, UK: Butterworth-Heinemann.

Clutterbuck, D. A., Kochan, F. K., Lunsford, L. G., Dominguez, N., & Haddock-Miller, J. (Eds.) (2017). *The Sage handbook of mentoring.* Thousand Oaks, CA: Sage.

Conklin, J. D. (2016, February). Meaningful mentorship: A three-step guide to successful mentor-mentee relationships. *Quality Progress, 49*(2), 58–59. Retrieved from http://asq.org/quality-progress/2016/02/career-corner/meaningful-mentorship.html

CQI. (2018). *Women in quality: It's good for business.* Retrieved from http://www.quality.org/event/branch/women-quality-it%E2%80%99s-good-business

Dawson, B. L., Thomas, K. M., & Goren, M. J. (2013). Career development. In Q. Roberson (Ed.), *The Oxford handbook of diversity and work* (pp. 300–314). New York: Oxford University Press.

Deloitte. (2016). *View from the top: What business executives really think about women leaders in the GCC.* Retrieved from htto://30percentclub.org/assets/uploads/Deloitte_and_30__Club_Study_-_View:from_the_top_(2).pdf

de Vries, J. (2011). *Mentoring for change.* Melbourne, Victoria: Universities Australia Executive Women & the LH Martin Institute for Higher Education Leadership and Management.

Dobbin, F., Schrage, D., & Kalev, A. (2015). Rage against the iron cage: The varied effects of bureaucratic personnel reforms on diversity. *American Sociological Review, 80*(5), 1014–1044. doi:10.1177/0003122415596416

Dubai Quality Group. (n.d.). http://www.dqg.org

Dunlop, I., Schreiber, C., & El Attar, M. (2015). *Women's careers in the GCC: The CEO agenda*. Pearl Initiative. Retrieved from http://www.pearlinitiative.org/resource-centre

Eagly, A. H. (1987). *Sex differences in social behavior: A social-role interpretation*. Hillsdale, NJ, U.S.: Lawrence Erlbaum Associates.

Eagly, A. H., & Carli, L. L. (2007). *Through the labyrinth: The truth about how women become leaders*. Brighton, MA, U.S.: Harvard Business School Publishing Corporation.

Eagly, A. H., & Diekman, A. B. (2005). What is the problem? Prejudice as an attitude-in-context. In J. Dovidio, P. Glick, & L. Rudman (Eds.), *On the nature of prejudice: Fifty years after Allport* (pp. 19–35). Malden, MA, U.S.: Blackwell.

Eby, L. T., Rhodes, J. E., & Allen, T. D. (2010). Definition and evolution of mentoring. In T. Allen, & L. Eby (Eds.), *The Blackwell handbook of mentoring: A multiple perspectives approach* (pp. 7–20). UK: Blackwell.

Eitzen, M., & Cunningham, J. (2009). The formation of a mentoring program as a mechanism to increase the knowledge of SQQ members. *Quality Assurance Journal, 12*, 139–146. doi:10.1002/qaj.460

Ellinger, A. M. (1997). *Managers as facilitators of learning in learning organizations* (Unpublished Doctoral dissertation). University of Georgia at Athens, GA.

Ellinger, A. D., Beattie, R., & Hamlin, R. (2014). The manager as coach. In E. Cox, T. Bachkirova, & D. Clutterbuck (Eds.), *The complete handbook of coaching* (2nd ed., pp. 256–270). London, UK: Sage.

Ellinger, A. D., & Kim, S. (2014). Coaching and human resource development: Examining relevant theories, coaching genres, and scales to advance research and practice. *Advances in Developing Human Resources, 16*(2), 127–138. doi:10.1177/1523422313520472

Ellinger, A. E., & Bostrom, R. P. (2002). An examination of managers' beliefs about their roles as facilitators of learning. *Management Learning, 33*(2), 147–179.

Ellinger, A. E., Ellinger, A. D., & Keller, S. B. (2005). Supervisory coaching in a logistics context. *International Journal of Physical Distribution & Logistics Management, 35*(9), 620–636. doi:10.1108/09600030510634562

Ely, R. J., & Thomas, D. A. (2001). Cultural diversity at work: The effects of diversity perspectives on work group processes and outcomes. *Administrative Science Quarterly, 46*, 229–273.

Farrell, F. (2008). Voices on Emiratization: The impact of Emirati culture on the workforce participation of national women in the UAE private banking sector. *Journal of Islamic Law and Culture, 10*(2), 107–165.

Feghali, E. (1997). Arab cultural communication patterns. *International Journal of Intercultural Relations, 21*(3), 345–378.

Ferdman, B. M. (2014). The practice of inclusion in diverse organizations: Toward a systemic and inclusive framework. In B. Ferdman, & B. Deane (Eds.), *Diversity at work: The practice of inclusion* (pp. 3–54). San Francisco, CA, U.S.: Wiley.

Fleig-Palmer, M. M., & Schoorman, F. D. (2011). Trust as a moderator of the relationship between mentoring and knowledge transfer. *Journal of Leadership & Organizational Studies, 18*(3), 334–343. doi:10.1177/1548051811408615

Foster, S. T., Jr. (2019). Research Note: Revisiting the future of quality management research. *Quality Management Journal, 26*(1), 65–67. doi:10.1080/10686967.2019.1542231

Gallant, M., & Pounder, J. S. (2008). The employment of female nationals in the United Arab Emirates (UAE): An analysis of opportunities and barriers. *Education, Business and Society: Contemporary Middle Eastern Issues, 1*(1), 26–33. doi:10.1108/17537980810861493

Garvey, B., Stokes, P., & Megginson, D. (2018). *Coaching and mentoring: Theory and practice* (3rd ed.). London, UK: Sage

Gelfand, M. J., Bhawuk, D. P., Nishii, L. H., & Bechtol, D. J. (2004). Individualism and collectivism. In R. House, P. Hanges, M. Javidan, P. Dorfman, & V. Gupta (Eds.), *Culture, leadership, and organizations: The GLOBE study of 62 societies* (pp. 437–512). Thousand Oaks, CA: Sage Publications, Inc.

Germain, M. L., Herzog, M. J., & Hamilton, P. R. (2012). Women employed in male-dominated industries: Lessons from female aircraft pilots, pilots-in-training, and mixed-gender flight instructors. *Human Resource Development International, 15*(4), 435–453. doi:10.1080/13678868.2012.707528

Giffi, C., Huelsman, T., Rodriguez, M. D., & McClelland, K. (2017). *Women in manufacturing: Stepping up to make an impact that matters.* Deloitte Development LLC. Retrieved from http://www.themanufacturinginstitute.org/Initiatives/Women-i n-Manufacturing/~/media/3B9BF94AEF0A46A5B755D17F1F1336BC.ashx

Gillies, A. C. (2015). Tools to support the development of a quality culture in a learning organization. *The TQM Journal, 27*(4), 471–482. doi:10.1108/TQM-03-2015-0039

Giscombe, K. (2007). Advancing women through the glass ceiling with formal mentoring. In B. Ragins, & K. Kram (Eds.), *The handbook of mentoring at work: Theory, research, and practice* (pp. 549–571). Thousand Oaks, CA: Sage.

Glick, P., & Fiske, T. (1997). Hostile and benevolent sexism: Measuring ambivalent sexist attitudes toward women. *Psychology of Women Quarterly, 21,* 119–135.

Goetsch, D. L., & Davis, S. (2015). *Quality management for organizational excellence: Introduction to total quality* (8th ed.). New York: Pearson.

Gotsis, G., & Grimani, K. (2016). The role of servant leadership in fostering inclusive organizations. *Journal of Management Development, 35*(8), 985–1010. doi:10.1108/JMD-07-2015-0095

GrantThorton. (2018). *Women in leadership: Beyond policy to progress.* Dubai, UAE: Grant Thorton UAE. Retrieved from https://www.grantthornton.ae/insights/ar ticles/women-in-leadership-2018/

Gray, D. E., Garvey, B., & Lane, D. A. (2016). *A critical introduction to coaching and mentoring.* London, UK: Sage.

Gray, J. D., Lee, M. J., & Totta, J. M. (1995). Mentoring at the Bank of Montreal: A case study of an intervention that exceeded expectations. *Human Resource Planning.*

Greenwood, B. N., Carnahan, S., & Huang, L. (2018). Patient-physician gender concordance and increased mortality among female heart attack patients. *PNAS, 115*(34), 8569–8574.

Gulf Research Center. (2015). *UAE: Estimates of population residing in the UAE by country of citizenship (selected countries, 2014).* Retrieved from http://www.gulfmigration. org/uae-estimates-of-population-residing-in-the-uae-by-country-of-citizensh ip-selected-countries-2014/

Gutierrez-Gutierrez, L. J., Barrales-Molina, V., & Kaynak, H. (2018). The role of human resource-related quality management practices in new product development: A dynamic capability perspective. *International Journal of Operations & Production Management, 38*(1), 43–66. doi:10.1108/IJOPM-07-2016-0387

Hagen, M. (2010). Black belt coaching and project outcomes: An empirical investigation. *Quality Management Journal, 17*(2), 54–67. doi:10.1080/10686967.2010.11918270

Hamlin, R. G., Ellinger, A. D., & Beattie, R. S. (2006). Coaching at the heart of managerial effectiveness: A cross-cultural study of managerial behaviours. *Human Resource Development International, 9*(3), 305–331. doi:10.1080/13678860600893524

Hassi, A. (2012). Islamic perspectives on training and professional development. *Journal of Management Development, 31*(10), 1035–1045. doi:10.1108/02621711211281816

Haynes, R. K., & Ghosh, R. (2012). Towards mentoring the India organizational woman: Propositions, considerations, and first steps. *Journal of World Business, 47*, 186–193. doi:10.1016/j.jwb.2011.04.005

Hegstad, C. D. (1999). Formal mentoring as a strategy for human resource development: A review of research. *Human Resource Development Quarterly, 10*(4), 383–390.

Heilman, M., & Eagly, A. (2008). Gender stereotypes are alive, well, and busy producing workplace discrimination. *Industrial and Organizational Psychology, 1*(4), 393–398. doi:10.1111/j.1754-9434.2008.00072.x

Henderson, J., & McAdam, R. (2000). Managing quality in project-based emerging network organisations. *International Journal of Quality & Reliability Management, 17*(4/5), 364–376. doi:10.1108/02656710010298391

Ho, D. Y. (1976). On the concept of face. *American Journal of Sociology, 81*, 867–884. doi:10.1086/226145

Hodgson, S., & Hanson, D. (2014). Enforcing nationalization in the GCC: Private sector progress, strategy and policy for sustainable nationalization. *Middle East Journal of Business, 9*(2), 17–24.

Hofstede, G. (1997). *Cultures and organizations: Software of the mind*. London, UK: McGraw-Hill.

Hofstede Insights. (n.d.). *Compare countries*. Retrieved from http://www.hofstede-insig hts.com/product/compare-countries/

Hoobler, J. M., Masterson, C. R., Nkomo, S. M., & Michel, E. J. (2018). The business case for women leaders: Meta-analysis, research critique, and path forward. *Journal of Management, 44*(6), 2473–2499. doi:10.1177/0149206316628643

Hopen. (2004). Editor's notebook: All work and no play. *The Journal for Quality and Participation, 27*(3), 3.

Hoyt, C. L. (2012). Gender bias in employment contexts: A closer examination of the role incongruity principle. *Journal of Experimental Social Psychology, 48*, 86–96.

Huizing, R. L. (2012). Mentoring together: A literature review of group mentoring. *Mentoring and Tutoring: Partnership in Learning, 20*(1), 27–55. doi:10.1080/13611 267.2012.645599

Hunt, J. M., & Weintraub, J. R. (2017). *The coaching manager: Developing top talent in business* (3rd ed.). Thousand Oaks, CA: Sage.

Hutchings, K., Metcalfe, B. D., & Cooper, B. K. (2010). Exploring Arab Middle Eastern women's perceptions of barriers to, and facilitators of, international management opportunities. *International Journal of Human Resource Management, 21*(1), 61–83. doi:10.1080/09585190903466863

Hyter, M. (2004). Diversity programs to grow? *The Journal for Quality and Participation, 27*(4), 52.

Ibarra, H., Ely, R. J., & Kolb, D. M. (2013). Women rising: The unseen barriers. *Harvard Business Review, 91*(9), 60–66.

ICF. (2016). *2016 ICF global coaching study executive summary*. ICF. Retrieved from https ://coachfederation.org/research/global-coaching-study

Jackson, P., & Cox, E. (2018). Developmental coaching. In E. Cox, T. Bachkirova, & D. Clutterbuck (Eds.), *The complete handbook of coaching* (pp. 215–230). London, UK: Sage.

Jagsi, R., Griffith, K. A., DeCastro, R. A., & Ubel, P. (2014). Sex, role models, and specialty choices among graduates of U.S. medical schools in 2006–2008. *Journal of the American College of Surgeons, 218*(3), 345–352. doi:10.1016/j.jamcollsurg.2013.11.012

Kalbfleisch, P. J. (2007). Mentoring enactment theory: Describing, explaining, and predicting communication in mentoring relationships. In B. Ragins, & K. Kram (Eds.), *The handbook of mentoring at work: Theory, research, and practice* (pp. 499–518). Thousand Oaks, CA: Sage.

Kaynak, H. (2003). The relationship between total quality management practices and their effects on firm performance. *Journal of Operations Management, 21*, 405–435. doi:10.1016/S0272-6963(03)00004-4

Kemp, L. J. (2015). Business women associations in the United Arab Emirates: Influence of the network and networking. In S. Madsen, F. Ngunjiri, K. Longman, & C. Cherrey (Eds.), *Women and leadership around the world* (pp. 43–64). Charlotte, NC: Information Age Publishing, Inc.

Khoja, S., & Thomas, S. (2017). *Promoting women in the workplace.* Clyde & Co. Retrieved from http://www.clydeco.com/insight/article/promoting-women-in-the-workplace

Kim, S., & Egan, T. (2011). Establishing a formal cross-cultural mentoring organization and program: A case study of international student mentor association in a higher education context. *Journal of European Industrial Training, 35*(1), 89–105. doi:10.1108/03090591111095754

Kirkpatrick, J. D., & Kirkpatrick, W. K. (2016). *Kirkpatrick's four levels of training evaluation.* Alexandria, VA: ATD Press.

Kram, K. E. (1985). *Mentoring at work: Developmental relationships in organizational life.* Glenview, IL: Scott, Foresman & Company.

Kram, K. E. (2014). *Strategic relationships at work: Creating your circle of mentors, sponsors, and peers for success in business and life.* New York: McGraw Hill.

Kram, K. E., & Hall, D. T. (1989). Mentoring in the context of diversity and turbulence. In S. Lobel, & E. Kossek (Eds.), *Managing diversity: Human resource strategies for transforming the workplace* (pp. 108–136). London, UK: Blackwell.

Korn Ferry. (2018). *Future of work: The Global Talent Crunch.* Retrieved from http://www.kornferry.com/challenges/future-of-work

Kovach, J. V. (2017, July). A powerful mechanism for success: The positive effect a mentor can have on your career. *Quality Progress.* Retrieved from http://asq.org/quality-progress/2017/07/career-coach/a-powerful-mechanism-for-success.html

Lankau, M. J., & Scandura, T. A. (2007). Mentoring as a forum for personal learning in organizations. In B. Ragins, & K. Kram (Eds.), *The handbook of mentoring at work: Theory, research, and practice* (pp. 95–122). Thousand Oaks, CA: Sage.

Lanza, M. (1997). Feminist leadership through total quality management. *Health Care for Women International, 18*(1), 95–106.

Lasrado, F. (2016). Business excellence in the United Arab Emirates through soft TQM. *Human Systems Management, 35*, 229–236. doi:10.3233/HSM-160871

Lasrado, F. (2018). *Achieving organizational excellence: A quality management program for culturally diverse organizations.* Cham, Switzerland: Springer.

Lasrado, F., & Pereira, V. (2018). *Achieving sustainable business excellence.* Switzerland: Palgrave Macmillan.

Leung, A. K., & Cohen, D. (2011). Within- and between-culture variation: Individual differences and the cultural logics of honor, face, and dignity cultures. *Journal of Personality and Social Psychology, 100*(3), 507–526. doi:10.1037/a0022151

Lin, C., & Wu, C. (2005). Managing knowledge contributed by ISO 9001:2000. *International Journal of Quality & Reliability Management, 22*(9), 968–985. doi:10.1108/02656710510625239

Lockwood, A. L., Evans, S. C., & Eby, L. T. (2010). Reflections on the benefits of mentoring. In T. Allen, & L. Eby (Eds.), *The Blackwell handbook of mentoring: A multiple perspectives approach* (pp. 7–20). UK: Blackwell.

Madsen, S. R. (2010). Leadership development in the United Arab Emirates: The transformational learning experiences of women. *Journal of Leadership & Organizational Studies, 17*(1), 100–110. doi:10.1177/1548051809345254

McDonald, K., & Hite, L. (2016). *Career development: A human resource development perspective.* New York: Routledge.

Megginson, D., Clutterbuck, D., Garvey, B., Stokes, P., & Garrett-Harris, R. (2006). *Mentoring in action: A practical guide* (2nd ed.). London, UK: Kogan Page.

Melan, E. H. (1998). Implementing TQM: A contingency approach to intervention and change. *International Journal of Quality Science, 3*(2), 126–146. doi:10.1108/13598539810370297

Metcalfe, B. D. (2006). Exploring cultural dimensions of gender and management in the Middle East. *Thunderbird International Business Review, 48*(1), 93–107. doi:10.1002/tie.20087

Metcalfe, B. D., & Murfin, T. (2011). Leadership, social development and political economy in the Middle East: An introduction. In B. Metcalfe, & F. Mimouni (Eds.), *Leadership development in the Middle East* (pp. 1–60). Northampton, MA: Edward Elgar.

Metz, I. (2009). Organisational factors, social factors, and women's advancement. *Applied Psychology: An International Review, 58*(2), 193–213 doi:10.1111/j.1464-0597.2008.00376.x

Metz, I., & Kulik, C. T. (2014). The rocky climb: Women's advancement in management. In S. Kumra, R. Simpson, & R. Burke (Eds.), *The Oxford handbook of gender in organizations* (pp. 175–199). Oxford, UK: Oxford University Press.

Mostafa, M. M. (2005). Attitudes towards women managers in the United Arab Emirates: The effects of patriarchy, age, and sex differences. *Journal of Managerial Psychology, 20*(6), 522–540. doi:10.1108/02683940510615451

Murphy, W. M., Gibson, K. R., & Kram, K. E. (2017). Advancing women through developmental relationships. In S. Madsen (Ed.), *Handbook of research on gender and leadership* (pp. 361–377). Northampton, MA: Edward Elgar.

Murrell, A. J., & Blake-Beard, S. (Eds.) (2017). *Mentoring diverse leaders: Creating change for people, processes, and paradigms.* New York, U.S.: Routledge.

Murrell, A. J., Crosby, F. J., & Ely, R. J. (Eds.) (1999). *Mentoring dilemmas: Developing relationships within multicultural organizations.* Mahwah, NJ: Lawrence Erlbaum Associates.

Murrell, A. J., Forte-Trammell, S., & Bing, D. A. (2009). *Intelligent mentoring: How IBM creates value through people, knowledge, and relationships.* Upper Saddle River, NJ, U.S.: IBM Press.

Nair, N., & Vohra, N. (2017). Mentoring as a means to achieve inclusion: A focus on practice and research on women in India. In A. Murrell, & S. Blake-Beard (Eds.),

*Mentoring diverse leaders: Creating change for people, processes, and paradigms* (pp. 124–144). New York: Routledge.

Ndihokubwayo, J. B., Maruta, T., Ndlovu, N., Moyo, S., Yahaya, A. A., Coulibaly, S. O., ... and Abrol, A. P. (2016). Implementation of the World Health Organization regional office for Africa stepwise laboratory quality improvement process towards accreditation. *African Journal of Laboratory Medicine*, 5(1), 280–288. doi:10.4102/ajlm.v5i1.280

Nishii, L. H. (2013). The benefits of climate for inclusion for gender-diverse groups. *Academy of Management Journal*, 56(6), 1754–1774. doi:10.5465/amj.2009.0823

Noland, M., Moran, T., & Kotschwar, B. (2016). *Is gender diversity profitable? Evidence from a global survey*. Washington, DC: Peterson Institute for International Economics.

Nugent, J. S., Dinolfo, S., & Giscombe, K. (2013). Advancing women: A focus on strategic initiatives. In S. Vinnicombe, R. Burke, S. Blake-Beard, & L. Moore (Eds.), *Handbook of research on promoting women's careers* (pp. 391–405). Northampton, MA: Edward Elgar.

O'Neill, R. (2002). Gender and race in mentoring relationships: A review of the literature. In D. Clutterbuck, & B. Ragins (Eds.), *Mentoring and diversity: An international perspective* (pp. 1–22). UK: Butterworth-Heinemann.

Ostry, J. D., Alvarez, J., Espinoza, R. A., & Papageorgiou, C. (2018). *IMF staff discussion note: Economic gains from gender inclusion: New mechanisms, new evidence*. IMF. Retrieved from http://www.imf.org/en/Publications/Staff-Discussion-Notes/Issues/2018/10/09/Economic-Gains-From-Gender-Inclusion-New-Mechanisms-New-Evidence-45543

Özdemir, P., & Albayrak, T. (2015). How to cope with second-generation gender bias in male-dominated occupations. In M. Kitada, E. Williams, & L. Froholdt (Eds.), *Maritime women: Global leadership*. New York: Springer Nature.

Palmer, T., & Arnold, V. J. (2013). Coaching in the Middle East. In J. Passmore (Ed.), *Diversity in coaching: Working with gender, culture, race and age* (pp. 111–126). London, UK: Kogan Page.

Panina, D. (2016). Women in global professional service firms: The end of the gentlemen's club? In N. Zakaria, A. N. Abdul-Talib, & N. Osman (Eds.), *Handbook of research on impacts of international business and political affairs on the global economy* (pp. 23–41). doi:10.4018/978-1-4666-9806-2.ch002

Passmore, J. (Ed.) (2013). *Diversity in coaching: Working with gender, culture, race and age*. London, UK: Kogan Page.

Perchiazzi, M. (2017). Intercultural relationships and mentoring: The Italian Air Force on an Afghanistan NATO training mission, Shindand. In D. Clutterbuck, F. Kochan, L. Lunsford, N. Dominguez, & J. Haddock-Millar (Eds.), *The Sage handbook of mentoring* (pp. 531–538). London, UK: Sage.

Perrone, L. A., Confer, D., Scott, E., Livingston, L., Bradburn, C., McGee, A., ... and Martin, R. (2016a). Implementation of a mentored professional development programme in laboratory leadership and management in the Middle East and North Africa. *Eastern Mediterranean Health Journal*, 22(11), 832–839.

Perrone, L. A., Voeurng, V., Sek, S., Song, S., Vong, N., Tous, C., ... and Martin, R. (2016b). Implementation research: A mentoring programme to improve laboratory quality in Cambodia. *Bulletin World Health Organization*, 94, 743–751. doi:10.2471/BLT.15.163824

Pollock, S., & Mott, D. (2015). *Coaching green belts for sustainable success*. Milwaukee, WI: Quality Press.

Psychogios, A. G., Atanasovski, J., & Tsironis, L. K. (2012). Lean Six Sigma in a service context: A multifactor application approach in the telecommunications industry. *International Journal of Quality & Reliability Management, 29*(1), 122–139. doi:10.1108/02656711211190909

Ragins, B. R. (2002). Differences that make a difference: common themes in the case studies of diversified mentoring relationships. In D. Clutterbuck, & B. Ragins (Eds.), *Mentoring and diversity: An international perspective* (pp. 161–172). UK: Butterworth-Heinemann.

Ramaswami, A., & Dreher, G. F. (2010). Dynamics of mentoring relationships in India: A qualitative, exploratory study. *Human Resource Management, 49*(3), 501–530.

Ramaswami, A., Huang, J.-C., & Dreher, G. (2014). Interaction of gender, mentoring, and power distance on career attainment: A cross-cultural comparison. *Human Relations, 67*(2), 153–173. doi:10.1177/0018726713490000

Riddle, D. D., Hoole, E. R., & Gullette, E. C. (Eds.) (2015). *The Center for Creative Leadership handbook of coaching in organizations.* San Francisco, CA: Jossey-Bass.

Rochetti, K. (2016, March). Culture shock: Addressing gender inequity in technical industries. *Qualityprogress.com,* 51–52.

Rock, A. D., & Garavan, T. N. (2006). Reconceptualizing developmental relationships. *Human Resource Development Review, 5*(3), 330–354. doi:10.1177/1534484306290227

Ross, K. (2019). *How to coach for creativity and service excellence: A lean coaching workbook.* Boca Raton, FL: CRC Press.

Rother, M. (2018). *The Toyota KATA practice guide.* New York: McGraw Hill Education.

Rother, M., & Aulinger, G. (2017). *Toyota KATA culture: Building organizational capability and mindset through KATA Coaching.* New York: McGraw Hill Education.

Rudman, L. A. (2005). Rejection of women? Beyond prejudice as antipathy. In J. Dovidio, P. Glick, & L. Rudman (Eds.), *On the nature of prejudice: Fifty years after Allport* (pp. 106–120). Malden, MA, U.S.: Blackwell.

Rugh, A. B. (2007). *The political culture of leadership in the United Arab Emirates.* New York: Palgrave Macmillan.

Salomaa, R. (2015). Expatriate coaching: Factors impacting coaching success. *Journal of Global Mobility, 3*(3), 216–243. doi:10.1108/JGM-10-2014-0050

Scandura, T. A., & Siegal, P. H. (1995, August). *Mentoring as organizational learning during a corporate merger.* Paper presented at the National Academy of Management Meeting, Vancouver, CA.

Schein, V. E. (1973). The relationship between sex role stereotypes and requisite management characteristics. *Journal of Applied Psychology, 57,* 95–100.

Schein, V. E. (1975). Relationships between sex role stereotypes and requisite management characteristics among female managers. *Journal of Applied Psychology, 60,* 340–344.

Schermerhorn, J. R., & Bond, M. H. (1997). Cross-cultural leadership dynamics in collectivism and high power distance settings. *Leadership & Organization Development Journal, 18*(4), 187–193. doi:10.1108/01437739710182287

Shen, Y., & Kram, K. E. (2011). Expatriates' developmental networks: Network diversity, base, and support functions. *The Career Development International, 16*(6), 528–552. doi:10.1108/13620431111178317

Smetana, J. B., Chakraborty, M., & Banerjee-Batist, R. (2018). Career development challenges for women pursuing leadership in India. In R. Ghosh, & G. McLean (Eds.), *Indian women in Leadership.* New York, U.S.: Palgrave MacMillan.

Smith, J. L. (2011, April 1). Face of quality: Mentoring improves organizations. *Quality Magazine*. Retrieved from http://www.qualitymag.com/articles/87877-face-of-q uality-mentoring-improves-organizations

Stokes, P., & Merrick, L. (2016). Designing mentoring schemes for organizations. In J. Passmore, D. Peterson, & T. Freire (Eds.), *The Wiley Blackwell handbook of the psychology of coaching and mentoring* (pp. 197–216). West Sussex, UK: John Wiley & Sons.

Sturges, S. T. (2012). Coaching and mentoring. In J. Wilson (Ed.), *International human resource development: Learning, education and training for individuals and organizations* (pp. 341–360). London, UK: Kogan Page.

Suliman, A. M. (2006). Human resource management in the United Arab Emirates. In P. Budhwar, & K. Mellahi (Eds.), *Managing human resources in the Middle East* (pp. 59–78). Abingdon, UK: Routledge.

Syed, J., & Özbilgin, M. (2009). A relational framework for international transfer of diversity management practices. *The International Journal of Human Resource Management, 20*(12), 2435–2453.

Tabbron, A., Macaulay, S., & Cook, S. (1997). Making mentoring work. *Training for Quality, 5,* 6–9.

Thiagaragan, T., Zairi, M., & Dale, B. G. (2001). A proposed model of TQM implementation based on an empirical study of Malaysian industry. *International Journal of Quality & Reliability Management, 18*(3), 289–306. doi:10.1108/02656710110383539

Tlaiss, H. A. (2013). Women managers in the United Arab Emirates: Successful careers of what? *Equality, Diversity, and Inclusion: An International Journal, 32*(8), 756–776. doi:10.1108/EDI-12-2012-0109

Triandis, H. C. (1995). *Individualism & collectivism: New directions in social psychology.* Boulder, CO: Westview Press.

Ulanovsky, M., & Perez, P. (2017). Peer mentoring: A powerful tool to accelerate the learning experience. In D. Clutterbuck, F. Kochan, L. Lunsford, N. Dominguez, & J. Haddock-Millar (Eds.), *The Sage handbook of mentoring* (pp. 582–586). London, UK: Sage.

Wasserman, I. C., Gallegos, P. V., & Ferdman, B. M. (2008). Dancing with resistance: Leadership challenges in fostering a culture of inclusion. In K. Thomas (Ed.), *Diversity resistance in organizations* (pp. 175–200). New York: Lawrence Erlbaum Associates.

Waterbury, T. (2015). Learning from the pioneers: A multiple-case analysis of implementing Lean in higher education. *International Journal of Quality & Reliability Management, 32*(9), 934–950. doi:10.1108/IJQRM-08-2014-0125

Waxin, M.-F., & Bateman, R. (2016). Human resource management in the United Arab Emirates. In P. Budhwar, & K. Mellahi (Eds.), *Handbook of human resource management in the Middle East* (pp. 123–140). Cheltenham, UK: Edward Elgar Publishing Limited. doi:10.4337/9781784719524.00015

Wilkof, M. V., & Schneer, J. (1995). *Journal for Quality and Participation, 18*(3), 66–69.

Zakaria, N. (2000). The effects of cross-cultural training on the acculturation process of the global workforce. *International Journal of Manpower, 21*(6), 492–510.

Zhuang, W., Wu, M., & Wen, S. (2013). Relationship of mentoring functions to expatriate adjustments: Comparing home country mentorship and host country mentorship. *The International Journal of Human Resource Management, 24*(1), 35–49. doi:10.10 80/09585192.2012.669784

# 6

# Why Does Quality Matter? The Impact of Green Supply Chain Management Practices on Corporate Performance

*Hassan Younis*

## CONTENTS

## INTRODUCTION

Global warming, carbon emissions, and the depletion of natural resources have heralded significant changes in the ways that organizations produce and deliver products and services. Within this context, the greening of supply chains has gained the attention of practitioners in many countries. In some countries, for example, carbon taxation has been introduced as a mandatory requirement. Some big firms are now mandating that their suppliers have environment management systems (EMS) in place and, in some cases, have their systems certified. According to a recent International Organization for Standardization (ISO) survey, there are more than 300,000 ISO certified organizations every year (Ozusaglam et al., 2017). However, the implementation of green supply chain management (GSCM) practices is still at a nascent stage and, therefore, the impact of these practices on corporate performance (CP) remains unclear.

Consequently, the aim of this chapter is to explore GSCM practices and their relationship to CP. The chapter will specifically highlight the relationship between implementing a set of GSCM practices—including eco-design, green purchasing, environmental cooperation, and reverse logistics—on different dimensions of CP—namely, environmental, operational, economic, and social outcomes.

I will define what GSCM entails and how it relates to sustainability. In the next section, I will discuss the most common GSCM practices adopted by international organizations. I will discuss CP and explain its different dimensions, which are always targeted in any green initiative. I will elaborate on the drivers of GSCM practices as well as the ISO 14001 environment management certification. In the next section, I will discuss three theoretical lenses that can improve our understanding of the relationship between green supply chain initiatives and overall CP. Subsequently, I will discuss the effects of the identified GSCM practices on CP from all perspectives. Finally, I will present the theoretical and practical implications, offer some recommendations for supply chain managers, and propose future research avenues.

## DEFINITION OF GREEN SUPPLY CHAIN MANAGEMENT

At the outset of this chapter, it is important to define what constitutes a green supply chain. This section presents a few definitions found in the literature. Hervani (2005, p.334) offered the following useful definition of a green supply chain: a "green supply chain is a concept that combines green procurement, environmental management of manufacturing materials, environmental circulation, marketing, and reverse logistics." According to Sarkis (2003, p.399), a green supply chain is "a combination of the activities that encompass product design, all stages of manufacturing and distribution and all aspects of reverse logistics, and emphasized the latter's importance." Sundarakani et al. (2010, p.43) added another dimension, asserting that "green supply chain management can be defined as the integration of environmental thinking into supply chain management, including product design, supplier selection and material sourcing, manufacturing processes, product packaging, delivery of the product to consumers, and end-of-life management of the product after its use."

These definitions build on earlier work by Beamon (1999, p.332), who defined a green supply chain as "the extension of the traditional supply chain to include activities that aim at minimizing environmental impacts of a product throughout its entire cycle, such as green design, resource saving, harmful material reduction and product recycle and reuse."

Kumar and Putnam (2008, p.305) proposed that the end-to-end supply chain process, which was called "cradle to grave" in the early 1980s, be called "cradle to cradle," which means that the product must be returned to its origin (the manufacturer) to be reused or properly disposed. Srivastava (2007), however, argued that GSCM practices need to be integrated across the supply chain, including the acquisition of raw materials, product design, manufacturing processes, finished product delivery, and finally the management of product disposal at the end of its lifecycle.

Large firms are currently mandating that their suppliers have EMS in place to continue doing business with them. For example, IBM, Xerox, Ford, GM, and Toyota require their suppliers to develop EMS consistent with ISO 14001 certification (Eltayeb et al., 2010).

Given these definitions, it can be clearly observed that greening must span the entire supply chain at all stages. Only then can it be reasonably claimed that a green supply chain is producing degradable products using minimum resources and generating minimal waste (Younis et al., 2016; Younis and Sundarakani, 2019).

## SUSTAINABILITY

In the literature, the terms "sustainability" and "green supply chain" have been considered to go hand-in-hand, and both have become buzzwords in the contemporary business environment (Carter and Easton, 2011). Sustainability is the endurance of systems and processes; however, in the business world, sustainability is used to refer to an organization's environmental, economic, and social actions. Nevertheless, scholars, such as Elkington (1994), have claimed that a sustainable supply chain encompassing environmental and social activities must not harm the economic performance of the firm. Thus, Elkington (1998) introduced his triple bottom line concept of sustainability, theorizing that sustainability is the intersection of the environmental, social, and economic performance of the firm.

Sustainability is a strategic, transparent integration and achievement of the organization's social, environmental, and economic goals in coordination with other supply chain members (Carter and Easton, 2011). GSCM includes sustainability and the operational component and, hence, it relates to a 360-degree performance improvement at both the chain and firm levels.

## ADOPTION OF A GREEN SUPPLY CHAIN INITIATIVE

Although there are many green initiatives that organizations can adopt, the four following practices have been found to be the most dominant

**FIGURE 6.1**
GSCM practices.

organizational practices, and they are integral to any certification for GSCM implementation, such as ISO 14001. These four practices can be adopted by any member within the supply chain, either on the upstream or downstream side of the chain. The next section will elaborate on each of the four practices. Figure 6.1 displays the conceived model for frequently adopted GSCM practices.

## Eco-Design

Johansson (2002) defined eco-design as actions taken during the product development stage targeted at minimizing a product's environmental impact during its lifecycle, starting from acquiring raw materials for manufacturing, to the use of the product, and finally to the disposal of the product, without compromising on other essential product criteria, such as performance and cost.

Eco-design is an important green supply chain initiative because, at this stage, every aspect of the product is determined, including the raw materials to be used, the energy consumed, and the waste generated. It can be argued that product design touches each stage of the supply chain regarding environmental impact, starting with production, through to consumption and, finally, disposal. Therefore, it is important to integrate environmental aspects in the product design at the early stage of development (Eltayeb, 2009).

Indeed, it is the product attributes and basic materials that determine how much energy the product needs to function, what waste it may generate, and how it can be disposed. Taking the above into consideration, one can claim that eco-design plays an integral role in any sustainable development effort, especially in the manufacturing industry. This, in turn, entails close collaboration among supply chain members to ensure that a product's life and afterlife are taken into account from the early stages of development.

Among the relevant studies, Eltayeb and Zailani (2009) surveyed 132 ISO 14001 certified organizations in Malaysia to investigate the adoption of green supply chain initiatives. Their study uncovered that eco-design is the most frequently adopted green supply chain initiative, followed by green purchasing and reverse logistics, respectively.

Eco-design as a GSCM initiative has been investigated by many researchers, such as Zailani et al. (2011) and Lee et al. (2012), who examined its impact on firms' environmental performance. However, Laosirihongthong et al. (2013) delved deeper and investigated the impact of product- and packaging-related eco-design practices on environmental, economic, and intangible aspects of firm performance.

Perotti et al. (2012) used semi-structured interviews with executives from 13 third-party logistics (3PL) providers in Italy to understand how eco-design along with other GSCM practices can affect CP. Similarly, Diabat et al. (2013) explored the relationship between a set of GSCM practices (including eco-design) and different performance outcomes. Furthermore, Eltayeb and Zailani (2009) administered a survey to ISO 14001 organizations in Malaysia to rank the adoption of different GSCM practices, and eco-design was one of the four GSCM practices selected for this study. In this work, eco-design was found to be the number one adopted GSCM initiative. Zhu et al. (2006) and Zhu and Sarkis (2004) used eco-design in addition to other GSCM practices in their studies to assess their impact on different CP dimensions. Zhu and Sarkis (2005) included eco-design in their survey to companies in three industrial sectors in China and consequently established the drivers of the implementation of GSCM practices.

Furthermore, Deutz et al. (2013) focused on eco-design practices in the UK manufacturing industry and assessed the environmental factors that designers consider during the product design stage in the selected companies. Additionally, Zhu and Sarkis (2007), Eltayeb et al. (2011), and Zhu et al. (2012) included eco-design (along with other GSCM practices) in their studies to test its relationship with different performance outcomes. Moreover, Vijayvargy et al. (2017) investigated the impact of organizational size on the adoption of GSCM practices, including eco-design in India, to determine how these GSCM practices impact organizational performance.

More recently, Namagembe et al. (2019) assessed the relationship between five green practices including eco-design and firm performance. The authors also investigated the influence of each green practice on environmental performance, economic benefits, and economic costs.

It can be concluded that eco-design is an important GSCM practice that is always considered in any CP improvement strategy involving green initiatives.

## Green Purchasing

Green purchasing can be defined as an environmental purchasing initiative aimed at ensuring that purchased products and materials meet environmental objectives set by the purchasing firm, such as reducing sources of waste and encouraging the recycling, reuse, and substitution of materials (Carter et al., 1998; Min and Galle, 2001; Zsidisin and Siferd, 2001). Green purchasing is receiving significant attention worldwide, and businesses have become keener to evaluate their suppliers' environmental performance before making any procurement decisions (Zhu and Sarkis, 2006). Some authors have gone further by evaluating second-tier suppliers' environmental performance as well. For example, Walton et al. (1998) ranked second-tier suppliers' environmental performance as the second most important criterion when evaluating the supplier's environmental performance. Furthermore, Green et al. (1998) found that implementing green purchasing practices in firms in the UK can help companies achieve "environmental excellence." In the same context, Schlegelmilch et al. (1996) found that environmental consciousness has a positive impact on pro-environmental purchasing behaviors.

Large organizations, such as Ford, General Motors, Xerox, and International Business Machines, consider green purchasing as a key element of their environmental management systems; as such, they ensure that their suppliers develop environmental strategies that encompass green purchasing and, thus, obtain ISO 14001 certification as a green label for their environmental responsibility (Eltayeb et al., 2010). Green purchasing has been used in different studies tackling the impact of GSCM practices on CP. For example, Zhu et al. (2010) used green purchasing as an independent variable along with other variables to measure its impact on the firm's economic and environmental performance. Furthermore, Eltayeb et al. (2010) selected green purchasing as the only dependent variable against two independent variables measuring CP including social responsibility and expected business benefits. Liang and Chang (2008) also employed green purchasing along with green production and green marketing to examine their impact on profit goals, sales goals, and return on investment.

More recently, Diabat et al. (2013) and Laosirihongthong et al. (2013) used green purchasing along with other green supply chain initiatives to examine their impact on a set of CP outcomes including environmental, economic, and intangible performance. Similarly, Green et al. (2012)

examined the effects of green purchasing together with internal environmental management, green information systems, cooperation with customers, investment recovery, and eco-design on different dimensions of CP—namely, environmental, operational, economic, and organizational performance. Green purchasing was also among the GSCM practices adopted by Zhu et al. (2006), along with eco-design, reverse logistics, and cooperation with customers, to examine their impact on economic, operational, and environmental performance. Zhu and Sarkis (2005) also incorporated a set of GSCM practices including green purchasing in an analysis of variance (ANOVA) to compare drivers and practices of GSCM in three typical sectors in China—namely, the automobile industry, thermal power plants, and the electrical/electronic industry.

Recently, Vijayvargy et al. (2017) and Namagembe et al. (2019) measured the impact of green purchasing along with other green practices on organizational performance, which they found to be an important green practice for improving operational and economic performance.

## Environmental Cooperation

Adopting green supply chain practices requires internal and external cooperation among different stakeholders. For example, in the manufacturing industry, cooperation aimed at achieving environmental objectives must exist among the organization's different departments, such as purchasing, marketing, production, and human resources. Similarly, external cooperation between different stakeholders within the supply chain, including the raw material supplier, manufacturer, logistics provider, and customer, must take place to introduce an ecologically responsible design for a product that is safe and easy to recycle (Gonzalez, 2008). It is possible to achieve sustainable growth when the supply chain members cooperate and forge trust-based relationships. Moreover, both internal and external cooperation entail "buy in," commitment, and support from the senior management in each organization to deliver on the environmental goals and objectives.

Environmental cooperation has been used as a GSCM initiative in several studies, but often in one of two forms—that is, either upstream with suppliers or downstream with customers. Cooperation with suppliers or customers will be referred to as environmental cooperation. Examples of extant studies that employed environmental cooperation include the work of Lee et al. (2012), who examined the impact of environmental cooperation on different performance dimensions within electronics firms in Korea, and Perotti et al. (2012), who used environmental cooperation along with other GSCM initiatives to examine how the adoption of GSCM practices by 3PLs in Italy can affect CP. Furthermore, Diabat et al. (2013) examined the effects of collaboration with suppliers and customers, in addition to other GSCM initiatives, on different CP measures.

Equally, environmental collaboration with suppliers was on Azevedo et al.'s (2011) list of GSCM initiatives in their investigation into the relationships between GSCM practices and supply chain performance in the automotive industry in Portugal. Another example of environmental cooperation is Ford Motors. The company offers seminars and training sessions for its suppliers to assist them in achieving their goals for environmental excellence (Rao, 2002).

Regarding cooperating with customers, Green et al. (2012), Zhu et al. (2006), Zhu and Sarkis (2007), and Namagembe et al. (2019) examined the effects of a set of GSCM practices, including cooperation with customers, on different CP outcomes, such as environmental and economic performance.

These studies demonstrate that environmental cooperation is a key practice in any green supply chain initiative because it brings all parties together to ensure that they work in harmony to achieve a common goal—namely, maximizing the efficiency and effectiveness of the supply chain as a whole. This chapter defines environmental cooperation as the activities that take place between supply chain members for eco-design, cleaner production, green packaging, use of less energy during the transportation of materials and goods, and working together toward mutual environmental responsibilities and objectives.

## Reverse Logistics

Carter and Ellram (1998, p.86) defined reverse logistics as "the return or take back of products and materials from the point of consumption to the forward supply chain for the purpose of recycling, reuse, remanufacture, repair, refurbishing or safe disposal of the products and materials." Like other green supply chain initiatives, reverse logistics play a key role in enhancing the organization's operational efficiency, improving its competitiveness, and reducing system-wide costs. Reverse logistics are one of the most commonly used GSCM practices in the extant literature. For example, Perotti et al. (2012) included reverse logistics along with other GSCM initiatives in their study on logistics providers in Italy to assess the adoption level of these initiatives and their potential impact on different CP dimensions. Likewise, Diabat et al. (2013) employed the fuzzy TOPSIS method to explore how reverse logistics, along with other GSCM initiatives, can lead to improved CP. Moreover, reverse logistics were among three GSCM practices that Eltayeb and Zailani (2009) ranked according to adoption levels in Malaysia.

Reverse logistics were also among the GSCM initiatives that Hervani et al. (2005) looked at from a performance measurement perspective to propose a model for a performance measurement system. Moreover, Azevedo et al. (2011) considered reverse logistics in their analysis of five case studies in the Portuguese automotive industry to examine its relationship with supply chain performance. Similarly, Eltayeb et al. (2011) assessed the environmental, economic, and intangible outcomes resulting from the adoption of different GSCM practices including reverse logistics. Additionally, reverse logistics were one of the green supply chain practices that Younis et al. (2016) included in their study, which they found to be a key factor in improving corporate social performance. More recently, Namagembe et al. (2019) investigated the effects of five green supply chain practices including reverse logistics on three performance dimensions— namely, environmental performance, economic benefits, and economic costs.

The studies presented here confirmed the importance of reverse logistics as a GSCM initiative either at the firm or supply chain level. This is because it acts as a commitment from the respective chain members to the customers and other stakeholder groups that the product in question will be returned to be processed, repaired, or properly disposed of in an environmentally friendly way.

## CORPORATE PERFORMANCE

CP represents the opposite side of the GSCM practices–performance equation and has been used as a dependent variable in most studies examining its relationship with GSCM. Indeed, GSCM initiatives might lead to tangible benefits, such as cost reduction (Orlitzky et al., 2003; Melnyk et al., 2003; Eltayeb et al., 2011), improved quality (Melnyk et al., 2003), waste reduction (Azevedo et al., 2011), reduction of lead times

(Melnyk et al., 2003), improved profitability (Darnall et al., 2008; Menguc and Ozanne, 2005), positive stock returns (Klassen and McLaughlin, 1996; Menguc and Ozanne, 2005), and energy conservation (Cordano et al., 2010). GSCM practices may also lead to intangible benefits, such as enhanced competitiveness (Rao, 2002; Rao and Holt, 2005), increased shareholder value (Bose and Pal, 2012), increased customer satisfaction (Azevedo et al., 2011), improved job satisfaction (Jun et al., 2006), enhanced efficiency (Azevedo et al., 2011), and new market opportunities (Diabat et al., 2013; Walley and Whitehead, 1994).

As discussed earlier, Elkington (1998) introduced the "triple bottom line" and claimed that sustainability is nothing but the intersection of economic, environmental, and social performance. However, this chapter adds another dimension—that is, operational performance—to allow for measuring the impact of GSCM practices from a 360-degree perspective. Consequently, 360-degree CP is the impact resulting from implementing GCSM practices on four different aspects of CP. These are environmental performance, such as waste reduction and resource savings; operational performance, such as enhanced efficiency and improved quality; economic performance, such as improved profitability and positive stock returns; and social performance, such as improved job satisfaction and increased customer satisfaction. The following section elaborates each dimension.

## Environmental Performance

Zhu et al. (2008) defined environmental performance as the organization's ability to reduce carbon emissions, effluent waste, consumption of hazardous and toxic materials, and frequency of environmental accidents.

Carbon footprint is a new term that has recently become a buzzword used interchangeably with corporate environmental performance. It is defined as the amount of carbon dioxide released into the atmosphere as a result of the activities of a particular individual, organization, or community.

Many studies have used environmental performance alone and sometimes with other performance dimensions to measure the impact of GSCM practices implementation. For example, Schlegelmilch et al. (1996) analyzed the link between pro-environmental purchase behavior and measures of environmental consciousness. Similarly, using green purchasing and environmental performance, Green et al. (1998) found that pursuing a green purchasing policy improved companies' environmental performance across the supply chain. Moreover, Zailani et al. (2011) examined the extent to which an internal proactive environmental strategy and external institutional drivers motivate firms to adopt eco-design, which influences environmental performance. The authors found that eco-design positively affected environmental performance.

Similarly, Kung et al. (2012) investigated the relationship between environmental performance and green management among manufacturing firms in Taiwan. Additionally, Adebanjo et al. (2016) investigated the direct effect of external pressure on environmental outcomes and manufacturing performance and examined the mediating effect of sustainable management practices.

Other studies used environmental performance along with other performance dimensions. For example, Zhu et al. (2010) and Jabbour et al. (2015) both used environmental and operational performance in their studies, while Al-Tuwaijiri et al. (2004), Zhu and Sarkis (2007), and Namagembe et al. (2019) added economic performance to environmental performance in their studies. Furthermore, Nakao et al. (2007), as well Moneva and Ortas (2010), evaluated the significance of the link between corporate environmental performance and financial performance.

## Operational Performance

Melnyk et al. (2003) and Zhu et al. (2008) defined operational performance as the organization's capability to more efficiently produce and deliver products to customers with improved quality and reduced lead times, which ultimately improves its position in the marketplace and increases its chances of selling its products in international markets.

Operational performance has been extensively studied by many researchers in the GSCM context either on its own or in conjunction with other performance dimensions. Examples of such studies include the work of Yu et al. (2014), which investigated the relationships between three dimensions of integrated GSCM and many dimensions of operational performance.

In addition, operational performance has been measured in conjunction with environmental performance. Examples include the work of Large and Thomsen (2011), who studied the effects of different approaches (green assessment and green collaboration) on multiple operational and environmental aspects.

Another example of a study that employed operational performance along with other performance outcomes is the work of Vijayvargy et al. (2017), who investigated the impact of organizational size on the adoption of GSCM practices in Indian industry and the effects of GSCM practices on operational, environmental, and financial outcomes. Finally, Treacy et al. (2019) studied the relationship between ISO 14001 adoption and operating performance for both certified and non-certified firms in the UK and Ireland.

## Economic Performance

Green and Inman (2005) and Zhu et al. (2005) defined economic performance as financial and marketing performance improvements resulting from the implementation of GSCM practices that enhance the firm's position compared with the industry average. Financial improvement encompasses decreased costs for material purchasing (Alberti et al., 2000), energy consumption (Arimura et al., 2016), waste discharge (Darnall and Kim, 2012), and environmental accidents (Delmas, 2009). The marketing-based improvements include increases in average return on sales (De Jong et al., 2014; Zutshi and Sohal, 2004), average profit and profit growth (Lo et al., 2012), and average market share growth (Jacobs et al., 2010).

Economic performance and financial performance have been used interchangeably in different studies relating to GSCM, and they have been used alone or in conjunction with other performance dimensions.

Examples of studies employing economic performance alone are those of Liang and Chang (2008) and Bose and Pal (2011), who measured the effects of selected GSCM practices on different aspects of the firm's economic performance.

Most studies have incorporated economic and environmental performance owing to the belief that they are closely interwoven. Examples include the works of Perotti et al. (2012), Green et al. (2012), Rao (2002), King and Lenox (2001), Zhu et al. (2010), Al-Tuwaijiri et al. (2004), Eltayeb et al. (2011), Nakao et al. (2007), Vijayvargy et al. (2017), and Namagembe et al. (2019).

Finally, studies that have measured both economic/financial and social performance include the study of Wahba (2008), who presented empirical evidence of the influence of engaging in environmental responsibility on corporate market value.

## Social Performance

Wood (1991, p.693) defined social performance as "a business organization's configuration of principles of social responsibility, processes of social responsiveness, and policies, programs and observable outcomes as they tell the firm's societal relationships."

Implementing GSCM practices leads to improving corporate image and reputation (Bansal and Bogner, 2002; Boiral, 2007; Heras-Saizarbitoria et al., 2011; Melnyk et al., 2002; Orsato, 2006; Schoenherr, 2012; Vastag, 2009; Vastag and Melnyk, 2002), increased customer satisfaction (Chiarini, 2017; Schoenherr, 2012; Zutshi and Sohal, 2004), and more credible communication with partners (Montiel et al., 2012; Bansal and Bogner, 2002; Heras-Saizarbitoria et al., 2011; Zutshi and Sohal, 2004).

Examples of studies that included or measured the impact of GSCM practices on corporate social performance include the works of Orlitzky et al. (2003), Wahba (2008), Ozusaglam et al. (2018), and Sartor et al. (2019).

## Drivers of Green Supply Chain Management

Firms may pursue different strategies for adopting GSCM practices and complying with tougher environmental statutes. Mutingi (2013) recognized this when developing a taxonomic framework that can be used to form strategies for green supply chain initiatives. The approach categorized green supply chain strategies into four types: compliance-based, eco-efficient, innovation-centered, and closed-loop. However, it is not only legislation that drives businesses to go green and implement EMS; there are other factors that motivate businesses to improve their environmental record and enhance their competitiveness in the marketplace. For example, Lo (2014) claimed that the drivers to go green can be either external, such as legislation, customers, and competitors, or internal, such as senior management support, firm reputation, and cost reduction. These findings echoed a previous study conducted by Walker et al. (2008), who sought to identify the drivers of, and barriers to, implementing environmental supply chain management practices within the public and private sectors in the UK. Using interviews with seven different private and public sector organizations, the authors found that both drivers and barriers can be either internal or external. Internal drivers include value champions and cost reduction, whereas external drivers include regulations, customers, competitors, and society.

Adopting a similar qualitative approach, Mollenkopf et al. (2010) examined the relationship between green, lean, and global supply chain strategies, including their convergence and divergence. Their findings revealed that four factors motivated businesses to adopt some combination of green, lean, and global supply chain strategies—namely, cost reduction, customer demand, ISO 9000 and ISO 14001 certification, and risk management.

In a quantitative vein, Lee (2008) explored the drivers for implementing green supply chain initiatives in small and medium-sized suppliers. Analyzing the data obtained through a questionnaire administered to 142 small and medium-sized suppliers in South Korea, Lee concluded that buyers played a key role in facilitating these suppliers' adoption of green supply chain initiatives. He also found that the government's involvement and support were linked to the suppliers' greater willingness to participate in green supply chain initiatives. Moreover, Lee found that the participation of small- and medium-sized suppliers in green supply chain initiatives was directly related to their readiness, including internal available resources and organizational capabilities.

In concluding this section, it is fair to state that businesses are driven by internal and external pressures to green their operations, but the question is how these actions affect their CP. It might be best to answer this question by looking at the ISO 140001 standard to understand the specific environmental management system and the green practices of supply chain management.

## ISO 14001 ENVIRONMENTAL MANAGEMENT SYSTEM CERTIFICATION

A commonly adopted measure for GSCM practices is ISO 14001. Some practitioners have referred to it as the "green seal," which breaks environmental barriers for international trade. ISO 14001 certified organizations are those firms that implement EMS and wish to have their system certified to the ISO 14001 standard, which was introduced in 1996 (Bansal and Hunter, 2003). The ISO 14001 standard requires organizations to develop an environmental policy with specific objectives, execute a program to achieve those objectives, measure its efficacy, rectify any problems, and evaluate the system with the aim of improving its overall performance (Tibor and Feldman, 1996).

As per Ozusaglam et al. (2018), having EMS in place serves three main purposes for organizations: reduction in the depletion of natural resources, minimization of operations' environmental impact, and compliance with environmental regulations. Baek (2018) claimed that although certifying EMS is voluntary, ISO 14001 certification entails achieving the following prior to obtaining the certification to develop the firm's own environmental policy and program to improve environmental quality: identify all environmental aspects of production and operation processes and then rank them in terms of the significance of their environmental effects; set environmental goals and objectives to develop the firm's own procedures to monitor environmental aspects; train employees on these monitoring procedures; demonstrate a commitment to following environmental laws and regulations; plan and organize third-party audits; and review the environmental management system on a regular basis.

In their study on the impact of implementing GSCM practices on CP, Younis et al. (2016) found that half the companies surveyed had certified EMS. However, these companies were motivated by different institutional drivers in their attempts to satisfy certain stakeholders. Nevertheless, such certification was associated with all dimensions of CP. This association provides a good indication that these firms are moving in the correct direction because EMS implementation and certification form the basis of any green initiative to drive CP. These findings were echoed by Melnyk et al. (2003), who identified a positive relationship between the presence of formal, certified EMS and improved performance, such as reduced costs (economic performance), improved quality (operational performance), reduction of waste in the design and equipment selection process (environmental performance), and reduction of lead times (operational performance). Additionally, Gonzalez et al. (2008) found a strong relationship between possessing certified EMS and the demand on suppliers to implement environmental practices. ISO 14001 also improves corporate social performance because this standard allows employees to be responsible for making choices about how to meet the organization's environment goals; they encounter more constraints, for which they are likely to develop innovative solutions (Link and Naveh, 2005).

## Drivers of ISO 14001 Implementation

Organizations seeking to obtain ISO 14001 certification are usually driven by many factors that can be either external, such as stockholders, senior management, and pressure from employees, or external, such as pressure from customers, regulatory agencies, or occasionally indirectly from competitors. Sartor et al. (2018) claimed that ISO 14001 drivers can also be economic, environmental, or a combination of both. The authors listed 16 different drivers cited in 36 journal papers published between 2000 and 2018. Among the economic drivers listed were increased efficiency, improvement in the company's image, and green incentives. The environmental drivers included reduction in toxic release, improved environmental sensitivity, and adherence to environmental legal requirements. Finally, Sartor et al. (2018) captured ten hybrid drivers, including reduced resource consumption, reduced packaging material, investor pressure, pressure from suppliers, improved customer satisfaction, enhancement of product and process quality, penetration of foreign markets, pressure from customers, pressure from competitors, and reduction of information asymmetry between buyers and suppliers.

## Barriers to ISO 14001 Certification

While there are many drivers motivating businesses to get their EMS certified, there are also barriers that hinder certifying EMS to ISO 14001. Among the most cited barriers are the cost of certification (Alberti et al., 2000; Bansal and Bogner, 2002; Chiarini, 2017; Orsato, 2006; Schoenherr and Talluri, 2013; Zhu, Tian, and Sarkis, 2012; Zutshi and Sohal, 2004), improper implementation (Boiral, 2007; Del Brio and Junquera, 2003; Ferron-Vilchez, 2016; Iatridis and Kesidou, 2018; Jiang and Bansal, 2003; Montiel, Husted, and Christmann, 2012; Testa et al., 2018), risk of confidential information dissemination (Zutshi and Sohal, 2004; Boiral, 2011; Delmas, 2009), difficulties in evaluating outcomes (Bansal and Bogner, 2002; Delmas, 2009; Sullivan, 2005; Vastag and Melnyk, 2002), productivity decrease due to allocating resources to complete the required tasks (Bansal and Bogner, 2002; Boiral, 2011; Zutshi and Sohal, 2004), decrease in overall efficiency (Jacobs, Singhal, and Subramanian, 2010; Schoenherr and Talluri, 2013; Zutshi and Sohal, 2004), risk of underestimating needed resources (Zutshi and Sohal, 2004; Boiral, 2011), limited perceived economic improvements (Chiarini, 2017; Melnyk, Sroufe, and Calantone, 2003), lack of employee commitment (Bansal and Bogner, 2002; Zutshi and Sohal, 2004), difficulties in assessing progress after EMS implementation (Bansal and Bogner, 2002; Boiral, 2007), and absence of cultural changes within the program (Kitazawa and Sarkis, 2000).

## Impact of ISO 14001 Certification on Performance

Some researchers have claimed that ISO 14001 may have a negative impact on organizational performance due to the relatively expensive certification costs (Alberti et al., 2000; Bansal and Bogner, 2002; Zutshi and Sohal, 2004; Orsato, 2006; Tian, Zhu and Sarkis, 2012; Schoenherr and Talluri, 2013; Chiarini, 2017), productivity decrease resulting from allocating resources to work on the certification process (Bansal and Bogner, 2002; Zutshi and Sohal, 2004; Boiral, 2011), and decrease in overall efficiency (Zutshi and Sohal, 2004; Jacobs, Singhal, and Subramanian, 2010; Schoenherr and Talluri, 2013). However, many studies have reported a positive impact. For example, Sartor et al. (2018), in their review of 52 studies, found that there were 23 benefits to certifying EMS to ISO 14001. These benefits can be classified into five main categories: operational, environmental, legal, financial, and socioenvironmental related benefits. ISO 14001 has a strong and direct effect on environmental performance (Bellessi et al., 2005; Habidin et al., 2017) because it can lead to reduced waste and consumption of resources, which were the most common benefits in studies that reported a positive relationship with ISO 14001. For example, Miles et al. (1997), Alberti et al. (2000), Bansal and Bogner (2002), Melnyk et al. (2002), Melnyk et al. (2003), Zutshi and Sohal (2004), Heras-Saizarbitoria et al. (2011), Darnall and Kim (2012), Lo et al. (2012), Zailani et al. (2012), Arimura et al. (2016), and Wiengarten et al. (2017) found that ISO 14001 certification can lead to reductions in both waste and resource consumption.

Similarly, several studies, including recent ones such as Fryxell and Szeto (2002), Kwon et al. (2002), Arimura et al. (2016), Ferron-Vilchez (2016), and Graafland and Smid (2016), have claimed that ISO 14001 led to reduced negative environmental impact (e.g., air pollution). Within the environmental vein, some scholars have argued that the benefits of ISO 14001 can be extended to cover the whole supply chain. For example, Miles et al. (1997), Melnyk et al. (2003), Boiral (2007), Gonzalez et al. (2008), and Arimura et al. (2010) reported that ISO 14001 certification can lead to the diffusion of environmental practices within the supply chain.

## Operational Benefits

Operationally, ISO 14001 can lead to increased process productivity and control, as reported by many researchers, such as Alberti et al. (2000),

Bansal and Bogner (2002), Zutshi and Sohal (2004), Boiral (2007), Delmas (2009), Vastag (2009), and De Jong et al. (2014). Moreover, it improves the quality of products and services offered (Melnyk et al., 2002; Melnyk et al., 2003; Schoenherr, 2012; Teixeira et al., 2012; Wiengarten et al., 2017).

Within the operational dimension, and from a business process related perspective, a few studies reported different performance improvements resulting from ISO 14001 certification. For example, it leads to the optimized use of raw materials (Alberti et al., 2000; Sullivan, 2005; Lo et al., 2012) and increased flexibility (Alberti et al., 2000; Melnyk et al., 2003; Schoenherr, 2012). Furthermore, Melnyk et al. (2003), Zutshi and Sohal (2004), Boiral (2007), Jacobs et al. (2010), Heras-Saizarbitoria et al. (2011), and Chiarini (2017) found that ISO 14001 EMS certification led to improvements in employee awareness and morale. Additionally, Melnyk et al. (2003), Gonzalez et al. (2008), Klassen and Vachon (2009), Arimura et al. (2010), Testa et al. (2012), and Prajogo et al. (2014) found that ISO 14001 can ease the implementation of other environmental practices.

A few other researchers, such as Melnyk et al. (2003), Zutshi and Sohal (2004), Link and Naveh (2006), Orsato (2006), Mijatovic and Stokic (2010), Heras-Saizarbitoria et al. (2011), Aravind and Christmann (2011), Darnall and Kim (2012), and Lo et al. (2012), found that the implementation of ISO 14001 led to the development of internal capabilities in the organization that reduce environmental effects. Finally, ISO 14001 can lead to increase on-time deliveries and decreased lead times (Melnyk et al., 2002; Melnyk et al., 2003; Schoenherr, 2012). Recently, Reis et al. (2018) found in their critical analysis that the implementation of ISO 14001 led to enhancements in internal processes, strengthening of results, and prevention of potential problems.

## Financial Benefits

ISO 14001 can improve the firm's financial performance. For example, Alberti et al. (2000), Muskin (2000), Melnyk et al. (2002), Zutshi and Sohal (2004), Gonzalez-Benito and Gonzalez-Benito (2005), Jacobs et al. (2010), and De Jong et al. (2014) found that ISO 14001 can lead to increased sales, while Delmas (2009), Lo et al. (2012), and De Jong et al. (2014) confirmed that it can lead to an improvement in the firm's profitability. Moreover, Alberti et al. (2000), Zutshi and Sohal (2004), and Delmas (2009) found that ISO 14001 can lead to reduced insurance costs.

More recently, Treacy et al. (2018) found a positive relationship between ISO 14001 adoption and fixed assets turnover, and that such adoption can lead to a decline in manufacturing costs, receiving payments earlier than non-certified organizations, and sustained long-term improvement in return on assets. Similarly, Reis et al. (2018) found a positive relationship between ISO 14001 implementation and organizational and financial performance. Within the financial performance dimension, Jacobs et al. (2010) and Xu et al. (2016) found that ISO 14001 can lead to improved organizational performance on the stock exchange, and a smaller decline might be reported after an environmental violation (Xu et al., 2016). Last, ISO 14001 can lead to more efficient research and development investment and innovation (Inoue et al., 2013; Lim and Prakash, 2014; Arnold, 2015; He and Shen, 2017).

## Legal Benefits

As far as legal performance is concerned, studies have shown that ISO 14001 can improve compliance with the law and regulations (Alberti et al., 2000; Muskin, 2000; Melnyk et al., 2003; Zutshi and Sohal, 2004; Gonzalez-Benito and Gonzalez-Benito, 2005; Delmas, 2009; Heras-Saizarbitoria et al., 2011; Lo et al., 2012; Zailani et al., 2012; McGuire, 2014; He et al.,2016). ISO 14001 can also enhance relationships with communities and authorities (Alberti et al., 2000; Bansal and Bogner, 2002; Zutshi and Sohal, 2004; Vastag, 2009; Heras-Saizarbitoria et al., 2011; He et al., 2016; Chiarini, 2017). Moreover, implementation of ISO 14001 can lead to decreased frequency of inspections (Delmas, 2009; Vastag, 2009; Lo et al., 2012; He et al., 2016) and improved health and safety conditions of the workplace (Graafland and Smid, 2016; Chiarini, 2017; Wiengarten et al., 2017).

## Societal Benefits

The societal benefits that ISO 14001 can bring to the organization are numerous. For example, it can lead to an improved corporate image and reputation (Alberti et al., 2000; Bansal and Bogner, 2002; Melnyk et al., 2002; Vastag and Melnyk, 2002; Zutshi and Sohal, 2004; Orsato, 2006; Boiral, 2007; Vastag, 2009; Heras-Saizarbitoria et al., 2011; Schoenherr, 2012). Furthermore, ISO 14001 can lead to increased customer satisfaction (Chiarini, 2017; Schoenherr, 2012; Zutshi and Sohal, 2004) and more credible communication with partners (Bansal and Bogner, 2002; Zutshi and Sohal, 2004; Heras-Saizarbitoria et al., 2011; Montiel et al., 2012). To summarize, ISO 14001 is not only a certification but an end-to-end system that requires resources, attention, and top management support to ensure a high performing organization that outperforms competitors.

## EFFECTS OF GREEN SUPPLY CHAIN MANAGEMENT PRACTICES ON CORPORATE PERFORMANCE

Broadly, I argue that four GSCM practices were found to be the most commonly adopted ones across businesses and, thus, were selected for inclusion in the chapter. These are eco-design, green purchasing, environmental cooperation, and reverse logistics. With respect to CP, this study adopted four dimensions that were found to be highly associated with green supply chain implementation and were previously assessed by several researchers in the field (although not collectively). These were environmental performance, operational performance, economic performance, and social performance.

### Green Supply Chain Management and Environmental Performance

Environmental performance is a key performance dimension and it should always be improved once a green initiative is implemented. However, several studies have shown no significant effects of the four green supply chain practices on environmental performance. From a resource-based view, and as claimed by Hart (1995), it may be that these firms adopted compliance-based strategies in these GSCM practices and not proactive strategies and, thus, they could not positively affect environmental performance. Similar findings were reported by Green et al. (2012), who found no significant relationship between green purchasing and environmental performance. Furthermore, Simpson et al. (2007) reported that there was no evidence of a significant relationship between environmental commitment and environmental performance. Moreover, Eltayeb et al. (2010) reported that green purchasing implementation must be stipulated and mandated by government regulations to be an effective tool for performance enhancement. This point was supported by the work of Zhu and Sarkis (2007), who showed that government regulations are the main driver of an organization's enhanced environmental performance. Another explanation might be that organizations implement GSCM practices without assessing which practices deliver the best outcomes.

For example, Lo (2014) claimed that reverse logistics practices might deliver better performance outcomes than eco-design practices for firms downstream of the supply chain. It is also noteworthy that such results differ from one industry to another. For example, green purchasing practices might lead to better performance outcomes than eco-design for firms in the textile manufacturing industry. In Younis et al.'s (2016) qualitative study, when firms' environment management representatives (EMRs) were asked why GSCM practices failed to improve corporate environmental performance, the answers varied. For example, the production managers of two companies manufacturing tiles and pipes, respectively, stated that eco-design practices might not impact corporate environmental performance if the practices are not properly implemented. However, the purchasing manager of a third company manufacturing pharmaceuticals advised that eco-design practices entail management support and commitment to lead for real performance improvements. Finally, the procurement manager of another company specializing in furniture manufacturing opined that eco-design practices are long-term initiatives and, thus, the benefits require some time to be realized. This, in effect, means that it can take some time for investments in GSCM to yield returns.

In the same study, when interviewees were asked why environmental cooperation did not impact corporate environmental performance, they presented four main reasons (Younis et al., 2016; Younis, and Sundarakani, 2019). For example, the production manager of one company manufacturing tiles asserted that non-adherence to EMS requirements might be a strong reason for this lack of relationship, while the quality control and assurance (QA) manager of another company manufacturing pre-insulated pipes felt that the cause was rooted in the lack of assignment of a dedicated staff member to manage environment-related matters within the firm. Additionally, both the procurement manager and HSE manager of another company producing ready-mix concrete claimed that it takes time for environmental cooperation practices to improve environmental performance. Another reason proffered for the lack of relationship between environmental cooperation and environmental performance was presented by the general manager of a building materials manufacturing business. He stated that recycling might generate some emissions and this, in turn, might hamper environmental performance improvements.

In some studies, green purchasing was found to have no relationship with environmental performance, the main reason for which was that firms did not assign a dedicated person to monitor the implementation of green purchasing practices and rectify any issues that arose during the implementation process (Younis et al., 2016). If organizations intend to improve their environmental performance, they must ensure that a qualified and certified environmental engineer is assigned to handle, monitor, and evaluate all green-related initiatives within the organization and report to management on a frequent basis. Similarly, reverse logistics practices need to be properly implemented for the results to improve the organization's environmental performance. Without an experienced and certified engineer with the responsibility to ensure the proper implementation of any green initiative, any environmental initiative will be a waste of money and a burden on the organization (Richey et al., 2005).

## Green Supply Chain Management and Operational Performance

Consistent with the resource-based view, many studies have shown that green purchasing and environmental cooperation are positively related to operational performance. Firms that meet this description tend to acquire and deploy innovative resources that proactively address environmental issues while working closely with their supply chain partners to prevent environmental accidents and improve product quality. For example, Diabat et al. (2013) found that environmental cooperation is one of the most important GSCM practices that can lead to better operational performance outcomes. In the United Arab Emirates, for example, the government has issued different regulations and initiatives, such as "Istedama," "Pearl Rating," and "Green Building," aimed at motivating supply chain members to work more closely to deliver more sustainable products and projects.

Regarding eco-design and reverse logistics, a few studies have found that these initiatives had no impact on operational performance. This is possibly because the level of implementation was insufficient to lead to better outcomes (Zhu et al., 2006). Similar findings were reported by Deutz et al. (2013), who identified that firms may not be effectively implementing eco-design due to the functional requirements, and this may, in turn, hamper any performance improvements.

In Younis's et al. (2016) qualitative study, some organizations provided similar reasons. For example, the production manager of a company said that if eco-design practices were not properly implemented, it may not lead to any operational benefits to the firm. Additionally, the QA manager of another company claimed that eco-design practices require a dedicated environmental management resource within the organization to monitor and manage its implementation, which is not currently the case in most companies.

Richey et al. (2005) reported similar results concerning reverse logistics. That is, the authors found that the implementation of reverse logistics procedures did not improve corporate operational performance. It may be that these firms implemented reverse logistics practices voluntarily and not due to legislation holding them responsible for the recovery and proper disposal of their products after use. Consequently, the implementation may not have been deep enough to lead to any improvement in the operational dimension (Mitra and Datta, 2014). It can also be argued that reverse logistics and eco-design require cooperation with other supply chain members for the benefits to be realized. Eltayeb et al. (2011) found that externally oriented GSCM practices, such as reverse logistics, had little impact on the internal (operational) performance of firms. Younis et al. (2016) also reported that they did not find a strong connection between reverse logistics and operational performance. Evidently, the operations manager of a company whom the authors interviewed stated that products from recycled materials are usually lower in quality than those from raw materials, and this might explain a lack of improvement in corporate operational performance. By the same token, when the general manager of another company was asked why reverse logistics failed to affect operational performance, he stated that it may be connected with issues in implementation. He also provided an example of a process used with one of their products—namely, bricks. The dust generated could be collected and recycled back into the production process, but this process requires proper control and implementation, which not all firms are good at.

## Green Supply Chain Management and Economic Performance

Studies have found evidence that green purchasing practices are having a significant impact on economic performance. Therefore, these practices are important for firms that have limited resources and want to realize short-term economic benefits. This is in keeping with Green et al. (2012), who found that green purchasing was positively linked to economic performance. Mitra and Datta (2014) reported similar results. They found that supplier collaboration was positively related to a sustainable product design, which, in turn, positively impacted economic performance. Furthermore, as Al-Tuwaijiri et al. (2004) uncovered, improvements in environmental performance may lead to an improvement in economic performance.

A possible reason why other green practices do not improve economic performance is that these practices might be long-term oriented and entail substantial initial investments, such as pollution prevention systems and R&D in eco-design products, which can take time to yield returns. At the same time, green purchasing has the benefit of being less capital intensive because it is an externally oriented green supply chain initiative. This was found to be the case in Malaysia, where Eltayeb et al. (2011) found that better economic performance was the main driver for Malaysian firms to adopt green purchasing practices. This was supported in the context of UAE firms, according to the findings reported by Younis et al. (2016). In their qualitative research, for example, a production engineer and technical manager of a company manufacturing glass reinforced plastic pipes and fittings stated that eco-design practices entail incurring extra costs to be properly implemented, and such costs require some time to be recovered. The same claim was made by another company manufacturing furniture items.

The procurement manager in that firm asserted that the three green supply chain practices of eco-design, environmental cooperation, and reverse logistics incur significant extra costs to implement, which is why the company's economic performance did not improve in the short term (Younis et al., 2016). In the same study, employees of firms in the pharmaceutical industry claimed that the eco-design of both the product and the packaging, as well as reverse logistics, will not improve economic performance in the short term, but this investment may be recovered in the long term. Finally, the environment management representative of a company producing and selling ready-mix concrete claimed that eco-design practices increase the product costs and can also lead to additional costs when working with other supply chain members (environmental cooperation). Therefore, he concluded that economic performance does not improve as a result of GSCM.

## Green Supply Chain Management and Social Performance

Among the four GSCM practices, it can be concluded that reverse logistics implementation significantly improves corporate social performance, consistent with the institutional theory perspective. Mitra and Datta (2014) obtained such results. In their study, the recovery of packaging and products improved corporate image. Drawing on institutional theory, therefore, it is rational to claim that improvements in the social performance of any firm are partially due to external drivers, such as firm image, but not linked to legislation or regulations, which were the major external drivers found in most previous studies. Instead, the main drivers of social performance found in other studies were internal reverse logistics pressures, and these findings echo Younis et al.'s (2016) and Lin and Sheu's (2012) conclusion that internally driven GSCM practices lead to performance improvements.

## THEORETICAL AND PRACTICAL IMPLICATIONS

This study adds to the body of knowledge by identifying the main GSCM practices adopted by most firms and their effects on different CP dimensions. The study also identified barriers to the implementation of a number of green supply chain practices while highlighting the importance of having a dedicated resource who is qualified and certified to handle all green initiatives in the organization. The findings also highlight the benefits of certifying EMS to ISO 14001 across different organizational dimensions.

This study contributes to business practice by presenting a stakeholder understanding of the relationship between the implementation of different green supply chain practices and CP, including the level of adoption that may identify the most appropriate GSCM practices for reaching the optimum performance level. Further, the results clarify the precautions that must be taken during any green initiative implementation in an attempt to assist organizations in successfully achieving their objectives.

## CONCLUSION AND FUTURE RESEARCH DIRECTIONS

Since this study focused on the manufacturing field, extending this research to other industrial sectors may allow researchers to understand how the performance of other firms is impacted by the implementation of GSCM practices and how they cope with mounting environmental issues in the construction sector, transportation sector, or other environmentally sensitive sectors.

As such, this study lays the foundation for future research in other sectors, such as services, construction, or aviation. Therefore, investigating firms' positions on the environmental radar and the different green practices implemented in that industry would be valuable. Further studies might also investigate the impact of EMS certifications, such as ISO 14001, on different CP dimensions to assess whether certification plays any role in improving firms' environmental performance and has any links with GSCM practices. The following recommendations are presented for firms interested in improving their carbon footprint and their environmental performance while implementing green supply chain practices:

(1) Ensure that senior management supports the initiative.
(2) Ensure that agreed practices are properly implemented and monitored.
(3) Ensure the adherence of EMS rules.
(4) Employ a dedicated environmental engineer to manage the implementation.
(5) Ensure that objective measures are in place to measure the outcomes.
(6) Ensure that all green initiatives are advertised to the public.

Consequently, this study presents insights for researchers proposing to study green supply chain practices in the future. Thus, the study contributes to both research and practice.

## REFERENCES

Adebanjo, D., Teh, P. and Ahmed, P. (2016). The impact of external pressure and sustainable management practices on manufacturing performance and environmental outcomes. *International Journal of Operations & Production Management*, 36(9):995–1013.

Alberti, M., Caini, L., Calabrese, A. and Rossi, D. (2000). Evaluation of the cost and benefits of an environmental management system. *International Journal of Production Research*, 38(17):4455–4466.

Al-Tuwaijri, S., Christensen, T. and Hughes, K. (2004). The relations among environmental disclosures environmental performance, and economic performance: A simultaneous equations approach. *Accounting Organizations and Society*, 29(5):447–471.

Alves Teixeira, A., Jabbour, C. J. C. and Jabbour, A. B. L. D. S. (2012). Relationship between green management and environmental training in companies located in Brazil:

A theoretical framework and case studies. *International Journal of Production Economics*, 140(1):318–329.

Aravind, D. and Christmann, P. (2011). Decoupling of standard implementation from certification: Does quality of ISO 14001 implementation affect facilities' environmental performance? *Business Ethics Quarterly*, 21(1):73–102.

Arimura, T. H., Darnall, N. and Katayama, H. (2010). Is ISO 14001 a gateway to more advanced voluntary action? The case of green supply chain management. *Journal of Environmental Economics and Management*, 61:170–182.

Arimura, T. H., Darnall, N., Ganguli, R. and Katayama, H. (2016). The effect of ISO 14001 on environmental performance: Resolving equivocal findings. *Journal of Environmental Management*, 166:556–566.

Arnold, M. (2015). The lack of strategic sustainability orientation in German water companies. *Ecological Economics*, 117:39–52.

Ayuso, S., Rodríguez, M., García-Castro, R. and Ariño, M. (2014). Maximizing stakeholders' interests: An empirical analysis of the stakeholder approach to corporate governance, *Business & Society*, 53(3):414–439.

Azevedo, S., Carvalho, H. and Machado, V. (2011). The influence of green practices on supply chain performance: A case study approach. *Transportation Research Part E-Logistics and Transportation Review*, 47(6):850–871.

Baek, K. (2018). Sustainable development and pollutant outcomes: The case of ISO 14001 in Korea. *Corporate Social Responsibility & Environmental Management*, 25(5):825–832.

Bansal, P. and Bogner, W. (2002). Deciding on ISO 14001: Economics, institutions, and context. *Long Range Planning*, 35(3):269–290.

Bansal, P. and Hunter, T. (2003). Strategic explanations for the early adoption of ISO 14001. *Journal of Business Ethics*, 46(3):289–299.

Barla, P. (2007). ISO 14001 certification and environmental performance in Quebec's pulp and paper industry. *Journal of Environmental Economics and Management*, 53(3):291–306.

Barney, J. (1986). Strategic factor markets: Expectations, luck and business strategy. *Management Science*, 32:1231–1241.

Beamon, A. (1999). Designing the green supply chain. *Logistics Information Management*, 12(4):330–353.

Bellessi, F., Lehrer, D. and Tal, A. (2005). Comparative advantage: The impact of ISO 14001 environmental certification on exports. *Environmental Science Technology*, 39:1943–1953.

Boiral, O. (2007). Corporate greening through ISO 14001: A rational myth? *Organization Science*, 18(1):127–146.

Bose, I. and Pal, R. (2011). Do green supply chain management initiatives impact stock prices of firms? *Decision Support Systems*, 52:624–634.

Chiarini, A. (2014). Strategies for developing an environmentally sustainable supply chain: Differences between manufacturing and service sectors. *Business Strategy and the Environment*, 23(7):493–504.

Chiarini, A. (2017). Setting strategies outside a typical environmental perspective using ISO 14001 certification. *Business Strategy and the Environment*, 26(6):844–854.

Campbell-Hunt, C. (2000). What have we learned about generic competitive strategy? A meta-analysis. *Strategic Management Journal*, 21(2):127–154.

Carter, C. and Easton, P. (2011). Sustainable supply chain management: Evolution and future directions. *International Journal of Physical Distribution and Logistics Management*, 41(1):46–62.

Carter, C. and Ellram, L. (1998). Reverse logistics: A review of the literature and framework for future investigation. *Journal of Business Logistics, 19*:85–102.

Conner, K. (1991). A historical comparison of resource based theory and five schools of thought within industrial organization economics: Do we have a new theory of the firm? *Journal of Management, 17*(1):121–154.

Cordano, M., Marshall, R. and Silverman, M. (2010). How do small and medium enterprises go "green"? A study of environmental management programs in the US wine industry. *Journal of Business Ethics, 92*(3):463–478.

Darnall, N., Jolley, G. and Handfield, R. (2006). Environmental management systems and green supply chain management: Complements for sustainability? *Business Strategy and the Environment, 18*:30–45.

Darnall, N. and Kim, Y. (2012). Which types of environmental management systems are related to greater environmental improvements? *Public Administration Review, 72*(3):351–365.

De Jong, P., Paulraj, A. and Blome, C. (2014). The financial impact of ISO 14001 certification: Top-line, bottom-line, or both? *Journal of Business Ethics, 119*(1):131–149.

Delmas, M. (2009). Stakeholders and competitive advantage: The case of ISO 14001. *Production and Operations Management, 10*(3):343–358.

Deutz, P., McGuire, M. and Neighbour, G. (2013). Eco-design practice in the context of a structured design process: An interdisciplinary empirical study of UK manufacturers. *Journal of Cleaner Production, 39*:117–128.

Diabat, A. and Govindan, K. (2011). An analysis of the drivers affecting the implementation of green supply chain management. *Resource, Conservation and Recycling, 55*:659–667.

Diabat, A., Khodaverdi, R. and Olfat, L. (2013). An exploration of green supply chain practices and performance in an automotive industry. *International Journal of Advanced Manufacturing Technology, 68*:949–961.

DiMaggio, P. and Powell, W. (1983). The iron cage revisited: Institutional isomorphism and collective rationality in organizational fields. *American Sociological Review, 48*(2):147–160.

Elkington, J. (1994). Towards the sustainable corporation: Win-win-win business strategies for sustainable development. *California Management Review, 36*(2):90–100.

Eltayeb, T. and Zailani, S. (2009). Going green through green supply chain initiatives towards environmental sustainability. *Operations and Supply Chain Management, 2*(2):93–110.

Eltayeb, T., Zailani, S. and Jayaraman, K. (2010). The examination on the drivers for green purchasing adoption among EMS 14001 certified companies in Malaysia. *Journal of Manufacturing Technology Management, 21*(2):206–225.

Eltayeb, T., Zailani, S. and Ramayah, T. (2011). Green supply chain initiatives among certified companies in Malaysia and environmental sustainability: Investigating the outcomes. *Resources Conservation and Recycling, 55*(5):495–506.

Ferron-Vilchez, V. (2016). Does symbolism benefit environmental and business performance in the adoption of ISO 14001? *Journal of Environmental Management, 183*:882–894.

Freeman, R. E. (1984). *Strategic Management: A Stakeholder Approach.* Pittman, Marshfield, MA.

Freeman, R. E. (2002). Stakeholder theory of the modern corporation, in T. Donaldson and P. Werhane (eds.), *Ethical Issues in Business: A Philosophical Approach*, 7th Edition, 38–48. Prentice Hall, Englewood Cliffs, NJ.

Frooman, J. and Murrell, A. J. (2005). Stakeholder influence strategies: The roles of structural and demographic determinants. *Business and Society*, 44:3–31.

Fryxell, E. and Szeto, A. (2002). The influence of motivations for seeking ISO 14001 certification: An empirical study of ISO 14001 certified facilities in Hong Kong. *Journal of Environmental Management*, 64(3):223–238.

Gonzalez, P., Sarkis, J. and Díaz, B. (2008). Environmental management system certification and its influence on corporate practices: Evidence from the automotive industry. *International Journal of Operations and Production Management*, 28(11):1021–1041.

Gonzalez-Benito, J. and Gonzalez-Benito, O. (2005). An analysis of the relationship between environmental motivations and ISO14001 certification. *British Journal of Management*, 16:133–148.

Gonzalez-Benito, J. and Gonzalez-Benito, O. (2008). Operations management practices linked to the adoption of ISO 14001: An empirical analysis of Spanish manufacturers. *International Journal of Production Economics*, 113(1):60–73.

Graafland, J. and Smid, H. (2016). Environmental impacts of SMEs and the effects of formal management tools: Evidence from EU's largest survey. *Corporate Social Responsibility and Environmental Management*, 23(5):297–303.

Green, K. and Inman, R. (2005). Using a just-in-time selling strategy to strengthen supply chain linkages. *International Journal of Production Research*, 43(16):3437–3453.

Green, K., Morton, B. and New, S. (1998). Green purchasing and supply policies do they improve companies' environmental performance. *Supply Chain Management*, 3(2):89.

Green, K., Zelbst, P., Meacham, J. and Bhadauria, V. (2012). Green supply chain management practices: Impact on performance. *Supply Chain Management: An International Journal*, 17(3):290–305.

Groenewegen, P. and Vergragt, P. (1991). Environmental issues as threats and opportunities for technological innovation. *Technology Analysis & Strategic Management*, 3(1):43–55.

Hart, S. (1995). A natural resource-based view of the firm. *Academy of Management Review*, 20:986–1014.

He, W. and Shen, R. (2017). ISO 14001 certification and corporate technological innovation: Evidence from Chinese firms. *Journal of Business Ethics*, 1:1–21.

He, W., Yang, Y. and Choi, S. (2016). The interplay between private and public regulations: Evidence from ISO 14001 adoption among Chinese firms. *Journal of Business Ethics*, 152(2):477–497.

Heras-Saizarbitoria, I., Arana Landín, G. and Molina-Azorín, J. (2011). Do drivers matter for the benefits of ISO 14001? *International Journal of Operations & Production Management*, 31(2):192–216.

Hervani, A., Helms, M. and Sarkis, J. (2005). Performance measurement for green supply chain management. *Benchmarking: An International Journal*, 12(4):330–353.

Inoue, E., Arimura, T. and Nakano, M. (2013). A new insight into environmental innovation: Does the maturity of environmental management systems matter? *Ecological Economics*, 94:156–163.

Jabbour, C. J. C., Neto, A. S., Gobbo Junior, J. A., Ribeiro, M. D. S. and de Sousa Jabbour, A. B. L. (2015). Eco-innovations in more sustainable supply chains for a low-carbon economy: A multiple case study of human critical success factors in Brazilian leading companies. *International Journal of Production Economics*, 164:245–257.

Jacobs, B., Singhal, V. and Subramanian, R. (2010). An empirical investigation of environmental performance and the market value of the firm. *Journal of Operations Management*, 28(5):430–441.

Johansson, G. (2002). Success factors for integration of eco-design in product development: A review of state of the art. *Environmental Management and Health*, 13(1):98–107.

Jun, M., Cai, S. and Shin, H. (2006). TQM practice in maquiladora: Antecedents of employee satisfaction and loyalty. *Journal of Operations Management*, 24(6):791–812.

Key, S. (1999). Toward a new theory of the firm: A critique of stakeholder theory. *Management Decision*, 37(3):317.

King, A., Lenox, M. and Terlaak, A. (2005). The strategic use of decentralized institutions: Exploring certification with the ISO 14001 management standard. *Academy of Management Journal*, 48(6):1091–1106.

Kitazawa, S. and Sarkis, J. (2000). The relationship between ISO 14001 and continuous source reduction programs. *International Journal of Operations & Production Management*, 20(2):225–248.

Klassen, R. and McLaughlin, C. (1996). The impact of environmental management on firm performance. *Management Science*, 42(8):1199–1214.

Klassen, R. and Vachon, S. (2009). Collaboration and evaluation in the supply chain: The impact on plant-level environmental investment. *Production and Operations Management*, 12(3):336–352.

Kumar, S. and Putnam, V. (2008). Cradle to cradle: Reverse logistics strategies and opportunities across three industries. *International Journal of Production Economics*, 15(2):305–315.

Kung, F., Huang, C. and Cheng, C. (2012). Assessing the green value chain to improve environmental performance: Evidence from Taiwan's manufacturing industry. *International Journal of Development Issues*, 11(2):111–128.

Kwon, D. M., Seo, M. S. and Seo, Y. (2002). A study of compliance with environmental regulations of ISO 4001 certified companies in Korea. *Journal of Environmental Management*, 65(4):347–353.

Laosirihongthong, T., Adebanjo, D. and Tan, K. (2013). Green supply chain management practices and performance. *Industrial Management and Data Systems*, 113(8):1088–1109.

Lee, S. (2008). Drivers for the participation of small and medium-sized suppliers in green supply chain initiatives. *Supply Chain Management*, 13(3):185–198.

Lee, S., Kim, S. and Choi, D. (2012). Green supply chain management and organizational performance. *Industrial Management and Data Systems*, 112(8):1148–1180.

Liang, S. and Chang, W. (2008). An empirical study on relationship between green supply chain management and SME performance in China. *Call of Paper Proceedings of 2008 International Conference on Management Science and Engineering*, 611–618.

Lim, S. and Prakash, A. (2014). Voluntary regulations and innovation: The case of ISO 14001. *Public Administration Review*, 74(2):233–244.

Lin, R. and Sheu, C. (2012). Why do firms adopt/implement green practices? – An institutional theory perspective. *Procedia – Social and Behavioural Sciences*, 57:533–540.

Link, S. and Naveh, E. (2006). Standardization and discretion: Does the environmental standard ISO 14001 lead to performance benefits? *IEEE Transactions on Engineering Management*, 53(4):508–519.

Lo, S. (2014). Effects of supply chain position on the motivation and practices of firms going green. *International Journal of Operations & Production Management*, 34(1):93–114.

Lo, C., Yeung, A. and Cheng, T. (2012). The impact of environmental management systems on financial performance in fashion and textiles industries. *International Journal of Production Economics*, 135(2):561–567.

McGuire, W. (2014). The effect of ISO 14001 on environmental regulatory compliance in China. *Ecological Economics*, 105:254–264.

Melnyk, S., Sroufe, R. and Calantone, R. (2003). Assessing the impact of environmental management systems on corporate and environmental performance. *Journal of Operations Management*, 21(3):329–351.

Melnyk, S., Sroufe, R., Calantone, R. and Montabon, F. (2002). Assessing the effectiveness of US voluntary environmental programmes: An empirical study. *International Journal of Production Research*, 40(8):1853–1878.

Menguc, B. and Ozanne, L. (2005). Challenges of the "green imperative": A natural resource-based approach to the environmental orientation-business performance relationship. *Journal of Business Research*, 58(4):430–438.

Mijatovic, I. and Stokic, D. (2010). The influence of internal and external codes on CSR practice: The case of companies operating in Serbia. *Journal of Business Ethics*, 94(4):533–552.

Miles, M., Munilla, L. and Russell, G. (1997). Marketing and environmental registration/certification, what industrial marketers should understand about ISO 14000. *Industrial Marketing Management*, 26(4):363–370.

Min, H. and Galle, W.P. (2001). Green purchasing practices of US firms. *International Journal of Production and Operations Management*, 21(9):1222–1238.

Mita, S. and Datta, P. (2014). Adoption of green supply chain management practices and their impact on performance: An exploratory study of Indian manufacturing firms. *International Journal of Production Research*, 52(7):2085–2107.

Mollenkopf, D., Stolze, H., Tate, W. and Ueltschy, M. (2010). Green, lean, and global supply chains. *International Journal of Physical Distribution & Logistics Management*, 40(1/2):14–41.

Moneva, J. and Ortas, E. (2010). Corporate environmental and financial performance: A multivariate approach. *Industrial Management and Data Systems*, 110(2):193–210.

Montiel, I., Husted, W. and Christmann, P. (2012). Using private management standard certification to reduce information asymmetries in corrupt environments. *Strategic Management Journal*, 33(9):1103–1113.

Muskin, J. (2000). Interorganizational ethics: Standards of behaviour. *Journal of Business Ethics*, 24(4):283–297.

Mutingi, M. (2013). Developing green supply chain management strategies: A taxonomic approach. *Journal of Industrial Engineering and Management*, 2:525.

Nakao, Y., Amano, A., Matsumura, K., Genba, K. and Nakano, M. (2007). Relationship between environmental performance and financial performance: An empirical analysis of Japanese corporations. *Business Strategy and the Environment*, 16(2):106–118.

Namagembe, S., Ryan, S. and Sridharan, R. (2019). Green supply chain practice adoption and firm performance: Manufacturing SMEs in Uganda. *Management of Environmental Quality*, 30(1):5–35.

Orlitzky, M., Schmidt, F. and Rynes, S. (2003). Corporate social and financial performance: A meta-analysis. *Organization Studies*, 24(3):403–441.

Orsato, R. (2006). Competitive environmental strategies: When does it pay to be green? *California Management Review*, 48(2):127–143.

Ozusaglam, S., Robin, S. and Wong, C. Y. (2018). Early and late adopters of ISO 14001-type standards: Revisiting the role of firm characteristics and capabilities. *Journal of Technology Transfer, 43*(5):1318–1345.

Paulraj, A. and de Jong, P. (2011). The effect of ISO 14001 certification announcements on stock performance. *International Journal of Operations & Production Management, 31*(7):765–788.

Perotti, S., Zorzini, M., Cagno, E. and Micheli, G. (2012). Green supply chain practices and company performance: The case of 3PLs in Italy. *International Journal of Physical Distribution and Logistics Management, 42*(7):640–672.

Post, J. E., Preston, L. E. and Sachs, S. (2002). Managing the extended enterprise: The new stakeholder view. *California Management Review, 45*(1):6–28.

Prajogo, D., Tang, A. K. Y. and Lai, K.-H. (2014). The diffusion of environmental management system and its effect on environmental management practices. *International Journal of Operations & Production Management, 34*(5):565–585.

Rao, P. (2002). Greening the supply chain: A new initiative in South East Asia. *International Journal of Operations Production Management, 22*(6):632–655.

Rao, P. and Holt, D. (2005). Do green supply chains lead to competitiveness and economic performance? *International Journal of Operations and Production Management, 25*(9):898–916.

Reis, A., Neves, F., Hikichi, S., Salgado, E. and Beijo A. (2018). Is ISO 14001 certification really good to the company? A critical analysis. *Production, 28*:1–16.

Richey, R., Chen, H., Genchev, S. and Daughert, P. (2005). Developing effective reverse logistics programs. *Industrial Marketing Management, 34*(8):830–840.

Russo, M. and Fouts, P. (1997). A resource-based perspective on corporate environmental performance and profitability. *Academy of Management Journal, 40*(3):534–559.

Sarkis, J. (2003). A strategic decision framework for green supply chain management. *Journal of Cleaner Production, 11*(4):397–409.

Sartor, M., Orzes, G., Touboulic, A., Culot, G. and Nassimbeni, G. (2019). ISO 14001 standard: Literature review and theory-based research agenda. *Quality Management Journal, 26*:132–164.

Schlegelmilch, B., Bohlen, G. and Diamantopoulos, A. (1996). The link between green purchasing decisions and measures of environmental consciousness. *European Journal of Marketing, 30*(5):35.

Schoenherr, T. (2012). The role of environmental management in sustainable business development: A multi-country investigation. *International Journal of Production Economics, 140*(1):116–128.

Schoenherr, T. and Talluri, S. (2013). Environmental sustainability initiatives: A comparative analysis of plant efficiencies in Europe and the U.S. *IEEE Transactions on Engineering Management, 60*(2):353–365.

Simpson, D., Power, D. and Samson, D. (2007). Greening the automotive supply chain: A relationship perspective. *International Journal of Operations and Production Management, 27*(1):28–48.

Srivastava, S. (2007). Green supply-chain management: A state-of the-art literature review. *International Journal of Management Reviews, 9*(1):53–80.

Stieb, J. (2009). Assessing Freeman's stakeholder theory. *Journal of Business Ethics, 87*(3):401–414.

Sullivan, R. (2005) Code integration: Alignment or conflict? *Journal of Business Ethics, 59*(1–2):9–25.

Sundarakani, B., Souza, R., Goh, M., Wagner, S. and Manikandan, S. (2010). Modelling carbon footprints across the supply chain. *International Journal of Production Economics*, *12*(1):43–50.

Testa, F., Iraldo, F., Frey, M. and Daddi, T. (2012). What factors influence the uptake of GPP (green public procurement) practices? New evidence from an Italian survey. *Ecological Economics*, *82*:88–96.

Tibor, T. and Feldman, I. (1996). ISO 14000: *A Guide to the New Environmental Management Standards*. Irwin Professional, Burr Ridge, IL.

Treacy, R., Humphreys, P., McIvor, R. and Lo, C. (2019). ISO14001 certification and operating performance: A practice-based view. *International Journal of Production Economics*, *208*:319–328.

Vastag, G. (2009). Revisiting ISO 14000 diffusion: A new "look" at the drivers of certification. *Production and Operations Management*, *13*(3):260–267.

Vastag, G. and Melnyk, S. A. (2002). Certifying environmental management systems by the ISO 14001 standards. *International Journal of Production Research*, *40*(18):4743–4763.

Vijayvargy, L., Thakkar, J. and Agarwal, G. (2017). Green supply chain management practices and performance: The role of firm-size for emerging economies. *Journal of Manufacturing Technology Management*, *28*(3):299–323.

Walker, H., Di Sisto, L. and McBain, D. (2008). Drivers and barriers to environmental supply chain management practices: Lessons from the public and private sectors. *Journal of Purchasing and Supply Management*, *14*:69–85.

Walley, N. and Whitehead, B. (1994). It's not easy being green. *Harvard Business Review*, *72*:46–46.

Walton, S., Handfield, R. and Melnyk, S. (1998). The green supply chain: Integrating suppliers into environmental management process. *International Journal of Purchasing and Material Management*, *2*:11–11.

Wernerfelt, B. (1984). A resource-based view of the firm. *Strategic Management Journal*, *5*(2):171–180.

Whiteman, G., Walker, B. and Perego, P. (2013). Planetary boundaries: Ecological foundations for corporate sustainability. *Journal of Management Studies*, *50*(2):307–336.

Wiengarten, F., Humphreys, P., Onofrei, G. and Fynes, B. (2017). The adoption of multiple certification standards: Perceived performance implications of quality, environmental and health & safety certifications. *Production Planning and Control*, *28*(2):131–141.

Wood, D. (1991). Corporate social performance revisited. *Academy of Management Review*, *16*:691–718.

Xu, X. D., Zeng, S. X., Zou, H. L. and Shi, J. J. (2016). The impact of corporate environmental violation on share-holders' wealth: A perspective taken from media coverage. *Business Strategy and the Environment*, *25*(2):73–91.

Younis, H. and Sundarakani, B. (2019). The impact of firm size, firm age and environmental management certification on the relationship between green supply chain practices and corporate performance. *Benchmarking: An International Journal*, *Vol. ahead-of-print* (No. ahead-of-print). doi:10.1108/BIJ-11-2018-0363.

Younis, H., Sundarakani, B. and Vel, P. (2016). The impact of implementing green supply chain management practices on corporate performance. *Competitiveness Review: An International Business Journal*, *26*(3):216–245.

Yu, W., Chavez, R., Feng, M. and Wiengarten, F. (2014). Integrated green supply chain management and operational performance. *Supply Chain Management,* *19*(5/6):683–696.

Zailani, S., Eltayeb, T., Hsu, C. and Tan, K. (2012). The impact of external institutional drivers and internal strategy on environmental performance. *International Journal of Operations and Production Management, 32*(6):721–745.

Zhu, Q., Geng, Y. and Lai, K. (2010). Circular economy practices among Chinese manufacturers varying in environmental-oriented supply chain cooperation and the performance implications. *Journal of Environmental Management, 91*(6):1324–1331.

Zhu, Q. and Sarkis, J. (2004). Relationships between operational practices and performance among early adopters of green supply chain management practices in Chinese manufacturing enterprises. *Journal of Operations Management, 22*(3):265–289.

Zhu, Q. and Sarkis, J. (2006). An inter-sectorial comparison of green supply chain management in China: Drivers and practices. *Journal of Cleaner Production, 14*(5):472–486.

Zhu, Q. and Sarkis, J. (2007). The moderating effects of institutional pressures on emergent green supply chain practices and performance. *International Journal of Production Research, 45*(18):4333–4355.

Zhu, Q., Sarkis, J. and Lai, K. (2012). Green supply chain management innovation diffusion and its relationship to organizational improvement: An ecological modernization perspective. *Journal of Engineering and Technology Management, 29*(1):168–185.

Zsidisin, G. and Siferd, S. (2001). Environmental purchasing: A framework for theory development. *European Journal of Purchasing and Supply Management, 7*(1):61–73.

Zutshi, A. and Sohal, A. (2004). Environmental management system adoption by Australasian organizations: Part 1: Reasons, benefits and impediments. *Technovation, 24*(4):335–357.

# 7

## Quality Management and Its Impacts on the Dynamics of Multinational Corporations' Center–Subsidiary Relationship

*Nizam Abdullah and Mohd Nazari Ismail*

### CONTENTS

### INTRODUCTION

The study of multinational corporations (MNCs) can be traced back to as early as the mid-1970s, when scholars Brandt and Hulbert (1976) conducted an empirical study on these firms. An MNC consists of a center that operates multiple subsidiaries in different geographical areas; therefore, the study of MNCs must inevitably involve their subsidiaries. Birkinshaw (2000) outlines three subsidiary management streams: the HQ and subsidiary relationship (Brandt & Hulbert, 1976; Hedlund, 1980); the subsidiary role (Bartlett & Ghoshal, 1986; White & Poynter, 1984); and subsidiary evolution (Birkinshaw, Braunerhjelm, Holm, & Terjesen, 2006; Jarillo & Martínez, 1990). The common theme among these draws upon an ever-evolving subsidiary role from the mere command and control of the most critical component of the MNC. Such a role involves being the center of excellence (Frost, Birkinshaw, & Ensign, 2002) as market satellites to strategic dependent units (White & Poynter, 1984). This entails research recognizing that subsidiary evolution can be driven from within and without. Subsidiary role evolution is the outcome of some combinations of the various roles that subsidiaries play as part of the MNC. However, when viewed at the micro level, subsidiary role evolution is a result of internal and external factors, such as the strategy of the MNC center and the manner in which subsidiary managers choose to respond to it (Birkinshaw, Bouquet, & Ambos, 2007). Hence, this brings forth a contemporary research stream that examines the interplay between MNC managers (Balogun, Fahy, & Vaara, 2017; Guiette & Vandenbempt, 2017).

A growing number of general management researchers have placed emphasis on the significance of the dialectic relationship between quality management and organizational culture (Kull & Wacker, 2010; Wu, 2015). In her study, Wu (2015) posits that certain national cultures display better implementation of quality programs than others. Abdullah and Ismail (2017) conducted a study of center-led change initiatives in different national settings. The various change initiatives, the primary units of analysis, suggest that the nationals of certain countries tend to be more engaged in the development of change. Based on the general IB literature, focus-driven change activities can take the form of the use of best practices, cost-saving initiatives, and some other kind of activity that is regarded as enhancing the effectiveness of the general MNC (Tempel, Edwards, Ferner, Muller-Camen, & Waechter, 2006). The research on change has thus far highlighted the importance of understanding the various interactions between individuals or key actors within the organization, all of which have some type of effect on the outcome of the change itself (Guiette & Vandenbempt, 2017; Kraft, Sparr, & Peus, 2016).

As we undertake a close examination of the change phenomenon from the perspectives of the actors involved, one powerful theoretical lens emerges as the most useful. Sensemaking and sensegiving can be powerful tools for examining which meanings and interpretations (Balogun & Johnson, 2004; Maitlis, 2005) are transmitted by actors during their negotiations with others. MNC managers have different worldviews about the organization, the subsidiary, and the relationship between the two. In organizational change situations, these managers interpret and evaluate the change processes. Sensemaking encourages researchers to understand and explore individuals' worldviews, as well as why they are seeing a change in the organization and reacting to it the way they are. A recent study by Abdullah and Ismail (2017) focused on the implementation of quality management in the form of center-led change initiatives at an MNC operating in Kuala Lumpur, Asia. MNCs that are involved in the telecommunications industry often refer to its fast-changing environment (Anand & Barsoux, 2017). This case study will shed some light on new and significant findings in several heterogeneous settings.

---

## LITERATURE REVIEW

Although some scholars (Birkinshaw & Morrison, 1995; Kostova & Roth, 2002) view the MNC center–subsidiary relationship as "relationalist," at the micro level of analysis, many still treat actors as faceless subjects when explaining the change processes involved. In fact, with regard to issues and conflicts within MNCs, many scholars conclude that organizational structure, practices, and culture eventually resolve these issues and conflicts over time. How actors conduct themselves, such as in negotiations, and the ways in which they respond to initiatives are likely to be affected by their personal interests and interpretations. The sensemaking, narrative, and discourse analysis perspectives are among the lenses that encourage us to explore phenomena from an epistemological perspective that is similar to that of a social constructivist. These perspectives encourage us to examine social actors' views of the world and how these affect their responses to initiatives. In MNC negotiations between centers and subsidiaries, the personal interests and interpretations of the actors, whom we know from the general change literature (Maitlis & Sonenshein, 2010), affect the ways in which they respond to initiatives. This raises the question of the role of politics in negotiations surrounding these implementation processes.

In the following section, several relevant theoretical perspectives—namely, institutional theory, sensemaking, narrative, and discourse analysis—will be discussed. It is important to note that the four theoretical perspectives that will be discussed next are not exhaustive. With the exception of institutional theory, these theoretical perspectives are most relevant to the study of the implementation of center-driven initiatives from a social constructivist worldview.

## Institutional Theory

The institutional approach is useful in delineating the complexity surrounding the MNC from a macro perspective. This complexity involves multiple domains of the institutional environment, varied country environments, and institutional distance (Kostova & Zaheer, 1999). Institutional distance can explain the many different dimensions of subsidiaries and their differentiated relationships with each other within the MNC. Certain subsidiaries (Bouquet & Birkinshaw, 2008a) are described as possessing different sets of capabilities and resources compared with others, thus enabling various levels of mandates (Birkinshaw, 1996) to be granted by the MNC center. The institutional perspective further recognizes that many of the MNC's environmental complexities have led to its complicated non-hierarchical structure; hence, some subsidiaries enjoy greater autonomy than others. Institutionalists tend to observe organization practices as "after the event" occurrences that are a result of environmental conditioning, ranging from history to people and their actions. In their study, Kostova and Roth (2002) measured the level of practice implementation versus internalization. An institutional profile is defined as an issue-specific set of regulatory, cognitive, and normative institutions in a given country. It implies that institutionalists treat organizational practice as a taken-for-granted assumption (Vaara, Tienari, & Laurila, 2006) that focuses on measuring any relative correlations, such as adoption. Many institutionalists (Kostova & Roth, 2002; Vora, Kostova, & Roth, 2007) use quantitative analysis to study the organization approach.

Although the institutional perspective presents an accurate description of the complex nature of the MNC center and subsidiary relationship, it has its limitations in regard to helping researchers to explore processes such as change involving subsidiary managers. Other researchers have adopted a different perspective when examining the micro-political processes that play out within this institutional context, such as through sensemaking, narrative, and discourse analysis.

## Sensemaking

Weick (1995) can be credited for his pioneering work on the notion of sensemaking, especially in the context of organizations. He defines sensemaking as a combination of varied individuals' interests and objectives based on their collaborative processes of shared awareness and understanding. It is often noted that the study of sensemaking in organizations concerns the state of uncertainty that arises when these organizations are in crisis mode or are involved in change situations. Weick further identified seven considerations that emerge when organizations face uncertain or ambiguous situations. These organizations (1) construct their identities; (2) are retrospective; (3) enact sensible environments; (4) social; (5) ongoing; (6) extract cues; and (7) become plausible. These seven properties form the core recipe for the process of sensemaking within Weick's work. While Weick's pioneering work has been accepted and recognized, others draw on sensemaking in more specific ways when exploring its role in strategic change. Gioia and Chittipeddi (1991), for instance, define sensemaking as a situation that involves meaning construction and reconstruction by involved people as they attempt to develop a meaningful platform to enable understanding of the intended objective. Sensegiving is further defined as being concerned with the process of attempting to influence sensemaking and meaning construction based on the intended redefinition of organizational reality. Gioia and his co-author (1991) embarked on this research using sensemaking as the core analytical framework focusing on strategic change initiation, which will be discussed in detail in the following sections.

Many scholars have performed a wide array of research on sensemaking in organizations. The most distinct areas can be grouped into two streams: (1) research on sensemaking and crisis (Christianson, Farkas, Sutcliffe, & Weick, 2009; Gephart, 1993; Weick, 1988, 1993) and (2) research on sensemaking and change (Balogun & Johnson, 2004; Gioia, Thomas, Clark, & Chittipeddi, 1994; Maitlis, 2005). While there is a strong research stream that examines sensemaking and crisis, it is not the most relevant here; rather, the research on sensemaking and change is more relevant.

The growing research on organizational change examines the phenomenon as an unfolding set of narratives that are shaped by power relationships that can capture the political processes involved (Buchanan & Dawson, 2007). Narrative studies of sensemaking are further explained in the article as a powerful method of examining the alternative meanings in political processes that evolve during crises and change events within organizations.

## Narratives

Narrative analysis is about how individuals in organizations construct the social world and attach meaning to it. Narratives shape meanings and can be used by actors to measure the game of organizational power and the politics surrounding organizational change (Buchanan & Dawson, 2007). Barry and Elmes' study (1997) shows that various levels of actors, such as employees, middle managers, and senior managers, have different sets of voices and perspectives. The authors, thus, argue that narratives are compilations of stories from one or many stakeholders, and they propose that the study of strategy can be examined using a narrative process. The approach to using narrative as a sensemaking tool can be viewed as being similar to the ways in which people use stories and narratives to understand the multivocal nature of organizations (Sonenshein, 2010).

Organizational change is a multivocal process by which different employees construct varied stories and then attach various meanings to change processes. The approach of using narrative as storytelling (Brown, Stacey, & Nandhakumar, 2008; Humphreys & Brown, 2008) is about embarking on a methodological exploration of people's storytelling from different perspectives. In organizational change, whoever creates the most credible narrative—the one that most people believe—affects the discourse about the change process and, therefore, the meaning attached to it. Narratives are the struggles among the stories told by employees who aim to dominate each other. The outcome of change is determined by the story that stands at the end of the narrative struggle.

Buchanan and Dawson (2007) suggest that narratives extend beyond mere description and that some can even highlight contrasting motives, evolving relationships, interpersonal tensions, hidden conflicts, and outcomes. Sonenshein (2010) sees both sensemaking and sensegiving as being closely related to narrative analysis, in that they are viewed as a discursive construction that actors use. Sensemaking is described by the author as a tool that is used to shape an individual's own understanding, while sensegiving is used to influence others, and the combination is an outcome of the collective construction of meanings. Maitlis and Sonenshein (2010) argue that in uncovering the different meanings that rarely surface, it is, therefore, crucial to understand how things unfold in organizations that are experiencing change, and narrative studies on sensemaking provide a method of exploring these. In another major study, Brown (2000) describes sensemaking as a narrative process in which meanings are constructed and shared, explaining that "the power to tell a story is itself hegemonic, and readers need constantly to be aware that even a story reflexively told is suffused with power" (2004, p.109).

While sensemaking encourages the researcher to explore individuals' evaluations and interpretations, narratives encourage him or her to go even further in regard to organizational change. Subsidiary managers bring with them stories about what this change means (Buchanan & Dawson, 2007), and others may also have heard stories about change from other sources, such as the center. The employees of subsidiaries are subjected to different stories and have their own, which come from different ones (Barry & Elmes, 1997; Sonenshein, 2010); the ones that they decide are the most plausible will determine what happens in the end. Therefore, narratives encourage us to understand not only how people respond and the stories they tell but also how these have shifted over time.

To date, research using narratives has tended to focus on senior managers rather than on lower-level employees. Maitlis and Sonenshein (2010) highlight that the lack of power and influencing skills existing among lower-level employees may preclude them from shaping the sensemaking of the individuals at the top of organizations. This concern is interesting, as it is similar to the tone of other scholars, such as Gioia and Chittipeddi (1991), Buchanan and Dawson (2007), Brown (2000), and Barry and Elmes (1997), in regard to the issue of the relationship between sensemaking and power. However, Bouquet and Birkinshaw (2008b) point out that strategies and methods exist to enable low-power actors to pursue their objectives through bottom-up approaches. Other scholars have also demonstrated how resistance against center-driven initiatives is manifested through several discourse approaches (Balogun, Jarzabkowski, & Vaara, 2011). Several levels of discourse exist, as described by Alvesson and Karreman (2000), and these range from the broader grand-discourse to the narrower micro-discourse approach. The meso-discourse approach, such as discourse analysis, will be discussed next.

## Discourse Analysis

In the field of strategy, narrative is only one subsection of many discursive approaches. The term "organizational discourse" refers to a collection of texts that are manifested from the practices of talking and writing that bring objects into being in the organization as texts are produced, disseminated, and consumed (Hardy & Phillips, 2004). In the study of organizational discourse, four domains are prevalent: conversation and dialogue; narratives and stories; rhetoric; and tropes. Discourse carries a vast number of debates from numerous perspectives, such as from the basic, naturally occurring talk, linguistic-based approaches to others that confine discourse to merely textual material. Other scholars, such as Hardy and her co-authors (2005), approach the study of discourse as a means by which actors draw on, reproduce, and transform discourses while simultaneously producing social reality that embeds constituted ideas discursively. Critical discourse analysis is an approach to examining language and the phenomena that are often due to social inequalities. Alvesson and Karreman (2000) and Vaara (2010) are among the few scholars who attempt to present the varieties of discourse within the organizational context.

Many researchers have used the term discourse loosely while it has also been used simultaneously in a wide array of studies on social sciences and organization (Alvesson & Karreman, 2000). According to these authors, the opposing spectrums represent (1) discourse determination, wherein discourse implies social and psychological consequences; and (2) discourse autonomy, wherein discourse is considered autonomous or perhaps linked loosely to the social aspect (individual). This interesting perspective of the discourse field demonstrates the variety of ways in which social sciences and research draw discourse from different perspectives. The authors focused the discussion on the analysis of middle-range discourse that was drawn primarily from Potter and Wetherell's (1987) work. Alvesson and Karreman (2000) highlight that one must critically evaluate empirical material in terms of situated meaning versus meaning, which allows for transportation beyond the local context and, thus, enables comparison. Vaara (2010) highlights that scholars' interests in the discursive aspects of strategy and strategizing are focused on understanding the micro-level activities and practices that are linked with strategizing (Knights & Morgan, 1991).

The broader macro level forms the essential ideas and ideological assumptions that tend to comprise the organizational discourse about strategy, while the micro level is the construct that gives life to the organizational-level discourses through narratives of strategy. Many of the author's works draw on secondary sources, such as publicly available texts (2000, 2003, 2010) and interviews (Vaara, Tienari, Piekkari, & Säntti, 2005). Most of the author's work does not explore inside the organization itself, thus drawing on a perspective that enables this research to use such data. Vaara's (2000) paper describes three intercultural sensemaking processes: the search for rational understanding,* emotional identification,[†] and sociopolitical manipulation.[‡] Through the critical discourse analysis approach, the author suggests that cultural sensemaking involves sociopolitical manipulation that can be used as a political tool when promoting or resisting organizational changes. Vaara and colleagues studied how key actors draw on and mobilize rationalistic and nationalistic discourses in public discussions (Tienari, Vaara, & Björkman, 2003) as a vehicle to challenge the forces of globalization. The study also revealed that actors can use different and sometimes contradictory discourses at various times to legitimize their positions while pursuing specific objectives. Vaara et al. (2005) describe the existence of the complex and ambiguous power associated with language policies in MNCs, leading to the idea of the strength of national identity images and nationalist ideology in multinational settings.

Maguire and Hardy (2009) examine the discursive dynamics associated with deinstitutionalization, focusing on data collection from varied sources: tape recordings, books, transcripts, government reports, and interviews. Using a combination of interviews and secondary sources, the authors analyze and capture "who did what and when," and, most importantly, they establish narrative accounts. Similar to the data collection by Maguire and Hardy, the longitudinal study of MNC subsidiary evolution involved conducting interviews from inside the organization, and it demonstrated the nuances related to resistance and control (Balogun et al., 2011). Many studies have found that leaders deliberately use language to legitimate the actions that they have taken in organizations (Tienari et al., 2003; Vaara, 2000; Vaara et al., 2005).

---

* Rational understanding is a process that mostly resembles the ideal and naïve view of cultural learning as involving the observation and analysis of "real" cultural differences (p.104).

[†] Emotional identification occurs when the news is seen as negative or the anticipated changes appear threatening. There is a tendency to increasingly identify with one's side and distance oneself from the other (p.98).

[‡] Sociopolitical manipulation refers to claims concerning cultural differences and incompatibility that can be used in particular as political tools when resisting specific changes (p.101).

Leaders often draw on all the general conversation, and others sometimes refer to sociopolitical manipulation to legitimate their actions. Therefore, discourse analysis encourages the researcher to understand how these people in change are attempting to use the broader context to legitimate their actions.

## Melding Theoretical Perspectives

Drawing on the transnational solution (Bartlett & Ghoshal, 2002) and differentiated network (Hedlund, 1986), subsidiary managers have developed significant autonomy due to the highly competitive and differentiated local markets within which they work. How subsidiary managers conduct themselves, such as in negotiations, and the ways in which they respond to initiatives are likely to be affected by their interpretations and evaluations of their work encounters. A useful method of unpacking managers' interpretations and how they construct their thoughts socially can be explored through sensemaking, narratives, and discourse analysis. Although these theoretical perspectives display differences in several dimensions, they share a distinct similarity in the context related to social constructionism. Managers' thinking and how they perceive things are some of the issues within the dimensions that these lenses are being used to explore.

Sensemaking encourages the researcher to explore the manager's evaluation and interpretation. In change situations, managers actively seek to understand the implications for them and what they should do. The sensemaking process encourages the researcher to recognize that managers have different worldviews, cognitive schemas (Balogun & Johnson, 2005), and mental maps; therefore, the ways in which they understand and see implications differ. Narrative perspectives alert the researcher to more than merely how the sensemaking process examines change through a multivocal process. In a multivocal change process, different managers have various perspectives and, thus, varied interests (Sonenshein, 2010). Therefore, they attach different meanings and implications to the change process. Due to the different worldviews of managers, the narratives in the change process mean that these individuals attach varied meanings to different events. Managers use narratives to convince others to interpret things the same way that they do (Buchanan & Dawson, 2007). As different people have different narratives, this creates what scholars refer to as a narrative struggle (Brown et al., 2008; Humphreys & Brown, 2008).

Certain meanings and narratives that matter prevail and, finally, determine the outcome of changes. Narratives encourage the researcher to take the sensemaking process further and to understand not only what different people are saying about the process in question but also how this influences it over time. Discourse analysis is about how people use language deliberately to legitimate things and how it is a tool of change (Hardy et al., 2005). Discourse analysis encourages the researcher to understand how in regard to organizational change, managers attempt to use the broader context to legitimate their actions.

Taken together, these theoretical perspectives present a formidable combination of tools that enable the exploration of change from within an organization, focusing on those that were involved. Although these three perspectives may have similarities in the social constructionism context, they also have differences in terms of the data collected. Whereas narrative studies emphasize the importance of "being there," understanding the participant's perspective, and detecting the multiple voices at play in different parts of the organization, discourse analysis tends more toward eliciting data from secondary sources, thereby emphasizing the broader context. Therefore, these theoretical perspectives serve as the basis for shaping the research methodology and the nature of the data collected.

## THE CASE STUDY: MNC CENTER-LED CHANGE INITIATIVE

The MNC CenCo is a mobile network operator (MNO) located in several geographically dispersed offices in Asia and headquartered in Kuala Lumpur. CenCo was chosen for this study because of its fast-changing environment and its different organizational cultures stemming from the diverse countries in which they operate. CenCo's subsidiary offices are located in Sri Lanka (LaCo), Indonesia (InCo), Malaysia (MyCo), and Bangladesh (BaCo). LaCo, which was established in 1993, is a wholly owned subsidiary of CenCo, while InCo was formerly part of a North American international joint venture (IJV) that was established in 1989. MyCo, which was established 1988, is a wholly owned subsidiary of CenCo, and finally, BaCo, which was established in 1997, was formerly a joint venture company between CenCo and a local entrepreneur. CenCo's staffing policy varies from mostly geocentric to polycentric.

CenCo had three center-led initiatives at different stages of implementation— (1) a central and electronic management system (CEMS); (2) a standard operating manual (SOM); and (3) a competency model framework (CMF)— all of which were explored in this study. These quality management initiatives were selected based on two criteria. First, the initiatives had to have been undertaken within the past three years, as individuals find it difficult to articulate contexts from which they have become detached. Second, the initiatives must have been significant, such as those requiring changes in major processes, realignment, or system upgrades.

Semi-structured interviews were chosen to allow the interviewees the freedom to express themselves regarding matters pertaining to their unique experiences and within their own meaning constructs. Confidentiality was conveyed as one of the most important aspects of data handling for this research. The interviewees were assured that all the names pertaining to the subsidiaries would be anonymized and that no individual names would be mentioned in this study. This part of the review was shared with the interviewees at the start of each session to encourage them to share their encounters openly. Considerable effort was put into making the sessions as casual as possible, and interviews were conducted in either formal or informal settings. The following important questions guided the study:

- Can you tell me about yourself and how you came to be doing this job?
- One of the things that I am particularly interested in is how strategic change initiatives unfold; can you share your knowledge about the history of the CenCo initiatives?
- Who else do you think might be able to help me with this matter that we have discussed?

The purpose of conducting semi-structured interviews was to allow managers the freedom to express their views on matters pertaining to their unique experiences. Additionally, semi-structured interviews provide researchers with a form of guidance throughout the data-gathering process (Kvale & Brinkmann, 2009). This research was based on sequential procedures, by means of which the researcher aimed to expand the findings from the face-to-face interviews with managers involved in center-led change initiatives. The change initiatives act, which was the primary unit of analysis for the study, was central to the interviews, which were replicated at the four MNC subsidiaries that were involved in the study.

One focus group discussion was conducted, followed by 18 individual, face-to-face interviews that yielded rich, thick descriptions of the events being investigated (Isabella, 1990). The managers or groups of managers who were interviewed had direct involvement in more than one stage of the initiative. First- and second-order analyses were conducted for this research data, which were similar to those used by Gioia and Chittipeddi (1991). The first-order analysis involved an ethnographic analytical technique that was performed to identify themes and patterns, including those that were meaningful to and used by the interviewees in the research. For the second-order analysis, which was more theoretical, the data, as well as the outcomes of the first-order analysis, were examined to identify their underlying meanings. These meanings might create patterns that are not necessarily apparent to the informants but are essential to this study. The implementation of the quality management initiatives across CenCo's subsidiaries required a mix of center and subsidiary managers within this multiple- and comparative case study (Yin, 2003). The replication technique applied to several organizational case studies is described by Yin (2003) as a multiple embedded case study.

Actors perceive, interpret, and evaluate each other's conduct when they engage in change processes. They use power and other means to enact their identities (e.g., in the subsidiary) and to enable them to respond meaningfully to and thereby influence others through the act of sensegiving. Thus, it is a political tool that actors use to shape the meanings of others or, in this case, the outcomes of changes. For example, by understanding the patterns of interaction, subsidiary managers enact (sensegive) to center managers. We can then understand how this enactment influences the development of change or the change outcome itself. Additionally, sensemaking allows us to identify the various potential dynamics between the patterns of interaction enacted by center and subsidiary managers (e.g., see Maitlis, 2005), as well as the outcomes of the center-led change initiatives. This brings "sensemaking" to the fore as the single most powerful analytical tool for this research and, thus, helps underpin the theoretical construct of this study.

## FINDINGS

Four different national cultures were interwoven throughout the development of the quality management initiatives. There was interplay between subsidiary and center actors, who were attempting to make sense of the change taking place and simultaneously seek to influence the development of the initiative and its overall outcome. The research findings suggest that the subsidiaries that made significant progress implementing one or more center-led change initiatives were those that engaged in both the sensemaking and sensegiving processes. Several patterns of sensemaking/sensegiving appeared to drive the development of the center-led change initiatives. However, the three most significant patterns that emerged from the study were (1) communication intensity; (2) the adoption of change; and (3) the resolution of barriers (Figure 7.1).

## Communication Intensity

Communication intensity refers to the intensity of the enacted sensemaking and sensegiving between actors involved throughout the change development process. Several layers of communication occur

**FIGURE 7.1**
The three patterns of sensemaking. (Adapted from Abdullah and Ismail, 2017.)

simultaneously: (1) center with subsidiary managers; (2) subsidiary managers with their internal teams; and (3) peer subsidiary managers. There are other forms of communication, such as between the center and subsidiary team members and between the team members and external parties; however, these are either insignificant or irrelevant to this study. In the CEMS initiative, InCo stands out as displaying the highest level of communication intensity. In the days following its establishment, InCo's American IJV partner instituted several key management positions, which were occupied by American expatriates. Therefore, it is not surprising that InCo's current organizational culture does not resemble the typical Asian culture. They display higher indices of individualism, with traits such as self-reliance, competitiveness, and equity (Trompenaars, 1994). For instance, from the start of the CEMS initiative, InCo displayed a highly combative approach to CenCo. Both were embroiled in an intense, heated debate about issues ranging from the legality of the CEMS to the non-resolution of several of its problems.

InCo displayed intense sensegiving and sensemaking activities, making sense of things before assigning meaning to them. Its self-reliance in regard to the preservation of its organizational culture consistently allows it to do things its own way. In the case of the CEMS, InCo managed to gain approval from CenCo to build a standalone system. Within the greater discourse of InCo's organizational culture, which is derived from the early period of the American IJV management, InCo is still Indonesian by nationality. Based on the nationalistic Pancaseela-based philosophical theory of the Indonesian state, InCo as a whole carries with it strong cultural values— such relationships, reputation, and cooperation—of which it is proud. This display of a strong national cultural value was among the primary factors that influenced the decision to allow InCo to implement the CEMS on a standalone basis. At the height of the disagreement with CenCo, InCo's manager had sought sanction from the local board. Under the guise that all information that belongs to an Indonesian company must reside within Indonesia, CenCo eventually had to concede, thereby allowing InCo to build its own system.

InCo was an active member of the rebel alliance* and provided insight about key information related to flaws of the CEMS. This led the alliance to pressure CenCo to perform the post-implementation review (PIR).† At

---

* An informal pact consisting of BaCo, InCo, and LaCo against CenCo.
† A post-implementation review of a project based on the deliverables.

the time, InCo was no longer directly involved in the CEM initiatives; however, it remains active in the alliance. Even later in the BAU stage, InCo helped the alliance with the post-remedial action plan based on the CEMS PIR report. Like the earlier planning stage, remnants of the American IJV organizational culture at InCo interplayed in the engagement between the center and subsidiary. The uncertainty avoidance index for Indonesia and the US is marginal compared, for example, with those of Germany and Japan (Hofstede, 1994). However, over the period under the American IJV management, InCo has adapted one of the strongest litigation cultures among American MNCs. In the rebel alliance example, InCo was instrumental in leading the pact to devise meticulous tactics, such as lobbying for PIR engagement to help steer the course of the change initiative. The reality is that many of CenCo's intended objectives were later derailed or transformed.

Conversely, BaCo appeared recalcitrant from the beginning, often being non-cooperative and, at times, skeptical of CenCo's ability to deliver the CEMS. Although, unlike InCo, BaCo was not directly confrontational, it was communicating actively with others and appearing to influence others' views of the CEMS (Maitlis & Sonenshein, 2010). Later in the rebel alliance, BaCo was chosen by the alliance members to lead the PIR engagement. With the support of other alliance members, BaCo was able to convince CenCo in a number of key action plans of the CEMS after implementation.

BaCo's communication intensity was not limited to the top echelon but, rather, transcended to its internal teams (Balogun & Johnson, 2004). Within these teams, BaCo held small workshops and awareness sessions, ultimately managing to produce several workaround solutions that minimized many of the CEMS' limitations and issues. BaCo has no specific corporate culture; rather, it is predominantly the Bangladeshi national culture that permeates the company. Bangladeshi national culture has a high power index relative to many other Asian cultures and brings with it the typical leadership style that tends to be authoritarian (Hofstede, 1994). The authoritarianism of BaCo's leadership relates to the recalcitrant behavior that was displayed during the CEMS episode. However, it is ironic that the same authoritarian approach adopted by BaCo's manager, combined with the collectivism of its team members, was able to elicit some of the best solutions to the CEMS barriers.

For LaCo, the communication intensity that was displayed was primarily in the rebel alliance and within its internal teams. LaCo's initial reaction to the CEMS was mostly characterized as contemplated but later became assertive when it became a part of the alliance. As part of the alliance, LaCo actively provided support regarding how the CEMS should strategize against CenCo. LaCo's manager's consistent push via a symbolic "Go Green" campaign kept the momentum going in regard to the CEMS initiative (Gioia et al., 1994). LaCo's organizational culture mirrors its national culture, which comprises high collectivism, a large power distance, moderate masculinity, and a strong uncertainty avoidance.

With regard to the SOM initiative, the subsidiaries appear to display a fair amount of communication intensity. They participated actively in the early planning stage undertaken by CenCo. With the later involvement of FAB* as the consultant, the subsidiaries again displayed strong collective participation. They actively provided both positive and negative inputs to FAB, and the high communication intensity continued to be evident even after FAB's departure. The CMF is another initiative that displayed subsidiaries' strong communication at both levels. Subsidiary managers communicated to their respective managers regarding the CMF and team members provided feedback about gaps in the CMF. With the exception of BaCo, which was implementing two versions of the CMF (an internal and a CenCo version), after several constructive discussions with the center, they eventually migrated to CenCo's CMF. In both initiatives, we see the extensive coopetition approach through the interplay between center and subsidiary actors (Lundgren-Henriksson & Kock, 2016).

### The Adoption of Change

The adoption of change refers to the level of change, which ranges from minimal to active adopters. Minimal adopters display low levels of both implementation and internalization, in essence disavowing the practice of change (Kostova & Roth, 2002). At the other end of the spectrum are the active adopters, who display the highest levels of both measures of change. Based on the three initiatives explored in this study, Table 7.1 depicts the various adoption levels for each entity.

In the CEMS example, both InCo and BaCo rank the highest for level of implementation. LaCo followed with medium implementation, and finally, CenCo and MyCo both ranked as low implementation. InCo's belief in the CEMS practice surpassed that of BaCo; therefore, it is appropriate to

---

* An external consultant appointed by CenCo to document the SOM.

**TABLE 7.1**

Adoption Levels of Initiatives

|  | CEMS | SOM | CMF |
|---|---|---|---|
| CenCo | Assent | Assent | Assent |
| MyCo | Minimal | Ceremonial | Minimal |
| InCo | Active | Active | Minimal |
| BaCo | Ceremonial | Ceremonial | Ceremonial |
| LaCo | Ceremonial | Ceremonial | Ceremonial |

label InCo an active adopter and BaCo a ceremonial adopter. Conversely, the term ceremonial adopter is best suited to LaCo because of the mild combination of internalization and CEMS implementation. In comparison with the CEMS, the implementation of the SOM and CMF initiatives was significantly less complex for subsidiaries. To deliver the SOM and CMF, subsidiaries require minimal investment in terms of time, manpower, and funds. This is the primary factor that suggests why the implementation of the two aforementioned initiatives was relatively better than that of the CEMS. Based on the adoption measure that was applied for CEMS, it was discovered that both BaCo and LaCo fitted the criteria for the ceremonial adopter terminology for the SOM and CMF initiatives. They both display significant levels of implementation compliance but lack belief in the initiative practices. Whereas MyCo is a ceremonial adopter of the SOM and a minimalistic adopter of the CMF, InCo is an active adopter of the SOM. It is interesting to note that, with the exception of CenCo, all the subsidiaries are active users of the SOM. However, only InCo is an active adopter, because of its strong belief in the SOM practice.

### The Resolution of Barriers

Finally, the resolution of barriers refers to the efforts taken to overcome obstacles to the change initiative. Anand and Barsoux (2017) define barriers or blockers as vital components of change that need to be targeted. When the data that were available from the three initiatives undertaken at the CenCo group were analyzed, it was discovered that BaCo and InCo were the two most active subsidiaries. They made consistent efforts to find ways to overcome the barriers in one or more initiatives and were quick to respond to change barriers at different levels both internally and externally.

BaCo, for instance, formulated innovative solutions to CEMS' predicament. These solutions took the form of the CEMS 101 checklist, Wi-Fi upgrade, and off-office work hours. BaCo's manager overcame the LR barrier by engaging senior management at the MC.* In regard to the CMF initiative, BaCo overcame the barrier by securing the endorsement of the board to implement a dual CMF version for 2014. InCo was highly active, seeking ways to overcome numerous barriers related to both the CEMS and SOM initiatives. In regard to the CEMS, the InCo manager's assertive approach to the center eventually gained InCo the right to operate the CEMS independently. Additionally, the manager identified potential internal barriers to CEMS, including those related to the CEMS' project management. He later hired a dedicated system administrator to ensure that his existing team members were not burdened with additional tasks related to CEMS delivery. Regarding the SOM initiative, InCo's manager overcame the formatting barrier by engaging his local board. This allowed InCo more than 10% flexibility to customize the SOM to suit local needs. InCo also managed to convince the center that it could operate the CEMS independently and should be allowed to further customize the CEMS section of the SOM. In the end, InCo's version of the SOM deviated more than 30% from that of the center (group).

### Knowledge

This study is perhaps the first to use the actor-centered approach to explore center-led change initiatives across subsidiaries and to do so in a "high-velocity industry" (Eisenhardt & Bourgeois, 1988)—an MNC operating in Asia. This study is among the few research projects applying the qualitative approach to the IB field (Birkinshaw, Brannen, & Tung, 2011). The quality of access to both the center and subsidiaries makes this study potentially the first of its kind to be undertaken. Hence, it has the potential to expand and further develop knowledge of how center and subsidiary managers contribute strategically to the process of undertaking center-led change initiatives.

This study explores how subsidiary managers as change recipients were at times in a state of confusion due to the imposed implementation by the center (Guiette & Vandenbempt, 2017; Lundgren-Henriksson & Kock, 2016). Here, subsidiary managers attempt to make sense of the situation

---

* The management committee members report directly to the CEO.

(Maitlis, 2005; Sonenshein, 2010) based on their different sets of individual views of it. Within this confusion, the managers are grouped together in what they call the "rebel alliance" to overcome the barriers set by the center. Consistent with Giuliani's (2016) work on sensebreaking (Vlaar, Van Fenema, & Tiwari, 2008), it was found that during change development, alliance members assign different meanings to CEMS, referring to it as "double work," a "failure," and a "repository system." This sheds light on how the rebel alliance played a more dominant role (Maitlis & Christianson, 2014). It further unraveled how the interplay between organizations and their members influences and steers the course of change.

According to Filstad (2014), the center's persistence in maintaining exclusivity in regard to decision-making processes may have led to a contradiction between its own sensemaking and sensegiving processes. Consistent with Kezar (2013), it was shown that not only were sensemaking and sensegiving prevalent throughout the development of the various initiatives but also that, along the way, their natures were altered slightly from what had been intended initially. The CEMS initiative, for instance, was meant to be a "real-time" system, but in the end, it was simply a "repository" system. InCo and BaCo made the most significant progress among the four subsidiaries. They were early adopters of change, and by addressing difficulties and pressure at an early stage (Higgins, Stubbs, & Love, 2014), they were able to shape the meanings of the initiatives. Other subsidiaries that were either part of the alliance in the CEMS case or were leading the initiative directly echo similar meanings about these.

## PRACTICAL IMPLICATIONS

The findings of this study should help center managers who were involved in delivering change initiatives. Corporate transformations have a miserable success rate, as 75% of change initiative end in failure (Anand & Barsoux, 2017). The current MNC structure is no longer the traditional command-and-control type; therefore, within their circle of influence, subsidiary managers have the power to decide on how to respond to center-led change initiatives (Ambos & Birkinshaw, 2010; Bouquet & Birkinshaw, 2008b). This study has explored three center-led change initiatives based on an actor-centered approach. The question of why individuals do what they do is examined through the sensemaking lens.

The three patterns of sensemaking/sensegiving that emerged from this study offer center managers a glimpse into how the development of change progresses over time. It was observed that the center manager appears to employ the coopetition* strategy (Luo, 2005), which was implemented by sensegiving the meaning of the initiatives (Maitlis & Lawrence, 2007). The center manager assigned meaning to the initiative; for instance, in the CEMS case, they sensegive to the subsidiary that it was about emulating established MNCs via office automation. The center carried a similar sensegiving message for the remaining two SOM and CMF initiatives. They were relatively more successful at deploying the SOM and CMF initiatives, compared with the CEMS. In regard to the development of the SOM and CMF initiatives, the center was more subsidiary-centric than in the case of the CEMS. They were attentive and collective in their decision making, and the approach was described as guiding, collaborating, and supporting. Another factor that needs to be considered is the extent of the resources needed for a certain initiative to be delivered.

The study was conducted from the end of 2013 to early 2017 in the real environment of an MNO MNC. InCo was by far the only one that achieved the active adoption level for both the CEMS and SOM initiatives. InCo was still using both initiatives at the end of this study. InCo's implementation surpassed the norm; for example, it is now using CEMS in business intelligence and for data analytics. BaCo and LaCo were second to InCo, with both showing high levels of implementation but lacking the internalization component. Therefore, we recommend that practitioners pay close attention to change recipients throughout the development phase of the change, especially any change that requires extensive resources to be obtained from subsidiaries.

Additionally, BaCo and InCo were the farthest from CenCo in terms of geographical distance, but this study's findings suggest that contextual distance is perhaps more prominent than geographical distance when it involves headquarter value creation (Beugelsdijk, Nell, & Ambos, 2017). Contextual distance, comprising cultural, administrative, and economic distance, is perhaps another area that needs to be further explored to enable a better understanding of the nuanced dynamics of the parent–subsidiary relationship.

---

* Refers to the simultaneous use of cooperation and competition strategies.

## CONCLUSION

The research findings suggest that subsidiaries that made significant progress in implementing one or more center-led initiatives were those that engaged in both sensemaking and sensegiving processes. Three patterns of sensemaking or sensegiving emerge from this study and help to drive the center-led initiatives from the planning/implementation of the BAU* phase. First, communication intensity refers to the level of sensemaking and sensegiving that is enacted by managers throughout the development of change. Second, the adoption of change refers to the level of change, which ranges from minimal to active adoption (Kostova & Roth, 2002). Finally, resolution to barriers refers to the efforts made to overcome the obstacles to the change initiative. The interplay between the center and subsidiaries in making sense of change might threaten the values and cultures of certain organizations. They might also be enablers that help to strengthen the culture of the firm—both the center and subsidiaries. When their optimal capabilities are harnessed, organizational culture and values can successfully influence and enable quality to be incorporated between the center and subsidiaries. The following points may highlight the expected development and outcomes of center-led change initiatives:

- The center needs to emphasize the behavior of key actors and cultural aspects throughout the development stage of the change; this should help ensure a higher number of active adopters of change.
- The center needs to pay attention to any negative cues from subsidiaries, and the issues need to be attended to as quickly as possible.

## REFERENCES

Abdullah, N., & Ismail, M. N. (2017). MNE center-subsidiary dynamic relationship of center-led change initiatives from an actor-centered approach. In Z. Bekirogullari, M. Y. Minas, & R. X. Thambusamy (Eds.), *4th Beci International Conference on Business and Economics 2017* (Vol. 1, pp. 106–118). Nicosia: Future Acad.

Alvesson, M., & Karreman, D. (2000). Varieties of discourse: On the study of organizations through discourse analysis. *Human Relations, 53*(9), 1125.

---

* Business as usual occurs when business practices reach the normal day-to-day operational state.

Ambos, T. C., & Birkinshaw, J. (2010). Headquarters' Attention and its effect on subsidiary performance. *Management International Review (MIR)*, *50*(4), 449–469.

Anand, N., & Barsoux, J.-L. (2017). What everyone gets wrong About change management. *Harvard Business Review*, *95*(6), 79–85.

Balogun, J., Fahy, K., & Vaara, E. (2019). The interplay between HQ legitimation and subsidiary legitimacy judgments in HQ relocation: A social psychological approach. *Journal of International Business Studies*, *50*(2), 223–249.

Balogun, J., Jarzabkowski, P., & Vaara, E. (2011). Selling, resistance and reconciliation: A critical discursive approach to subsidiary role evolution in MNEs. *Journal of International Business Studies*, *42*, 765–786.

Balogun, J., & Johnson, G. (2004). Organizational restructuring and middle manager sensemaking. *The Academy of Management Journal*, *47*(4), 523–549.

Balogun, J., & Johnson, G. (2005). From intended strategies to unintended outcomes: The impact of change recipient sensemaking. *Organization Studies*, *26*(11), 1573–1601.

Barry, D., & Elmes, M. (1997). Strategy retold: Toward a narrative view of strategic discourse. *The Academy of Management Review*, *22*(2), 429–452.

Bartlett, C. A., & Ghoshal, S. (1986). Tap your subsidiaries for global reach. *Harvard Business Review*, *64*(6), 87–94.

Bartlett, C. A., & Ghoshal, S. (2002). *Managing Across Borders: The Transnational Solution* (2nd ed.). Boston, MA: Harvard Business School Press.

Beugelsdijk, S., Nell, P. C., & Ambos, B. (2017). When Do Distance Effects Become Empirically Observable? An Investigation in the Context of Headquarters Value Creation for Subsidiaries. *Journal of International Management*, *23*(3), 255–267.

Birkinshaw, J. (1996). How multinational subsidiary mandates are gained and lost. *Journal of International Business Studies*, *27*(3), 467–495.

Birkinshaw, J. (2000). *Entrepreneurship in the Global Firm* (1st ed.). London: SAGE.

Birkinshaw, J., Bouquet, C., & Ambos, T. C. (2007). Managing executive attention in the global company. *MIT Sloan Management Review*, *48*(4), 39.

Birkinshaw, J., Brannen, M. Y., & Tung, R. (2011). From a distance and generalizable to up close and grounded: Reclaiming a place for qualitative methods in international business research. *Journal of International Business Studies*, *42*(5), 573–581.

Birkinshaw, J., Braunerhjelm, P., Holm, U., & Terjesen, S. (2006). Why do some multinational corporations relocate their headquarters overseas? *Strategic Management Journal*, *27*(7), 681–700.

Birkinshaw, J., & Morrison, A. (1995). Configurations of strategy and structure in subsidiaries of multinational corporations. *Journal of International Business Studies*, *26*(4), 729–753.

Bouquet, C., & Birkinshaw, J. (2008a). Managing power in the multinational corporation: How low-power actors gain influence. *Journal of Management*, *34*(3), 477–508.

Bouquet, C., & Birkinshaw, J. (2008b). Weight versus voice: How foreign subsidiaries gain attention from corporate headquarters. *Academy of Management Journal*, *51*(3), 577–601.

Brandt, W. K., & Hulbert, J. M. (1976). Patterns of communications in the multinational corporation: An empirical study. *Journal of International Business Studies (pre-1986)*, *7*(1), 57–64.

Brown, A. D. (2000). Making sense of inquiry sensemaking. *Journal of Management Studies*, *37*(1), 45–75.

Brown, A. D. (2004). Authoritative sensemaking in a public inquiry report. *Organization Studies*, *25*(1), 95–112.

Brown, A. D., Stacey, P., & Nandhakumar, J. (2008). Making sense of sensemaking narratives. *Human Relations, 61*(8), 1035–1062.

Buchanan, D., & Dawson, P. (2007). Discourse and audience: Organizational change as multi story process. *Journal of Management Studies, 44*(5), 669–686.

Christianson, M. K., Farkas, M. T., Sutcliffe, K. M., & Weick, K. E. (2009). Learning through rare events: Significant interruptions at the Baltimore & Ohio Railroad museum. *Organization Science, 20*(5), 846–860.

Eisenhardt, K., & Bourgeois, L. J. (1988). Politics of strategic decision making in high-velocity environments: Toward a midrange theory. *The Academy of Management Journal, 31*(4), 737–770.

Filstad, C. (2014). The politics of sensemaking and sensegiving at work. *Journal of Workplace Learning,* (1), 3.

Frost, T. S., Birkinshaw, J., & Ensign, P. C. (2002). Centers of excellence in multinational corporations. *Strategic Management Journal, 23*(11), 997–1018.

Gephart, R. P. (1993). The textual approach: Risk and blame in disaster sensemaking. *The Academy of Management Journal, 36*(6), 1465–1514.

Gioia, D. A., & Chittipeddi, K. (1991). Sensemaking and sensegiving in strategic change initiation. *Strategic Management Journal, 12*(6), 433–448.

Gioia, D. A., Thomas, J. B., Clark, S. M., & Chittipeddi, K. (1994). Symbolism and strategic change in academia: The dynamics of sensemaking and influence. *Organization Science, 5*(3), 363–383.

Giuliani, M. (2016). Sensemaking, sensegiving and sensebreaking: The case of intellectual capital measurements. *Journal of Intellectual Capital, 17*(2), 218–237.

Guiette, A., & Vandenbempt, K. (2017). Change managerialism and micro-processes of sensemaking during change implementation. *Scandinavian Journal of Management, 33*(2), 65–81.

Hardy, C., Lawrence, T. B., & Grant, D. (2005). Discourse and collaboration: The role of conversations and collective identity. *The Academy of Management Review, 30*(1), 58–77.

Hardy, C., & Phillips, N. (2004). Discourse and power. In D. Grant, C. Hardy, C. Oswick, & L. Putnam (Eds.), *The Sage Handbook of Organizational Discourse* (pp. 299–313). London: Sage.

Hedlund, G. (1980). The role of foreign subsidiaries in strategic decision-making in Swedish Multinational Corporations. *Strategic Management Journal (pre-1986), 1*(1), 23–36.

Hedlund, G. (1986). The hypermodern MNCA heterarchy? *Human Resource Management (1986–1998), 25*(1), 9–35.

Higgins, C., Stubbs, W., & Love, T. (2014). Walking the talk(s): Organisational narratives of integrated reporting. *Accounting, Auditing & Accountability Journal, 27*(7), 1090.

Hofstede, G. (1994). The business of international business is culture. *International Business Review, 3*(1), 1–14.

Humphreys, M., & Brown, A. D. (2008). An analysis of corporate social responsibility at credit line: A narrative approach. *Journal of Business Ethics, 80*(3), 403–418.

Isabella, L. A. (1990). Evolving interpretations as a change unfolds: How managers construe key organizational events. *Academy of Management Journal, 33*(1), 7–41.

Jarillo, J. C., & Martínez, J. I. (1990). Different roles for subsidiaries: The case of multinational corporations in Spain. *Strategic Management Journal, 11*(7), 501–512.

Kezar, A. (2013). Understanding sensemaking/sensegiving in transformational change processes from the bottom up. *Higher Education, 65*(6), 761–780.

Knights, D., & Morgan, G. (1991). Corporate strategy, organizations, and subjectivity: A critique. *Organization Studies, 12*(2), 251.

Kostova, T., & Roth, K. (2002). Adoption of an organizational practice by subsidiaries of multinational corporations: Institutional and relational effects. *The Academy of Management Journal, 45*(1), 215–233.

Kostova, T., & Zaheer, S. (1999). Organizational legitimacy under conditions of complexity: The case of the multinational enterprise. *The Academy of Management Review, 24*(1), 64–81.

Kraft, A., Sparr, J. L., & Peus, C. (2018). Giving and Making Sense About Change: The Back and Forth Between Leaders and Employees. *Journal of Business and Psychology, 33*(1), 71–87.

Kull, T. J., & Wacker, J. G. (2010). Quality management effectiveness in Asia: The influence of culture. *Journal of operations management, 28*(3), 223–239.

Kvale, S., & Brinkmann, S. (2009). *InterViews: Learning the Craft of Qualitative Research Interviewing* (2nd ed.). Thousand Oaks, CA, London: Sage Publications.

Lundgren-Henriksson, E.-L., & Kock, S. (2016). Coopetition in a headwind – The interplay of sensemaking, sensegiving, and middle managerial emotional response in coopetitive strategic change development. *Industrial Marketing Management, 58*, 20–34.

Luo, Y. (2005). Toward coopetition within a multinational enterprise: A perspective from foreign subsidiaries. *Journal of World Business, 40*(1), 71–90.

Maguire, S., & Hardy, C. (2009). Discourse and deinstitutionalization: The decline of DDT. *The Academy of Management Journal (AMJ), 52*(1), 148–178.

Maitlis, S. (2005). The social processes of organizational sensemaking. *The Academy of Management Journal, 48*(1), 21–49.

Maitlis, S., & Christianson, M. K. (2014). Sensemaking in organizations: Taking stock and moving forward. *Academy of Management Annals, 8*(1), 57–125.

Maitlis, S., & Lawrence, T. B. (2007). Triggers and enablers of sensegiving in organizations. *Academy of Management Journal, 50*(1), 57–84.

Maitlis, S., & Sonenshein, S. (2010). Sensemaking in crisis and change: Inspiration and insights from Weick (1988). *Journal of Management Studies, 47*(3), 551–580.

Potter, J., & Wetherell, M. (1987). *Discourse and Social Psychology: Beyond Attitudes and Behaviour.* London, Newbury Park, CA: Sage Publications.

Sonenshein, S. (2010). We're changing—Or are we? Untangling the role of progressive, regressive, and stability narratives during strategic change implementation. *The Academy of Management Journal (AMJ), 53*(3), 477–512.

Tempel, A., Edwards, T., Ferner, A., Muller-Camen, M., & Waechter, H. (2006). Subsidiary responses to institutional duality: Collective representation practices of US multinationals in Britain and Germany. *Human Relations, 59*(11), 1543–1570.

Tienari, J., Vaara, E., & Björkman, I. (2003). Global capitalism meets national spirit. *Journal of Management Inquiry, 12*(4), 377–393.

Trompenaars, F. (1994). *Riding the Waves of Culture: Understanding Diversity in Global Business.* IRWIN.

Vaara, E. (2000). Constructions of cultural differences in post-merger change processes: A sensemaking perspective on Finnish-Swedish cases. *Management, 3*(3), 81–110.

Vaara, E. (2003). Post-acquisition integration as sensemaking: Glimpses of ambiguity, confusion, hypocrisy, and politicization. *Journal of Management Studies, 40*(4), 859–894.

Vaara, E. (2010). Taking the linguistic turn seriously: Strategy as a mulitfaceted and inter-discursive phenomenon. In J. A. C. Baum, & J. Lampel (Eds.), *The Globalization of Strategy Research* (Vol. 27, pp. 30–47). United Kingdom: Emerald.

Vaara, E., Tienari, J., & Laurila, J. (2006). Pulp and paper fiction: On the discursive legitimation of global industrial restructuring. *Organization Studies, 27*(6), 789–813.

Vaara, E., Tienari, J., Piekkari, R., & Säntti, R. (2005). Language and the circuits of power in a merging multinational corporation. *Journal of Management Studies, 42*(3), 595–623.

Vlaar, P. W. L., Van Fenema, P. C., & Tiwari, V. (2008). Cocreating understanding and value in distributed work: How members of onsite and offshore vendor teams give, make, demand, and break sense. *MIS Quarterly: Management Information Systems, 32*(2), 227–255.

Vora, D., Kostova, T., & Roth, K. (2007). Roles of subsidiary managers in multinational corporations: The effect of dual organizational identification. *Management International Review, 47*(4), 595–620.

Weick, K. E. (1988). Enacted sensemaking in crisis situations. *Journal of Management Studies, 25*(4), 305–317.

Weick, K. E. (1993). The collapse of sensemaking in organizations: The Mann Gulch Disaster. *Administrative Science Quarterly, 38*(4), 628–652.

Weick, K. E. (1995). *Sensemaking in Organizations*. Sage Publications.

White, R. E., & Poynter, T. A. (1984). Strategies for foreign-owned subsidiaries in Canada. *Business Quarterly* (pre-1986), *49*(2), 59–69.

Wu, S. J. (2015). The impact of quality culture on quality management practices and performance in Chinese manufacturing firms. *International Journal of Quality & Reliability Management, 32*(8), 799–814.

Yin, R. K. (2003). *Case Study Research: Design and Methods*. Sage Publications.

# 8

# Creating a Culture of ISO 26000 (CSR) for the Mining Industry: A Review

*Flevy Lasrado and Faisal Hai*

## CONTENTS

## INTRODUCTION

In recent decades, the International Organization for Standardization (ISO) has added the development of generic standards to improve the consistency of organizational and management systems. The ISO 9000 series was introduced in 1988 as a way for organizations to implement quality management and quality assurance, while the ISO 14000 series was introduced in 1996 to provide practical tools for organizations to manage their environmental responsibilities. ISO 26000, launched in 2010, provides guidelines for social responsibility (Castka and Balzarova, 2007). In fact, over the last decade, corporate social responsibility (CSR) has grown from being criticized as a mere management fad to being endorsed as a good business practice by the majority of the world's leading companies (Moratis and Cochius, 2017). Moreover, quality management can significantly contribute to the deployment and uptake of the CSR agenda, although it needs to reinvent and rejuvenate key areas, such as management systems; integration of strategy, operations, technology, CSR, and quality; incorporation of corporate governance; and improvements in third-party certification and internal auditing practices (Castka and Balzarova, 2007). Interestingly, it has now been observed that there is an urgency for concerted efforts by the private sector, public sector, and non-governmental organizations to develop structures and institutions that contribute to social justice, environmental protection, and poverty eradication (Dobers and Halme, 2009).

ISO 26000 provides guidance on how businesses and organizations can operate in a socially responsible way. This means acting in an ethical and transparent way that contributes to the health and welfare of society. According to ISO, it has thousands of standards that help users contribute to the UN 2030 Agenda and its sustainable development goals, covering everything from sustainable communities and quality management to safety and measuring greenhouse gases. Almost any activity can be described in an ISO standard if relevant stakeholders meet and work toward consensus (ISO, 2018). Since there is no consistent understanding of what corporate sustainability and social responsibility encompass, one standard of ISO 26000 aims to provide guidance on social responsibility and help all types of organizations contribute to sustainable development (Hahn, 2013).

Numerous initiatives, guidelines, and tools have been made available for CSR practice, but very little is known about the usefulness of the new CSR standard, ISO 26000, in the mining industry (Ranängen et al., 2014). The mining industry has a major impact on society—from an economic, environmental, and social perspective—due to a vast number of criteria (Ranängen and Lindman, 2017). CSR has become particularly important due to the nature of activities carried out by mining companies associated with the mining of coal or metal, a high level of employment, and especially a strong impact on the social environment. In fact, according to Solomon et al. (2008), understanding the social aspect in the mining sector is an increasingly necessary and critical requirement for successful business. Moreover, mining industries receive significant global attention due to the nature of their environmental and social responsibilities (Govindan et al., 2014). Overall, ISO 26000 executes quality management and environmental management standards to provide management with standards of social responsibility (Castka and Balzarova, 2007). So, this indicates that ISO 26000 assists companies to perform well in their social obligation to society.

Given this growing importance, it is important to understand how the mining industry is creating a culture for CSR and how the adoption of the standard has been used. In order to review this aspect, first we discuss the contemporary background of the mining industry, and then we explore the extent to which CSR is practiced and what the future holds for the mining industry to create a culture for ISO-related standards.

## CSR AND ISO 26000

The concept of CSR has gone through a significant development. We can find many definitions that share the belief that companies hold some responsibility for the public good; however, they emphasize different elements of this (Gurská and Válová, 2013). In fact, CSR initiatives are often promoted as a means of contributing to the sustainability and development of the nation (Mutti et al., 2012). However, CSR is a means by which companies can frame their attitudes and strategies toward, and relationships with, stakeholders, investors, employees, or, as is salient here, communities within a popular and acceptable concept. A more recent definition of ISO 26000 defines *social responsibility* (SR) as the responsibility of an organization for the impact of its decisions and activities on society and the environment through transparent and ethical behavior that:

- Contributes to sustainable development, including the health and welfare of society.
- Takes into account the expectations of stakeholders.
- Is in compliance with applicable law and consistent with international norms of behavior.
- Is integrated throughout the organization and practices in its relationships (www.iso.org/sr).

In fact, ISO 26000 provides a shared understanding on CSR: it minimizes the confusion of and dispute about what SR means; what issues an organization needs to address in order to operate in a socially responsible manner; and what the best practices are in implementing social responsibility (Bustami et al., 2013). The main role of CSR for mining companies is to ensure a responsible business venture to reduce potential risks arising from safety issues, to minimize a potential negative environmental footprint, and to attract qualified employees and gain acceptance among local society (Wirth et al., 2016). According to Dżoga et al. (2010), some of the important benefits of CSR are shown in Table 8.1.

A further study from an Australian perspective shows that CSR has increased the commitment to the management of labor in two Australian mining industry companies (Jones et al., 2007).

ISO 26000 sets forth seven guiding principles and core subjects of social responsibility. These are presented in Table 8.2.

Organizations can assess their CSR initiatives that reflect these principles. For example, evaluating the seven principles of ISO 26000 in an Iranian context, significant relationships between CSR practices and organizational performance were found and it was observed that community involvement and development plays an important role in enhancing the organizational performance of organizations (Valmohammadi, 2014). Moreover, as Herciu (2016) notes, ISO 26000 will be able to: (a) create value for the organization and for others; (b) increase, decrease, or transform capital (financial, human, social, natural,

**TABLE 8.1**

Benefits of CSR

- Positive image of the company
- Mission credibility in the eyes of customers
- Increase in competitiveness
- Gaining consumer loyalty
- Increase in trust among stakeholders
- gaining the favor of the local community
- A positive image of the company among employees
- Building positive relationships with local authorities and the local community
- Increased investor interest
- Attracting and retaining the best employees
- Increased organizational culture within the company

**TABLE 8.2**

Guiding Principles and Core Subjects in ISO 26000

| Accountability | Organizational governance |
| --- | --- |
| <ul><li>Transparency</li><li>Ethical behavior</li><li>Respect for stakeholder interest</li><li>Respect for the rule of law</li><li>Respect for international norms of behavior</li><li>Respect for human rights</li></ul> | <ul><li>Human rights</li><li>Labor practices</li><li>Environment</li><li>Fair operating practices</li><li>Consumer issues</li><li>Community involvement and development</li></ul> |

and intellectual); (c) emphasize performance results and improvements; (d) enhance credibility; and (e) attract investors.

## THE MINING INDUSTRY, CSR, AND THE ROLE OF ISO 26000

Australian legislations such as the Protection of the Environment Operations Act 1997 (NSW) and the Environmental Protection Act (QLD) place rules and restrictions on what environmental modifications mining companies are allowed to make in order to extract ore. Once a mine has been exhausted of its resources, rehabilitation of the site to a certain standard is required by law, but as studies show, abandoned sites still remain a significant problem. Thus, measures to control pollution in coastal rivers and estuaries by mining activities cannot be only technical.

Interestingly, in recent years, concerns about the sustainability of CSR in businesses have become an increasingly high-profile issue in many countries and industries, none more so than the mining industry (Jenkins and Yakovleva, 2006). In fact, mining provides input for other industrial sectors that is vital for sustaining the population's wellbeing and the functioning of global economies (Mancini and Sala, 2018). Thus, responsible mining requires a company to engage with local communities throughout all stages of their operations, from exploration through to post-mining planning (Adey et al., 2011). In fact, the mining industry has started to pay serious attention to its environmental and social impacts. This has recently manifested itself in the formulation of CSR policies and strategies and a proliferation of CSR, environmental, sustainability, and community reporting (Jenkins, 2004).

Multinational mining companies have remodeled themselves as good corporate citizens and, for mining companies, CSR is the manifestation of a move toward greater sustainability in the industry (Jenkins and Obara, 2006). CSR is not necessarily simply "greenwashing," but there is a need to engage business critically toward more sincere versions of CSR in the mining industry (Hamann and Kapelus, 2004). Ranängen et al. (2014) conducted a study to explore how a mining and construction company practices CSR within the health area and to discuss the possible merits of ISO 26000 for CSR development in the mining industry in the developing world. The results of the study provide the following insights: (a) the standard can be used to evaluate and improve a company's CSR practices even if that company is already considered a frontrunner within CSR; (b) the standard can give valuable advice when designing community development programs and allocating the use of charity donations; and (c) traditional management systems based on occupational health and safety standard 18001 and ISO 14001 can rather effectively support actions and expectations in ISO 26000.

Similarly, another study by Bluszcz and Kijewska (2015) investigated the involvement of Polish companies from the mining and metallurgical industry in activities for sustainable development. It was observed that ISO 26000 is the most recognized international standard for CSR and it forms the basis for sustainable development. In fact, most Polish mining companies are quite active in the areas of environmental protection as well as relations with their employees (Majer, 2013). However, it is not yet all good for the mining industry when it comes to the reporting of results. A case study by Jenkins and Yakovleva (2006) of the world's ten largest mining companies found that there is considerable variation in the maturity of reporting content and styles of these mining companies. They suggest that stronger leadership and co-operation from the top reporting companies is necessary to support the laggards of the industry.

Interestingly, empirical findings by Catalan companies highlight a commitment to CSR and mining companies' engagement with stakeholders (Vintró et al., 2012). From a Swedish perspective, it is evident that certified management systems are effective tools for CSR in the mining industry (Ranängen and Zober, 2014a, 2014b).

Among the good practices, what is evident is that companies that have a good social policy are the ones that help educate people, openly communicate, support children, and conduct all activities according to the current needs in the country or area in which they are located (Gurská and Válová, 2013). Studies further observe that CSR widely implemented by large copper mining companies should focus on local or regional aspects. Active governmental policy is needed for implementation of CSR among small and medium-sized enterprises (SMEs) (Wirth et al., 2016).

In the short term, no clear relationship between CSR and financial performance could be identified when measured by return on assets (ROA), return on equity (ROE), and return on sale (ROS). However, in the long term, the findings show that there is a relationship between CSR activities and corporate value (Maki and Feng, 2018). Specific to the mining industry, the role of CSR indicates that relationships with stakeholders are important to mining companies in obtaining relevant social performance and in acquiring local legitimacy from surrounding communities. This highlights the importance of the elaboration, dissemination. and quality of social reports, particularly concerning credibility (Rodrigues and Mendes, 2018).

Environmental duties were noted to be the critical element of CSR in the mining sector in Argentina as well (Yakovleva and Vazquez-Brust, 2012); thus, they can help to create a strong SR culture for the mining industry. Overall, as rightly pointed out by Sethi et al. (2017), ISO 26000 is a good policy document about CSR and its main content areas. Its use, however, in enabling organizations to implement its principles and manage its core subject areas with high quality and integrity is still evolving.

However, in general, CSR consists of distinct types of responsibilities, and stakeholders give those responsibilities different relative importance in the mining industry (Yakovleva and Vazquez-Brust, 2012). As rightly pointed out in the study of Vázquez and White (2012), all mining companies should engage in permanent dialogue and involve the communities adjacent to the mines. The local communities have rights, claims, or specific interests that should be taken into account, and the companies must recognize and have due regard for the interests and legal rights of the people and respond to their expressed concerns. The CSR agenda in the mining industry in Malawi is strongly influenced by externally generated pressures, such as civil society organization activism and community expectations; however, it is clear that other drivers, such as public and private regulations and pressure from financial markets, also played a role in pressurizing Paladin to adopt a CSR agenda (Mzembe and Meaton, 2014).

Overall, the studies provide a good level of evidence that mining companies understand the CSR perspective and have activities to strengthen their position on this agenda. In fact, they agree with the linkages of implementation of CSR to the ISO standard and apply the standard for reporting. However, it is important for the mining companies to develop relationships with local communities to strengthen their standing by developing these "win-win" relationships. Development of good communication strategies would be an ideal way forward (Claasen and Roloff, 2012).

The earlier discussion points out that ISO 26000 is a robust standard that is guiding companies to sustainability through social responsibility. It is a guidance standard for organizations wanting to implement CSR. CSR is inevitable for organizations that want to classify themselves as high performing organizations. On the one hand, CSR can help reap several intangible benefits for an organization: a link between sustainability and organizational performance is already being established. A way forward, therefore, is to create a culture for internalizing ISO 26000. Just like the internalization of "quality culture" requires a major change in the mindset of management, as well as employees, there is a need to create a culture for adapting to sustainable development practices. "Going green" is now increasingly recognized as an important good practice by sustainable organizations, and there are several changes that organizations can seek to achieve (Lasrado and Zakaria, 2019).

Further, in the literature, it has also been discussed how ISO 26000 fits within two predominant CSR instruments: global reporting initiatives (GRI) and the United Nations Global Compact (UNGC). Zinenko et al. (2015) reports that some of these instruments may appear as redundant, but they complement each other. They have different goals and are useful in different parts of an organization's CSR infrastructure. These instruments help organizations to implement different CSR tools at different stages of integrating sustainability issues into their strategies and operations.

Broadly speaking, the internalization of the standard would also require behavioral change among employees. Consciousness of their workplace behavior, in terms of using natural resources responsibly, is an important first step. Second, senior management has a role to create the awareness and benefits of CSR that are to be incorporated in light of ISO standards, which must be communicated throughout the organization. Educational programs that can teach the values of sustainability must also be initiated. When the work environment becomes conducive to and educated about environmental concerns, the internalization of the CSR will begin to shape up. This soft approach will indeed help to reap the benefits of the standards in the long run.

## CONCLUSION

CSR must be implemented into every organizational level to have any meaningful impact. Truly, the majority of socially responsible practices are related to environmental issues and, therefore, there is a relationship between CSR and the application of environmental management systems. Moreover, stakeholders want to see a more comprehensive environmental approach; hence, future CSR initiatives must target these aspects. Overall, ISO 26000 aims at an institutionalization process that will lead to transformative change. CSR practices, ISO 26000 efforts, and CSR performance have become more important in order to achieve success and sustained quality improvement in the mining industry. With committed leadership and the right approach, the mining industry can adapt to a high-quality CSR culture.

CSR, in fact, could mean different things, for example, provision of reliable products and services or being a good corporate citizen. In a mining project, for example, a CSR could have an expectation of the company providing infrastructure, employment, and economic development for local communities. So it is the responsibility of the organization to choose the CSR agenda that has a developed process to monitor the same. The ISO 26000 standard in particular defines seven principles of social responsibility, which are accountability, transparency, ethical behavior, respect for stakeholder interests, respect for the rule of law, respect for international norms of behavior, and respect for human rights. Each of these guiding principles can be considered in an organization in relation to organizational governance, human rights, labor practices, the environment, fair operating practices, consumer issues, and community involvement and development. The mining industry in particular can give strategic importance to the environment and community involvement and development areas. This could be achieved, for example, by engaging in constant dialogue and engaging the communities adjacent to the mines. Finally, by focusing on the overall governance aspect, it can aim to address human rights and a healthy environment, which are of paramount importance to the mining workforce.

## ACKNOWLEDGMENT

This work has been funded by the Global Challenges seed funding scheme 2018 (Grant number: 136) of the University of Wollongong, Australia.

# REFERENCES

Adey, E.A., Shail, R.K., Wall, F., Varul, M., Whitbread-Abrutat, P., Baciu, C., Ejdemo, T., Lovric, I. and Udachin, V. (2011). Corporate social responsibility within the mining industry: Case studies from across Europe and Russia. In *Sustainable Development in the Minerals Industry*: 14/06/2011-17/06/2011 (pp. 153–170). Aachen University, Germany.

Bluszcz, A. and Kijewska, A. (2015). Challenges of sustainable development in the mining and metallurgy sector in Poland. *Metalurgija*, 54(2), pp.441–444.

Bustami, R., Na, D., Nasruddin, E. and A'mmaari, S.R. (2013). Exploring ISO 26000 and Global Reporting Initiatives (GRI): A neo-institutional analysis of two CSR institutions. *International Economics Letters*, 2(2), pp.10–18.

Castka, P. and Balzarova, M.A. (2007). A critical look on quality through CSR lenses: Key challenges stemming from the development of ISO 26000. *International Journal of Quality & Reliability Management*, 24(7), pp.738–752.

Castka, P. and Balzarova, M.A. (2008). ISO 26000 and supply chains—On the diffusion of the social responsibility standard. *International Journal of Production Economics*, 111(2), pp.274–286.

Claasen, C. and Roloff, J. (2012). The link between responsibility and legitimacy: The case of De Beers in Namibia. *Journal of Business Ethics*, 107(3), pp.379–398.

Deepankar, Sharma and Bhatnagar, Priya. (2015). Corporate social responsibility of mining industries. *International Journal of Law and Management*, 57(5), pp.367–372.

Dobele, A.R., Westberg, K., Steel, M. and Flowers, K. (2014). An examination of corporate social responsibility implementation and stakeholder engagement: A case study in the Australian mining industry. *Business Strategy and the Environment*, 23(3), pp.145–159.

Dobers, P. and Halme, M. (2009). Corporate social responsibility and developing countries. *Corporate Social Responsibility and Environmental Management*, 16(5), pp.237–249.

Fuzi, N.M., Habidin, N.F., Desa, A.F.N.C., Zamri, F.I.M. and Hibadullah, S.N. (2013). Corporate social responsibility practices, ISO 26000 efforts and CSR performance in Malaysian automotive industry. *International Journal of Managerial and Financial Accounting*, 5(3), pp.277–293.

Govindan, K., Kannan, D. and Shankar, K.M. (2014). Evaluating the drivers of corporate social responsibility in the mining industry with multi-criteria approach: A multistakeholder perspective. *Journal of Cleaner Production*, 84, pp.214–232.

Gurská, S. and Válová, A. (2013). Corporate social responsibility in mining industry. *Acta Universitatis Agriculturae et Silviculturae Mendelianae Brunensis*, 61(7), pp.2163–2170.

Hahn, R. (2013). ISO 26000 and the standardization of strategic management processes for sustainability and corporate social responsibility. *Business Strategy and the Environment*, 22(7), pp.442–455.

Hamann, R. (2003). Mining companies' role in sustainable development: The 'why' and 'how' of corporate social responsibility from a business perspective. *Development Southern Africa*, 20(2), pp.237–254.

Hamann, R. and Kapelus, P. (2004). Corporate social responsibility in mining in Southern Africa: Fair accountability or just greenwash? *Development*, 47(3), pp.85–92.

Helena, Ranängen, Thomas, Zobel and Andrea, Bergström. (2014). The merits of ISO 26000 for CSR development in the mining industry: A case study in the Zambian Copperbelt. *Social Responsibility Journal*, 10(3), pp.500–515.

Herciu, M. (2016). ISO 26000 – An integrative approach of corporate social responsibility. *Studies in Business and Economics*, 11(1), pp.73–79.

https://www.iso.org/files/live/sites/isoorg/files/store/en/PUB100401.pdf

Jenkins, H. (2004). Corporate social responsibility and the mining industry: Conflicts and constructs. *Corporate Social Responsibility and Environmental Management*, 11(1), pp.23–34.

Jenkins, H. and Obara, L. (2006). *Corporate Social Responsibility (CSR) in the Mining Industry – The Risk of Community Dependency.* Queen's University Belfast, Northern Ireland.

Jenkins, H. and Yakovleva, N. (2006). Corporate social responsibility in the mining industry: Exploring trends in social and environmental disclosure. *Journal of Cleaner Production*, 14(3–4), pp.271–284.

Jones, M., Marshall, S. and Mitchell, R. (2007). Corporate social responsibility and the management of labour in two Australian mining industry companies. *Corporate Governance: An International Review*, 15(1), pp.57–67.

Lasrado, F., and Zakaria, N. (2019). Go green! Exploring the organizational factors that influence self-initiated green behavior in the United Arab Emirates. *Asia Pacific Journal of Management*, pp.1–28.

Majer, M. (2013). The practice of mining companies in building relationships with local communities in the context of CSR formula. *Journal of Sustainable Mining*, 12(3), pp.38–47.

Maki, T. and Feng, L. (2018). From the ISO26000 perspective: Does corporate social responsibility influence corporate value? *Asian Journal of Management Science and Applications*, 3(2), pp.97–116.

Mancini, L. and Sala, S. (2018). Social impact assessment in the mining sector: Review and comparison of indicators frameworks. *Resources Policy*, 57, pp.98–111.

Moratis, L. and Cochius, T. (2017). ISO 26000: *The Business Guide to the New Standard on Social Responsibility*. Routledge.

Mutti, D., Yakovleva, N., Vazquez-Brust, D. and Di Marco, M.H. (2012). Corporate social responsibility in the mining industry: Perspectives from stakeholder groups in Argentina. *Resources Policy*, 37(2), pp.212–222.

Mzembe, A.N. and Meaton, J. (2014). Driving corporate social responsibility in the Malawian mining industry: A stakeholder perspective. *Corporate Social Responsibility and Environmental Management*, 21(4), pp.189–201.

Ranängen, H. and Lindman, Å. (2017). A path towards sustainability for the Nordic mining industry. *Journal of Cleaner Production*, 151, pp.43–52.

Ranängen, H. and Lindman, Å. (2018). Exploring corporate social responsibility practice versus stakeholder interests in Nordic mining. *Journal of Cleaner Production*, 197, pp.668–677.

Ranängen, H. and Zobel, T. (2014a). Exploring the path from management systems to stakeholder management in the Swedish mining industry. *Journal of Cleaner Production*, 84, pp.128–141.

Ranängen, H., Zobel, T. and Bergström, A. (2014b). The merits of ISO 26000 for CSR development in the mining industry: A case study in the Zambian Copperbelt. *Social Responsibility Journal*, 10(3), pp.500–515.

Rodrigues, M. and Mendes, L. (2018). Mapping of the literature on social responsibility in the mining industry: A systematic literature review. *Journal of Cleaner Production*, 181, pp.88–101.

Sethi, S.P., Rovenpor, J.L. and Demir, M. (2017). Enhancing the quality of reporting in Corporate Social Responsibility guidance documents: The roles of ISO 26000, Global Reporting Initiative and CSR-Sustainability Monitor. *Business and Society Review*, 122(2), pp.139–163.

Solomon, F., Katz, E. and Lovel, R. (2008). Social dimensions of mining: Research, policy and practice challenges for the minerals industry in Australia. *Resources Policy*, 33, pp.142–149.

Valmohammadi, C. (2014). Impact of corporate social responsibility practices on organizational performance: An ISO 26000 perspective. *Social Responsibility Journal*, 10(3), pp.455–479.

Vázquez, L.G. and White, R.G. (2012). Can mining be sustainable? ISO 26000 SR for responsible exploration and sustainable mining. *Ideas CONCYTEG*, 7(81), pp.323–341.

Vintró, C., Fortuny, J., Sanmiquel, L., Freijo, M. and Edo, J. (2012). Is corporate social responsibility possible in the mining sector? Evidence from Catalan companies. *Resources Policy*, 37(1), pp.118–125.

Wirth, H., Kulczycka, J., Hausner, J. and Koński, M. (2016). Corporate Social Responsibility: Communication about social and environmental disclosure by large and small copper mining companies. *Resources Policy*, 49, pp.53–60.

Yakovleva, N. and Vazquez-Brust, D. (2012). Stakeholder perspectives on CSR of mining MNCs in Argentina. *Journal of Business Ethics*, 106(2), pp.191–211.

Zinenko, A., Rovira, M.R. and Montiel, I. (2015). The fit of the social responsibility standard ISO 26000 within other CSR instruments: Redundant or complementary?. *Sustainability Accounting, Management and Policy Journal*, 6(4), pp.498–526.

# Index